JULIAN AND HELLENISM

Νικολάῳ καὶ Σοφίᾳ
τοῖς ἐμοὶ παρασχοῦσι
τό τε ζῆν καὶ τὸ εὖ ζῆν

Julian and Hellenism

An Intellectual Biography

POLYMNIA ATHANASSIADI-FOWDEN

CLARENDON PRESS · OXFORD
1981

Oxford University Press, Walton Street, Oxford OX2 6DP

London Glasgow New York Toronto
Delhi Bombay Calcutta Madras Karachi
Kuala Lumpur Singapore Hong Kong Tokyo
Nairobi Dar es Salaam Cape Town
Melbourne Auckland

and associate companies in
Beirut Berlin Ibadan Mexico City

Published in the United States by
Oxford University Press, New York

British Library Cataloguing in Publication Data
Athanassiadi-Fowden, Polymnia
Julian and Hellenism.
1. Julian, Emperor of Rome
2. Roman emperors—Biography
I. Title
937'.08'0924   DG317   80-41209

ISBN 0-19-814846-1

Printed in Great Britain by
Latimer Trend & Company Ltd Plymouth

PREFACE

I have attempted in this book to trace the various phases of the emotional, intellectual and spiritual itinerary followed by Julian in a life which began in AD 331 in the city of Constantinople and was extinguished thirty-two years later in the wastes of Mesopotamia. Against the complex and variegated background of a changing *oikoumene*, Julian emerges as a dynamic—not static—figure constantly at grips with practical and theoretical problems to which he is urgently called to give answers and solutions. Approaching him as a living and unpredictable man, I have sought to understand the tensions and conflicts which resulted from his confrontation with challenges within and challenges without. This preoccupation inevitably led me to concentrate on the motivation of Julian's actions rather than on their outcome, so that in this study certain areas of his activity, especially in the military sphere, to which considerable space would have been allotted in a conventional biography, have been merely alluded to.

In the dangerous journey through the labyrinth of Julian's inner development, I sometimes had the reassuring feeling that I was following an Ariadne's thread left by Julian himself; yet much more frequent were the moments of alarm when I had precipitately to retrace my steps at the sudden realization that too much familiarity with Julian's words could become a barrier to understanding him. To avoid that danger, I have always tried to examine Julian's statements minutely in the light of contemporary evidence. In dealing with the testimony of those who knew Julian—like Ammianus Marcellinus, Mamertinus, Libanius, Himerius and Gregory of Nazianzos—and those who lived close to Julian's age—like Eunapius, Zosimus, Socrates and Sozomen—I have been careful to keep constantly in mind the mentality, professional integrity, specific aims, idiosyncrasies and ideological affiliation of each. Even before the end of his brief life Julian had become a legendary figure, and all these writers had their share in the fostering of his myth. While writing this book, I discovered

with amazement how difficult it is for the historian to block his
ears completely against the persistent voice of legend. Unable
to ignore this problem, I have coped with it by endeavouring
to detect the elements in the historical Julian which could give
rise to some of the Julianic ghosts with which Byzantium lived.

I hope that, by the nature of its subject, this book may
be of some interest to a wider public. As a general rule, I
have translated or paraphrased all Greek and Latin quotations
in the text, though, very occasionally, single words, which I
hold to be absolutely untranslatable, appear in the text in
Greek without an adequate explanation, for I felt that such an
explanation would have required a whole volume.

Though I have made a conscious effort to evaluate Julian's
character by concentrating on the sources for his reign rather
than relying on the achievement of modern scholarship, I feel
obliged to mention here at least one scholar, without whose
contribution in the field of Julianic studies the present book
could not even have been undertaken. Joseph Bidez was not
only the author of a fine conventional biography of the
Emperor Julian, but, most importantly, he produced (in
collaboration with Franz Cumont) a masterly edition of the
bulk of Julian's writings.

Over the long period between its conception and its birth
this study benefited enormously from being submitted to the
cool eye of knowledgeable and sensitive critics. I could never
thank adequately Dr J. F. Matthews of Queen's College,
Oxford, for his iron determination to make me capable of
putting my ideas across to an English public. At the time of his
sojourn on this side of the Atlantic, Professor Peter Brown supported my labour over a critical period of self-doubt; his
instinctive sympathy with my approach proved an endless
source of inspiration for me. Dr Oswyn Murray of Balliol
College, Professor Robert Browning, and Dr J. H. W. G.
Liebeschuetz were sympathetic though acute critics of this
work at different stages of its development; only they and
myself know how much the book in its present form owes to
their erudition and expert advice on methodological issues. It
is extremely difficult even to begin to assess my debt of gratitude
to the Reverend Professor Henry Chadwick: he was the *deus ex*

machina who offered help over scholastic and essential matters alike just when help was needed. I should also record here my warmest thanks to Professor Constantine Tsatsos, that *homo universalis*, who has guided me ever since my first steps in the academic world. Professor George Babiniotis of Athens University has been for many years a teacher, a collaborator and a friend, and his genuine interest in my work, as well as the practical help that he lent me during the period of my research in a field so different from his own, evoke in me an uncommon sense of obligation.

Hardest of all is to define my debt to Oxford, where I wrote most of this book. During the years spent in that city I came to understand how much emotionally involved Julian could become with particular towns, and why.

It is customary on similar occasions to thank one's husband for his understanding and unfailing moral support. But I am in the privileged position of being able to say without exaggeration that this book belongs to him as much as it belongs to myself, for he did much more than argue over every single page in an often unsuccessful attempt to persuade me to comply with the objective rules of his mother tongue: he became for me, over the years of a twin career, a source of inspiration and information, an indefatigable worker and a μουσηγέτης, till this book was completed.

Athens, December 1980   POLYMNIA ATHANASSIADI-FOWDEN

CONTENTS

ABBREVIATIONS AND NOTES

CIL	*Corpus Inscriptionum Latinarum*, Berlin 1863–
CIMRM	M. J. Vermaseren, *Corpus inscriptionum et monumentorum religionis Mithriacae*, The Hague 1958
C.Just.	*Codex Iustinianus* (*Corpus Iuris Civilis* II, ed. P. Krueger), Berlin 1906[8]
C.Th.	*Theodosiani Libri XVI cum constitutionibus Sirmondianis* (ed. T. Mommsen), Berlin 1954[2]
ELF	Imperatoris Caesaris Flavii Claudii Iuliani *Epistulae Leges Poematia Fragmenta Varia* (edd. J. Bidez, F. Cumont), Paris 1922
ILS	H. Dessau, *Inscriptiones Latinae selectae*, Berlin 1892–1916
Julien	L'empereur Julien, *Œuvres complètes* I–II (edd. J. Bidez, G. Rochefort, C. Lacombrade), Paris 1932–64
MMM	F. Cumont, *Textes et monuments relatifs aux mystères de Mithra* I–II, Brussels 1896–9
OGIS	W. Dittenberger, *Orientis graeci inscriptiones selectae*, Leipzig 1903–5.
PG	J.-P. Migne, *Patrologia Graeca*
PL	J.-P. Migne, *Patrologia Latina*
PLRE	A. H. M. Jones, J. R. Martindale, J. Morris, *The Prosopography of the Later Roman Empire, A.D. 260–395*, Cambridge 1971

Titles of periodicals are abbreviated according to the conventions of *L'Année Philologique*.

References to Julian's works are not preceded by the name of their author. The orations are numbered according to the Budé edition. The numbering of the epistles is that of Bidez–Cumont; the references to *Contra Galilaeos* are always preceded by the initials *C.G.*

References to Libanius' orations are given without the abbreviation *or.* preceding the number of the oration. Where a reference is given to a declamation the abbreviation *Decl.* precedes the number.

INTRODUCTION:
HELLENISM: UNITY OR DIVERSITY?

What! Was it not the gods themselves who revealed to Homer, Hesiod, Demosthenes, Herodotus, Thucydides, Isocrates and Lysias all their learning? Did not these men think that they were consecrated, some to Hermes, others to the Muses? I think it is absurd that men who expound the works of these writers should dishonour the gods those authors honoured. Yet, though I think this absurd, I do not say that they ought to change their opinions and then instruct the young. Rather I give them this choice: either not to teach what they do not take seriously or, if they wish to teach, to practise what they preach and to persuade their pupils that neither Homer nor Hesiod nor any of these writers whom they expound and have declared to be guilty of impiety, folly and error in regard to the gods, is such as they declare. For since they make a livelihood and receive pay from the works of those writers, they thereby confess that they would put up with anything ... for the sake of a few drachmas.[1]

The problem to which Julian's edict on education addresses itself can be reduced to a simple choice of alternatives: Hellenism: unity or diversity? Rich in feeling and crystalline in its logic, Julian's law proclaims an unambiguous answer: unity!— a view shared by not a few Christian thinkers. 'What is the use of sending our children to the grammarian, where, before learning their texts, they will acquire wickedness and, in their desire to receive a trifle, they will lose the most important thing, all the vigour and health of their soul?',[2] was the anxious enquiry of John Chrysostom, a man in whom culture, literary talent and rhetorical skill combined to form the ideal late antique intellectual. Yet his older contemporary Gregory of Nazianzos—an Athenian by education and a born poet—held, theoretically at least, the opposite view and, when the edict on education appeared, he was so scandalized that he undertook (admittedly, after Julian's death) to refute the assumptions on

---

[1] *Ep.* 61. 423ab. The Law on Education, forbidding Christian participation in learning, was severely criticized even by those of Julian's contemporaries who were sympathetic to his attempt at a pagan restoration, cf. Ammianus XXII. 10. 7.

[2] *Adv. oppugn. vit. mon.*, PG 47. 367.

which it rested. 'Is Hellenism, is Atticism, your own personal chattel?',[3] Gregory angrily asked his dead enemy. But in equating Hellenism with Atticism Gregory allowed himself to make a grave linguistic error: he ignored the semantic evolution that the term 'Hellenism' had undergone since the fourth century BC, when it was actually coined.

The attempts to speak Greek made by an ever increasing number of foreigners at the dawn of the Hellenistic era provoked the righteous indignation of the native speakers who, wishing to put a stop to the maltreatment of their language, sought to formulate rules for a Greek free of barbarisms and solecisms. The Greek quality *par excellence*—Hellenism—was the correct use of the language.[4]

Yet is it possible to learn a foreign language without acquiring another personality in the process? Those oriental élites in the Hellenistic kingdoms who were from childhood steeped in Greek letters soon found out how deeply their entire world-view had been affected by a way of thinking and living distinctly alien from their own. During the Maccabean revolt chauvinistic Jews seized upon the word 'Hellenism' and used it pejoratively to describe the imitation of Greek ways by their coreligionists.[5] Indeed to such an extent were these Ἑλληνισταί alienated from their own cultural and religious heritage that for some of them 'Hellenism' became a stepping stone to a new religion; for the very first men to be known in history as Christians were converts from the community of Hellenists in Antioch.[6]

'Hellenism' as an adopted way of thought and life had now entered the stream of Christianity, innocently, unobtrusively, as the gift of outsiders to a new religion, which, needless to say, was eminently receptive to its influence, having itself sprung up in Hellenistic soil. The first Christian preachers and apologists stretched out their arms to clasp the gift of the Danaans—the linguistic phenomenon that had spread over most of the Mediterranean world together with the culture that it ex-

---

[3] *Or.* IV. 107.

[4] As in J. Stroux, *De Theophrasti virtutibus dicendi*, Pars I, Leipzig 1912, 13 ff. On the origins of the word Ἑλληνισμός, in the sense of 'correct postclassical Greek', cf. R. Laqueur, 'Hellenismus', *Schriften der hessischen Hochschulen* i (1924), 22 ff.

[5] 2 Macc. 4:13.

[6] Acts 11:26.

pressed—without suspecting all the subtle dangers to which they were exposing themselves. Actively they propagated the role of the Greek philosophical tradition as the best 'pedagogue in Christ', in the hope of gaining over the élites to their cause. At the same time they themselves became the living embodiment of their theory, for in order to put their own message across cogently they had recourse to the Hellenic manner. 'The many fear Greek philosophy, just as children are afraid of hobgoblins, lest it should kidnap them',[7] they declared, and urged their contemporaries to follow their own example and spoil the Egyptians: the spirit of Hellenism had to go, but the letter was to be retained. Men like Justin the Martyr, Clement of Alexandria and, above all, Origen undertook to teach the world how to set this process in motion and, with a superb confidence in the superiority of their revelatory religion, they presented Christianity as the catalyst of Hellenism.

But their edifying monologue was not to remain unanswered by those whom the apologists called the 'Hellenes'—the adepts of the religion that had from the earliest times grown in constant cross-fertilization with Greek culture. In reaction against the irreverent attitude of Christian intellectuals, these men argued that Hellenism, far from being a simple synonym for paganism, was a spiritual force, simple and unalloyed, in which culture and religion were coextensive categories for ever destined to mock the attempts of presumptuous alchemists. This view, put forward with uncommon vigour by Celsus in the second century, seems to have held some attractiveness for at least a limited number of Christians, as Tatian's impassioned attack *Against the Greeks* testifies.

Yet in his rejection of Hellenism *in toto* as something truly evil Tatian seems to have been more a man of the future than a typical product of his age. For his hatred of Hellenism was to find an active response only among the representatives of the ascetic movement, men who, in their deep contempt for any cultural and aesthetic achievement of Man, opted consciously for the desert against civilized life, against culture and history. 'Beasts or gods' in the eyes of a Hellene (and the emperor Julian was more inclined to see in them the former than the

---

[7] Clement, *Strom.* VI. 10. 80. 4.

latter[8]), the anchorites, with their categorical denial of the values of Hellenism, remained a permanent feature of the Byzantine world.[9]

To the mind of a rigorist Hellene the attitude of the Christian hermit towards his culture was at least ideologically consistent. It was the attitude of a man like Origen that he found infuriating; for Origen succeeded in refuting Celsus' argument that Hellenic culture and religion were indivisible. Origen though was a unique phenomenon. With his intuitive gift, his uncommon broadness of view and tremendous self-confidence, the third-century apologist made a distinction for which he could not possibly set any norms applicable by posterity; and the very validity of his distinction was called in doubt by the sharp debates on his own orthodoxy which divided theologians for centuries after his death. Perhaps the best measure of Origen's achievement was the rage that his memory provoked in Porphyry: not just an apostate, but a profaner of Hellenism too, this man had gone as far as any Christian could possibly go towards the amalgamation of Christian religion and Greek culture.[10] And predictably enough, neither camp thanked Origen for this: the Hellenes denounced him as a traitor and the Christians as a heretic.

Yet Origen was not the only spiritual genius the third century produced. In his counterpart, Plotinus, Hellenism found the man who redefined its religious core. Henceforth the dialogue between the two creeds was to be set on a new foundation. Basing his teaching on the Greek concept of *logos*, Plotinus at the same time revolutionized the history of Platonism by con-

---

[8] *ep.* 89b.288b; cf. IX. 201c.

[9] It is true that Byzantium produced cultured monastic figures, such as John Moschus and Theodore the Studite, and, what is more important, a substantial number of anonymous monks whose patient labour transmitted to us many a classical text. Yet one should not forget the armies of 'imbecile monks', the σαλοί of Psellus (cf. his *ep.* 166 in C. N. Sathas, Μεσαιωνικὴ βιβλιοθήκη v, Paris–Venice 1876, 424), who still in the eleventh century were running throughout Greece destroying whatever remained of the ancient temples in the name of a 'sacred war' (cf. Eustathius of Thessalonica, Ἐπίσκεψις βίου μοναχικοῦ ἐπὶ διορθώσει τῶν περὶ αὐτόν, *PG* 135. 729–909, esp. 868 ff., where these monks are presented as a well organized army and characterized by the bishop as λοιμῶδες κακόν, an 'infectious evil').

[10] Porphyry, *Contra Christianos* (= A. von Harnack, 'Porphyrius, "Gegen die Christen" 15 Bücher—Zeugnisse, Fragmente und Referate' *Abh. der kön. preuss. Akad. der Wiss., phil.-hist. Kl.* 1916, no. 1), fr. 39.

tributing to it his notion of mystical experience as the ultimate object of all philosophy. 'Our concern is not to be sinless, but to be God',[11] was his profession of faith. This deeply rooted belief illuminates the most powerful pages of the *Enneads*, where Plotinus vividly describes how the νοῦς in Man, at the end of a long process of conscious moral and intellectual effort, is at last gratified with a vision of the divine in which subject and object are fused in one.[12] Yet *unio mystica* is to be achieved—if at all—only by the steep path of noetic ascent, not through irrationality, for 'to set oneself above νοῦς is to fall away from it.'[13] These words, addressed to the Gnostics, contain a warning of which Plotinus' own followers did not always take heed.

In the next generation his system was to be associated with the theology of the *Chaldean Oracles* and begin gradually to move away from *logos*, now regarded as a secondary virtue, irrelevant to, and even incompatible with, the mystical soarings of the inner Man towards the One. Its place within the context of Neoplatonism was imperceptibly taken over by the fervour of faith, hope and love;[14] on another level, *logos* gave way before *mythos*, and all the wealth of the Hellenic revelatory tradition suddenly overwhelmed Neoplatonism. Like a snow-ball Neoplatonism rolled downwards into the Hellenic past, absorbing whatever it found in its way. Thanks to the loving labour of subtle commentators and allegorizers, Homer and Orpheus now became all-important figures, while the whole of Greek philosophy, with the exception of Scepticism and Epicureanism, was integrated within this last creative construction of Hellenism.

This process started with Porphyry. Yet, despite his evident fascination with the wisdom of the Orient and a certain taste for extreme forms of asceticism,[15] the Tyrian philosopher proved a genuine pupil of Plotinus, not only in the minute care that he bestowed on his edition of the *Enneads*, but also in more independent ways. In a text dating from his mature years, which

---

[11] *Enn.* I. 2. 6. 2–3.
[12] Porph. *V. Plot.* 23; Plotinus, *Enn.* I. 6. 7–9, IV. 8. 1, V. 8. 11, VI. 7. 34 (the clearest account of the mystic union given by Plotinus); see also VI. 9. 8–11.
[13] *Enn.* II. 9. 9. 51–2.
[14] Porph. *Marc.* 24; Proclus, *Theol. Plat.* I. 25 for the triad ἔρως, ἀλήθεια, πίστις.
[15] e.g. *Abst.* I. 36 and 45, *Marc.* 7, 34–5, etc.

ranks among the most beautiful products of late antique religious thought, Porphyry exhorts his belatedly acquired wife,
Marcella, to pursue zealously the narrow path that brings us to
bliss through the labours of the spirit, in a language that would
have met with his master's full approval. 'The mind of the sage
alone is the temple of God *par excellence* in human societies' (11)
is Porphyry's guiding principle as he urges Marcella to 'let the
nous in herself be God's temple' (19).

Porphyry's single-minded search after the divine had rendered
religious practice superfluous. His mind was too full of God and
of the mysteries of the spiritual life for him to need the faint
stimulus of ritual—a view he did not refrain from expressing in
bold language to his coreligionist Iamblichus. Yet at the same
time he felt that less fervent or less philosophical natures than
his own ought to be sustained in their struggle by a pious
routine: 'for such is the greatest fruit of piety, to honour divinity
according to tradition—κατὰ τὰ πάτρια' (18). Starting from this
presupposition, Porphyry wrote the most formidable of all
attacks on Christianity, in which he criticized the new religion
on social, cultural and dogmatic grounds. As 'a band of outlaws'
the Christians could not possibly make any claim whatever to
participate in the traditional culture of the empire,[16] which in
the spiritual sphere was now finding a new dynamic expression
thanks to the teaching of the Neoplatonists. These 'new men's'
redefinition of the religious core of Hellenism set the whole
cultural debate on a new basis, as the Christians themselves
were quick to understand.[17]

The critical initiative was taken by the Syrian Iamblichus,
who made the first steps towards crystallizing Neoplatonism
into a dogma and endowing it with a ritual—a process which
Julian was to continue and amplify. The new dimension that
the master of Apamea introduced into Neoplatonism was
theurgy,[18] a spiritual discipline derived from the theology of the
Chaldean Oracles and founded on the exploitation of the laws of

---

[16] *C. Christ.* frs. 1, 39, 49.

[17] Eusebius, *Praep. Ev.* II. 6. 16 ff., who refers contemptuously yet anxiously
to the Neoplatonists as νέοι τινές, ἐχθὲς καὶ πρώην ἐπιφυέντες.

[18] On the origins, essence and historical evolution of theurgy (θεουργία,
ἱερατική, τελεστική), as the science by which mystic union was achieved, see
H. Lewy, *Chaldaean Oracles and theurgy: mysticism, magic and Platonism in the later
Roman empire*, Paris 1978², with E. R. Dodds's review in *HThR* liv (1961), 263–73.

universal sympathy. It consisted in the performance of ritual actions, followed by the utterance of magic sounds or names,[19] which caused the appearance of gods and demons on earth (θεοφάνειαι), and ultimately brought the purified soul of the officiant to union with the divine.[20] But especially at this last stage, divine intervention—the factor of Grace—was vital. Thus the Syrian Iamblichus, in tune with the spirit of his age, introduced into Hellenism elements that appealed to Man's emotional part, an innovation for which he was vehemently attacked by Porphyry, who had, nevertheless, himself trespassed on the limits of orthodoxy as defined by his master.

Yet Porphyry's feeble opposition did nothing to arrest the tide. All he achieved by his ardent defence of philosophy was to be classified himself by future generations of Neoplatonists as a notional and temporary landmark in the history of the School:

There are those who prefer philosophy, like Porphyry and Plotinus and many other philosophers, and those who prefer ἱερατική, like Iamblichus and Syrianus and Proclus and the rest of the ἱερατικοί.[21]

Also Dodds's 'Theurgy and its relationship to Neoplatonism', *JRS* xxxvii (1947), 55–69 (= *The Greeks and the Irrational*, Berkeley 1951, repr. 1966, Appendix II). Theurgy was introduced into the Roman world by Julianus the so-called 'theurgist', who lived in Rome under Marcus Aurelius (Suda I. 434), and is presumed to have been the author of the *Chaldean Oracles*, a collection of hexameter verses, the surviving fragments of which expound a theological system that was largely accepted by Iamblichus and the later Neoplatonists (see Lewy, *Chaldaean Oracles*, 3–5; Dodds, *JRS* xxxvii, 55; E. des Places, *Oracles chaldaïques*, Paris 1971, 7). Theurgy owed much to Chaldean theology, from which it adopted its astrological system and the principle of universal sympathy, according to whose laws the numerous superimposed spheres of existence—mineral, animal, astral—were closely linked through a system of correspondences (cf. Iamblichus, *Myst.* V. 24), and were all (with the exception of the astral sphere) subject to the power of fate (δεσμοῖς ἀλύτοις ἀνάγκης, ἣν εἱμαρμένην καλοῦμεν, ἐνδέδεται πάντα, ibid. VIII. 7). By its very nature, Man's divine soul participated, at least potentially, in the First Principle, which was free from the bonds of Εἱμαρμένη. By theurgic action the divine soul was capable of abolishing Εἱμαρμένη, thus reaching unity with the First Principle (ibid. VIII. 6, 8 and X. 5).

[19] Cf. the definition of theurgy in *Orac. Chald.* 110. On theurgy as ἡ τῶν [θείων] ἔργων τέχνη see Iambl. *Myst.* I. 9. 33. On the importance of σύμβολα and συνθήματα in connection with theurgy see ibid. I. 11, 15, 21; II. 11; IV. 2; VII. 4–5. See also Lewy, *Chaldaean Oracles*, 462.

[20] An account of the way in which the theurgist brings about mystic union is given by Iambl. *Myst.* VI. 5–7.

[21] [Olympiodorus], *In Phaed.* (Norvin), 123, lines 3 ff.; cf. Suda I. 159: ἱερατικὴ καὶ φιλοσοφία οὐκ ἀπὸ τῶν αὐτῶν ἄρχονται ἀρχῶν.

Characterized by the lack of subtlety proper to any generalization, this distinction none the less points in the right direction
as regards the development of Neoplatonism. Iamblichus was
indeed the first to maintain that the mystic union was not to be
achieved by contemplation alone: 'The theurgic union is
achieved both through the performance of actions ineffable,
beyond intellection and accomplished in a manner worthy of
the gods (θεοπρεπῶs), and through the power of unutterable
symbols, which are understood by the gods alone' (*Myst.* II.
11). Such was the solemn verdict of the hierophant of the new
times.

Pupils flocked to Iamblichus from all over the Mediterranean
world, and stayed to drink at the springs of his divinely inspired
knowledge.[22] Thanks to Eunapius we get a glimpse of the
seemingly unremitting religious fervour that possessed these
men: they lived more in the domain of the supernatural than in
real life. One of them has left us a revealing correspondence
with Iamblichus, which has long been attributed to the Emperor Julian himself.[23] Apart from the hysterical rapture induced
in the pupil by the mere reception of a letter from his master,
what strikes the reader of this correspondence is the peculiar
usage of the term τὸ 'Ελληνικόν. So far τὸ 'Ελληνικὸν had meant
either the Greek nation or Greek culture. Now it acquires a
heavily and almost exclusively religious value, and the same
usage is extended to the word "Ελλην in this context. We have
to do with a kind of religious society, whose threatened creed
was revivified and redefined by Iamblichus. The pagan Father
is described as 'the saviour of τὸ 'Ελληνικόν",[24] 'the common
blessing of the Hellenes' or even 'the great delight of the
oikoumene'.[25]

It was in this atmosphere of exalted mysticism that in the
second quarter of the fourth century the belief gained ground
that all Greek culture was literally a product of divine inspira-

[22] Eunapius, *V. Phil.* V. 1. 4.

[23] F. Cumont, *Sur l'authenticité de quelques lettres de Julien*, Gand 1889, contested
the attribution of this collection of letters to the emperor Julian and suggested
that the author of *epp.* 181–7 was the sophist Julian of Caesarea (pp. 27–9). This
view was followed by J. Bidez (*Julien* I(2), 235) and criticized by T. D. Barnes,
'A correspondent of Iamblichus', *GRBS* xix (1978), 99–106, who sees in Ps.-Julian
a Syrian pupil of Iamblichus who visited the court of Licinius.

[24] [Julian], *ep.* 184. 419a.

[25] [Julian], *ep.* 181. 449b.

tion and, therefore, of a sacred character. This mentality is nowhere else as clearly articulated as in Julian's edict on education. In this document the emperor expressed with clarity and consistency his horror at the profanation of what to him was his very *raison d'être*. At the same time he put his finger on the great conflict that the contemporary Christian conscience was facing, and men like Gregory of Nazianzos hated him for exactly this reason.

It is clear that the Christian theologian did not believe in the intrinsic value of the feeble arguments that he put forward in his invectives against Julian, for his own attitude towards Greek culture was one of regretful half-denial.[26] At the moment when he was forced to choose between Christianity and his love of Greek letters, Gregory was caught on the horns of a sharp dilemma. 'A terrible tempest raged in my mind',[27] he confessed. Momentarily he thought that he had renounced Hellenism and done away with his sinful ἔρως τῶν λόγων,[28] an impression that he hastened to express in unambiguous terms:

Ἑλλὰς ἐμή, νεότης τε φίλη, καὶ ὅσα πέπασμαι,
Καὶ δέμας, ὡς Χριστῷ εἴξατε προφρονέως![29]

Yet nothing could be more Greek than this distich, in which Gregory vainly tries to exorcise the charms of Hellenism. The enumeration of all the things that make up the beauty and glamour of this world—Hellas, youth, affectionate memories of childhood, worldly pleasures, all laid down earnestly at the altar of Jesus—conveys the magnitude of his sacrifice in the Greek tragic manner. His sense of sacrifice becomes all the more intense as Hellenism is inevitably associated with the lost paradise of youth. Everywhere in his poetry Athens appears as the symbol of lost youth.[30] Ἀθῆναι καὶ λόγοι stand for his buried life, representing the world of *il gran rifiuto*—yet not an entirely extinct world, but one which at times may become painfully real and tantalize the striver after sanctity. What really

---

[26] See my discussion of Gregory's reaction to the edict on education in 'The Idea of Hellenism', *Philosophia* vii (1977), 349–51.
[27] *Historica*, PG 37. 1049.
[28] *In laudem Basili Magni, or.* XLIII. 15, 24.
[29] *Historica*, PG 37. 1449.
[30] Ibid. 1029–1166 and 1353–78.

frightened Gregory and his fellow Christians in Julian's law on
education was its ominous confirmation of what they had dimly
grasped themselves.[31]
    Yet not all educated Christians knew the tensions to which
Gregory's sensitive and passionate nature was subject. Among
Julian's contemporaries there were pragmatic men, endowed
with an infuriating common sense, men with a blunt aesthetic
awareness and the capacity to bridle what few emotions welled
up from the depths of their hearts. Even if educated in Greek
letters from an early age, such men succeeded in dissociating
themselves from that culture and came to look at Hellenism
afresh from the Christian point of view. In their works they
advocated for their coreligionists an attitude of reasoned acceptance of part of the Greek cultural heritage. Basil of Caesarea
is a crucial example of a man who succeeded in proving to the
vast majority of his contemporaries the irrelevance of the claim
made by Julian in his edict on education. Admitting the existence of a Hellenic religion in constant antagonism with
Christianity, Basil excludes large parts of the Greek philosophical heritage from the list of books allowed to be read by Christian children. The 'classics', as he defined them, were the
relatively harmless authors who survived into Byzantine
school-programmes and thus influenced the official intellectual
life of the empire and of modern Greece. Other men followed
in Basil's footsteps and became the spokesmen of Byzantine
humanism—the kind of baroque Hellenism which in time was
to win the West too.[32]
    The attempt to rob the Hellenes of their culture had indeed
been crowned with success. But only apparently, for in the
compromise something inevitably had to be sacrificed. And
triumphant Christianity's choice was the exact opposite of
Origen's. The Byzantine world opted for the letter, without of
course realizing it, believing in all sincerity that theirs was a
direct contact with the spirit of texts, which they could only

---

[31] Gregory's indignation against Julian's measures in *orr.* IV and V was really
for public consumption. In a private letter to a friend (in all probability Gregory
of Nyssa, who had apparently neglected his clerical duties for the sake of Greek
letters), Gregory says bluntly that a good Christian cannot be a rhetor: *ep.* 11
(Gallay).
[32] For further details see my article in *Philosophia* vii. 351–3.

read after having fitted them into the Church's Procrustean bed.[33] And yet, there were exceptions. Julian's Hellenism did not die with the cessation of philosophical teaching in Athens. It lived through Byzantium as a hidden underground current, and found dynamic expression at the very moment when the Byzantine empire was disintegrating politically. Pletho's reaction to this disintegration, and his dreams of a revived Hellenism, as expressed in his book of *Laws*, offer many striking parallels with Julian's programme.[34] It would indeed be an exaggeration to say that the Byzantines saw the problem of what attitude to adopt towards Platonism in exactly the same light as the Fathers,[35] but what remains certain is that, although the overwhelming majority of educated Byzantine people had the same attitude towards classical texts as Photius and Anna Comnena—an attitude which stemmed directly from Basil's teaching—there always existed the possibility for a lay élite to opt for Hellenism against the Christian dogmas. Despite, or rather because of, the compromise made by the Fathers of the fourth century, thanks to which a place was reserved in Byzantium for the ghosts of the classical authors,[36] there was still room

[33] Cf. P. Lemerle, *Le Premier Humanisme byzantin—Notes et remarques sur enseignement et culture à Byzance des origines au Xe siècle*, Paris 1971, 45, 47; C. Mango, *Byzantine Literature as a Distorting Mirror*, Inaugural lecture, Oxford 1975, esp. p. 18.

[34] On Mistra as an important intellectual centre in the Palaeologan period see D. Zakythenos, *Le Despotat grec de Morée* ii, Athens 1953, repr. London 1975, 310 ff. On the Hellenic reaction and Pletho see F. Masai, *Pléthon et le platonisme de Mistra*, Paris 1956, 48 ff. The parallel between Pletho's and Julian's ideals is made explicitly by George Gennadius Scholarius, Ἐπιστολὴ τῇ βασιλίσσῃ περὶ τοῦ βιβλίου τοῦ Γεμιστοῦ (= L. Petit et al. (edd.), *Œuvres complètes* iv, Paris 1935, 152). C. N. Sathas, *Documents inédits relatifs à l'histoire de la Grèce au Moyen-Age* vii, Paris 1888, throws further light on the survival of the Neoplatonic tradition in Byzantium; in this volume Sathas gathered texts in support of his thesis that Neoplatonic Hellenism as the rival of Christianity remained alive in Byzantium and was secretly transmitted from generation to generation.

[35] As does P. E. Stéphanou, *Jean Italos, philosophe et humaniste*, Rome 1949, 19.

[36] F. Masai, op. cit. 34, has expressed this very well: 'Si, par contraste avec la Turcocratie, Byzance paraît "grecque", c'est parce qu'elle garde l'expression extérieure de l'antiquité. Mais la langue n'était pas le tout, ni même l'essentiel du patrimoine hellénique. En réalité l'empire byzantin ne fut plus comme ses prédécesseurs un défenseur de l'hellénisme, il en a même été le premier enemi déclaré.' It should be remembered that 'Hellenism' remained a term of abuse throughout the Byzantine period; Photius, for example, a man of phenomenal Greek erudition, uses the word 'Hellene' as a simple synonym for 'pagan': *Bibl.* 77. 54a. Cf. G. Gennad. Schol. *Œuvres complètes* IV. 1 n.**.

in the Christian empire for people like Psellus, whose exegesis of Plato shocked the Christian establishment,[37] or John Italus, who was declared a heretic by both Christians and Hellenes.[38]

Anathema to those who devote themselves to Greek studies not simply for the sake of education, but who also adopt the foolish doctrines of the ancients and accept them for the truth; anathema to those who so firmly believe such doctrines that they unhesitatingly teach them and commend them to others, both secretly and openly.[39]

Condemned by Church and State alike, often persecuted, the spiritual progeny of Julian somehow made its difficult way through Byzantium to modern times; and perhaps, so long as there are men able to combine an austere religious sense with the cult of beauty, the indignant tones of the edict on education may yet continue to find a sympathetic audience.

[37] On the imprisonment of Psellus in the monastery Τὰ Ναρσοῦ on the order of the Patriarch Lichoudes, see P. Joannou, 'Psellos et le Monastère Τὰ Ναρσοῦ', *ByzZ* xliv (1951), 283–90.

[38] On the trial of John Italus and the reasons for his condemnation by the emperor Alexis I see P. E. Stéphanou, op. cit. 63–80. On the denunciation of Italus as a heretic by the Hellenes themselves see the anecdote quoted by F. Masai, op. cit. 288–90.

[39] J. Gouillard, 'Le Synodicon de l'orthodoxie: édition et commentaire', *T&MByz* ii (1967), 59, lines 214–18; transl. by J. M. Hussey, *Church and Learning in the Byzantine Empire (867–1185)*, Oxford 1937, 94 (slightly modified).

I. THE GARDENS OF ALCINOUS

Homer's world, not ours. AUDEN

When, after his vision at the Milvian Bridge, the emperor Constantine declared Christianity a 'religio licita', and even went so far as to embrace it publicly himself, he broke in one important respect with the millenial Roman cultural and religious tradition of which, as *imperator*, he was the living embodiment. 'It must never be forgotten that Constantine's revolution was perhaps the most audacious act ever committed by an autocrat in disregard and defiance of the vast majority of his subjects.' Bury's reminder is worth paying some attention to, for it voices a sentiment that many of Constantine's contemporaries felt more passionately and, often, expressed in less mild prose.

Yet a despot's religious policy, however sensitive and even brilliant, can never significantly alter the course of the spiritual history of his age. As the centuries-long dialogue between pagans and Christians shows, the stream of religious ideology flowed very slowly in the Roman world, and the intellectual landscape through which it passed changed but imperceptibly. Still in the fourth century both the syllabus and the educational methods available to the young remained substantially the same as they had been two centuries before; and when the time came for Constantine's nephew to embark on his studies, he was faced with a very traditional programme indeed. That Julian imbibed what he was taught in the particular way he did was the most natural thing in the world, especially in view of the peculiar circumstances that attended his earliest years.

On 9 September 337 the three sons of Constantine were proclaimed Augusti. Just before that date there took place the military uprising during which all the male members of the imperial family were murdered, with the exception of Julian and his elder half-brother Gallus.[1] Of this massacre Julian, who

[1] See Amm. XXI. 16. 8; also E. Stein, *Histoire du Bas-Empire* i, Bruges 1959, 131, who reads correctly the passage from Eus. *V. Const.* IV. 69. For an inter-

was then less than six years old,[2] retained a persistent memory, which haunts many an otherwise serene page of his.[3] Twenty-five years later the emperor will try to mitigate the poignant memory of the slaughter of his kindred by merging it into his profoundly familiar world of Greek culture. In words borrowed from Euripides he will then remember how 'there was suddenly murder everywhere as the demon brought the tragic curse weighing upon us to its fulfilment, "for our patrimony was divided by the pointed edge of the sword" and utter confusion reigned around':[4] after so many years Julian distinctly recalled the taste of murky smoke in his throat and the ῥύπος—the filth—that surrounded him before anybody had the presence of mind to retrieve the child 'from the blood and the din of battle and the slaughter of men'.[5]

The new emperor of the eastern provinces, Constantius, took care to send Julian away from the capital, to Nicomedia, where Eusebius, a bishop well trusted at Court, was charged with teaching him the Scriptures and imbuing the child with a Christian spirit.[6] Nicomedia was a good choice, because of its ambiguous character as a capital city of the empire,[7] but an obscure and forgotten one. It was indeed the ideal residence for a member of the imperial family whom the Court desired to keep away alike from childhood associations and from popularity.

It must have been one year later, when Eusebius left Nicomedia to become bishop of Constantinople, that Mardonius, the tutor of Julian's dead mother Basilina, came to the young prince.[8] Julian was seven years old and, having already received the rudiments of a Christian education, he was now first introduced to the world of Homer by a man who had been brought

---

pretation of the massacre in the light of the 'political theology' propagated by Eusebius, see S. Calderone, 'Teologia politica, successione dinastica e *consecratio* in età costantiniana', *Entretiens Hardt* xix (1972), 253–4.

[2] XII. 352c; Amm. XXV. 3. 23.
[3] VII. 228b; 230a; V. 270cd; 274d; 281b.
[4] VII. 228b and Euripides, *Phoen.* 68.
[5] VII. 229d–230a and Homer, *Iliad* Λ 164.
[6] Amm. XXII. 9. 4.
[7] Ibid. 3; see C. C. Vermeule, *Roman Imperial Art in Greece and Asia Minor*, Cambridge, Mass. 1968, 330 ff.
[8] XII. 352c.

up in the bosom of the imperial family.[9] The personality of Mardonius, who left a decisive mark on Julian's character, can easily be brought to life thanks to all the details his pupil gives about him. He was a Goth[10] and a eunuch, devoted to the family whose servant he had been since his early years. He had been trained from childhood by Basilina's father to be a παιδαγωγός and he did not fail to respond to the expectations of his master, developing both a genuine fascination for his profession and a strong affection for the family whose children were entrusted to him.[11] Naturally enough, this man, excluded from the activities of a normal existence, sought to find some other sphere where he would be able to lead a full life. Through his occupation with literature, he came to discover an ideal world— one which indeed provided a substitute for everyday reality to many a more talented and fortunate contemporary.[12] Little by little, he withdrew into the world that Homer had created, and sincerely despised all that lay without its boundaries. When Julian was entrusted to his care, Mardonius infected his pupil with this enthusiasm, while for his part Julian showed an absolute trust in his new master who, at that moment, was the only person capable of reproducing for the orphan something of the atmosphere of home life. In later years Julian remembered how Mardonius would say to him:

[9] XII. 352b. The main biographers of Julian seem to believe that Eusebius and Mardonius were teaching him at the same time; see N. H. Baynes, 'The early life of Julian the Apostate', *JHS* xlv (1925), 251 ff.; J. Bidez, *La Vie de l'empereur Julien*, Paris 1930, 16–21; R. Browning, *The Emperor Julian*, London 1975, 36.

[10] In the fourth century, Goths were commonly referred to as 'Scythians' (cf. Asterios of Amasea, *Homm.* IX. 12. 2; XIV. 11. 4 (Datema)). As Dr Augusto Guida has pointed out to me, Julian, who was well aware of the differences between the two races, must be using the word 'Scythian' in XII. 352a as a stylistic device. With the over-refined Antiochenes, whose life-style he finds incompatible with their Greek descent and *paideia*, the emperor contrasts a Scythian —the barbarian *par excellence*—to whom he owes his mastery of Hellenism. That Anacharsis the Scythian was a paragon of all Hellenic virtues is a *topos* of the Second Sophistic (cf. Diog. Laert. *V. Phil.* I. 102 ff.; Lucian, *Anacharsis*; the Letters of [Anacharsis] in *Epistolographi Graeci* (R. Hercher), Paris 1873, 102–5), which Julian did not disdain to use elsewhere (V. 269a). Indeed such references helped him to bring home the point that, though of barbarian descent himself, he had become the arbiter of Hellenism through his own efforts.

[11] XII. 351 ff.; cf. IV. 241c; V. 274d; VII. 235a; IX. 198a.

[12] Cf. the condemnation of this attitude by Plutarch as ridiculous, sterile and even dangerous, *Mor.* 814a–c. On this aspect of the psychology of late antique intellectuals, see E. L. Bowie, 'Greeks and their past in the Second Sophistic',

Never let the crowd of your playmates who flock to the theatres lead
you into the mistake of craving for such spectacles as these. Have you
a taste for horse races? There is one in Homer, very skilfully described. Take the book and study it. Do you hear them talking about
dances in pantomime? Leave them alone! Among the Phaeacians
the youths dance in more manly fashion. And for citharode you
have Phemius; for singer Demodocus. Indeed, there are in Homer
many plants more delightful to hear of than those we can see. *Yet
perhaps once in Delos, by the altar of Apollo, I did see the like, a young
shoot of a palm tree.* And the wooded island of Calypso and the caves
of Circe and the gardens of Alcinous . . . be assured that you will
never see anything more delightful than these. (XII. 351c–352a)

Himself indifferent to worldly pleasures and despising all the
tawdry honours attached to social position, Mardonius took
great care to shape his pupil's moral upbringing according to
his own beliefs and principles. His ambition was to make the
young prince able to appreciate the grandeur of simplicity.[13]
'My tutor taught me to keep my eyes fixed on the ground when
I was on my way to school' (XII. 351a). Julian cannot help
recalling with pride how the courtiers at Constantius' palace
in Milan were filled with shocked amusement at the sight of one
who 'did not walk like them, staring about me and strutting
along, but gazing on the ground as I had been trained by the
tutor who brought me up' (V. 274d). Slowly Mardonius infused
in Julian his own sober conservatism and impressed on him the
danger of adopting extreme attitudes, such as those professed
by certain Cynics of the fourth century.[14]

The far-reaching consequences of such a training can be
traced in Julian's 'unkingly' conduct,[15] for Mardonius' ideal
of Homeric simplicity took deep root in his pupil and should
be seen as the main factor accounting for Julian's inconsistent
behaviour, once he had fully developed his own imperial
theology. While he came spontaneously to evolve the theocratic
conception of kingship on which the Byzantine world rested,
his actions, reflecting his education, were never quite consistent
with his theory. This divergence between Julian's behaviour as

---

P&P xlvi (Feb. 1970), 3–41, and F. Millar, 'P. Herennius Dexippus: the Greek
world and the third-century invasions', *JRS* lix (1969), 12–29.
[13] V. 274d; XII. 351; Lib. XVIII. 11.
[14] IX. 198a; see below, pp. 129–30.
[15] See below, pp. 35, 79, 112–13.

a man nourished in the archaic and classical Greek tradition, and his ideology as a statesman was denounced by Ammianus and by the whole city of Antioch, while it caused both his contemporaries and modern scholars to misunderstand his notion of *imperium*.[16] Yet there was a time when Julian had not yet experienced any of these tensions, when he simply rejected all that was at variance with the spirit of his education.

This moment is caught in Ammianus' description of Julian's election to the rank of Caesar, an event that took place before the conviction that he was called to save the Roman empire had grown on the young prince. The highly disdainful manner in which he faced the situation reflects the particular training that he had received from Mardonius, and the particular way in which he had imbibed Homer and his ideal of simplicity. Any descendant of Constantine would have faced that moment as a turning-point in his existence, and would have lived to the full the ceremony, whose smallest details were rich in symbolic significance.[17] Not so Julian. When commenting later on this experience, he sums up the whole procedure in the manner of Marcus Aurelius, by using one contemptuous diminutive— χλανίδιον.[18] As for Ammianus, he describes at length all the ritual details, dwells upon the deep impression that the prince's eyes produced upon the soldiers and concludes by conveying Julian's attitude in the following words: 'When finally he was taken up to sit with the emperor in his carriage and conducted to the palace, he whispered this verse from the Homeric song: ἔλλαβε πορφύρεος θάνατος καὶ μοῖρα κραταιή, "the purple death and a mighty destiny have seized me" ' (XV. 8. 17).

At the heart of Julian's 'irreverent' attitude, Mardonius' influence can easily be detected. Julian came to understand Homer so well, and to grasp so fully the set of distinctive values that allows his universe to stand for all ages as a coherent and truthful cosmos, that even when faced with the possibility of death his mind instinctively had recourse to Homer in order to realize and express the situation. This is an extreme example

[16] See below, p. 35, p. 113 n. 132, p. 221.
[17] Cf. Constantius' attitude during his entry into Rome, as depicted by the same historian (XVI. 10) and Julian's disapproving comments on it (II. 129b–d). See also L. Warren Bonfante, 'Emperor, God and Man in the IV Century: Julian the Apostate and Ammianus Marcellinus', *PP* xix (1964), 410 n. 22.
[18] V. 277a, diminutive of χλανίς, *paludamentum*.

of what Homer meant to Julian: he really was the great educator according to whose precepts the prince fashioned his life, as had so many of the men of classical Greece.[19] That Julian absorbed the Homeric epic in the particular way he did is admittedly a circumstance for which Mardonius is not to be held solely responsible,[20] and the fact that Julian's mother, who turned out a fervent Christian,[21] had read the same texts with the same tutor provides an eloquent illustration of the potential ambivalences of a classical education in late antiquity. Mardonius doubtless started teaching his precocious pupil by reading Homer and Hesiod, asking him to memorize long passages, according to the custom of the age, and then analysing them grammatically, syntactically and stylistically.[22] Thus he acted unawares as Augustine's *ebrius doctor*[23] and it was here that Julian was trapped (as the Christians would have it), for he saw clearly that no merely aesthetic analysis could possibly be applied to a work as catholic as Homer's epic, which gives expression to a whole world with its politics, ethics, aesthetics and metaphysics. In the words of a great scholar:

It was the Christians who finally taught men to appraise poetry by a purely aesthetic standard—a standard which enabled them to reject most of the moral and religious teaching of the classical poets as false and ungodly, while accepting the formal elements in their work as instructive and aesthetically delightful ... But poetry cannot be really educative unless it is rooted in the depths of the human soul, unless it embodies a moral belief, a high ardour of the spirit, a broad and compelling ideal of humanity. And the greatest

---

[19] Plato, *Rep.* 606e.

[20] O. Seeck, *Geschichte des Untergangs der antiken Welt*, iv, Berlin 1911, 206, and F. Schemmel, 'Die Schulzeit des Kaisers Julian', *Philologus* lxxxii (1927), 459–60, even regard Mardonius as a Christian.

[21] Basilina bequeathed her large estates to the Church: see O. Seeck, *RE* iii. 98–9.

[22] On Julian's precociousness see Eunap. *V. Phil.* VII. 1. 7. For the role of the memory in education from the fourth century BC onwards, cf. Plato, *Leg.* 810e ff.; *Rep.* 486d: ἐπιλήσμονα ἄρα ψυχὴν ἐν ταῖς ἱκανῶς φιλοσόφοις μή ποτε ἐγκρίνωμεν, ἀλλὰ μνημονικὴν αὐτὴν ζητῶμεν δεῖν εἶναι; Philostratos, *V. Apoll.* II. 30, 41; III. 16, 43; Plut. *Mor.* 711c; *Pan. Lat.* II. 18. 3. Also H.-I. Marrou, *Histoire de l'éducation dans l'antiquité*, Paris 1965⁶, 251–2. For the great importance attached by the ancients to the faculty of memory, which ultimately constituted the attribute *par excellence* of the educated man and was considered to be the major factor in strengthening individual identity see Brown *Religion*, 133 and notes.

[23] See the famous passage from Augustine's *Conf.* I. 16.

of Greek poetry does more than show a cross-section of life taken at random. It tells the truth; but it chooses and presents its truth in accordance with a definite ideal.[24]

The subtler among the Christians tried to dissociate this truth from its ideal, then to substitute for the latter examples drawn from the field of Christian teaching. Yet the number of scholars who have been able to see through this process is distressingly small. The myth propagated by official Byzantium, that its baroque Hellenism was animated by the breath of classical Greece, is still much more appealing than the sober truth, in whose light Byzantium appears as the systematic persecutor of the spirit of Hellenism. For the standard policy of the Eastern empire towards Hellenism adopted all the techniques of *the letter that killeth*. The honest warning of John Chrysostom, that the price of a cultivated mind was for the Christian the loss of his soul,[25] was a dangerous precept for the Greek-speaking empire to espouse; the road of compromise was far safer, and cunning men like Basil of Caesarea, Socrates Scholasticus and Theodoret of Cyrrhus duly set about the task of ensuring a place in the Byzantine intellectual firmament for the ghosts of the classical authors. Their Bible might have been Basil's Πρὸς τοὺς Νέους, a homily on the dangers of the classics and on the ways Christians could circumvent them, either by interpreting the poets in the light of the Scriptures, or by censoring them.[26]

Unlike Basil's ideal teacher, Mardonius was a man who had grasped to the full the spirit of the Homeric epic and had felt very strongly the attraction of the poet's universe. The furtive glimpse into Mardonius' understanding of Homer which his exhortations to his pupil allow us leaves no doubt that he would have whole-heartedly agreed with Macaulay's pronouncement on the *Iliad* and the *Odyssey*: 'having survived ten thousand capricious fashions, having seen successive codes of criticism become obsolete, they still remain to us, immortal with the immortality of truth, the same when perused in the study of an English scholar, as when they were first chanted at the banquets of the Ionian princes.' Through his teaching Mardonius transmitted

---

[24] W. Jaeger, *Paideia: The Ideals of Greek Culture* i, Oxford 1939, 35–6.

[25] See above, p. 1.

[26] Cf. Marrou, op. cit. 462; Lemerle, *Le Premier Humanisme byzantin*, 45. See also above, p. 10.

to Julian his own religious reverence for the world of
Homer.[27] That was possibly the first expression of truth and
beauty with which the child came in contact; he then saw how
everything in the epic—gods, moral and aesthetic values, social
conditions, landscapes and colours—were fused together to
create a complete human world.

Indeed it was only thanks to this deeply felt sense of the unity
and completeness of the Homeric universe that Julian could
begin to feel a person; by a clear—if unconscious—process,
which we can trace stage by stage, he began to absorb himself
in a world that was in no danger of collapsing overnight, a
world in which there was no room for the absurd. Death itself,
moral and physical pain and emotional disturbance were here
explicable in terms of divine justice. Whenever in later life
clouds gathered in the sky above his head, Julian knew where to
seek a patch of sunshine. When as Caesar he was treacherously
deprived of a close friend and collaborator, he wrote a self-
consolation in which he identified with the most subtle of the
Homeric heroes, Odysseus:—οἰώθη δ᾽ ᾽Οδυσσεύς, 'and Odysseus
was left alone'[28]—and through this game he managed to overcome depression, bolster his courage and stand up again to face
the tempests that were to come.[29] The 'drug of forgetfulness'
for which he had searched at the moment of separation from
his friend was to be found in the profoundly reassuring world of
Homer. It comes as no surprise at all to the reader that as the
Self-consolation on the Departure of the Excellent Salutius progresses,
the tone becomes more optimistic and the Homeric quotations
begin to convey hope. Thus the last words of this therapeutic
text are words of joy: they reproduce the warm greeting that
Odysseus received once he was restored to his hearth,[30] even
though the implication of the very last line is that the beloved
friend would have to go through the realm of Hades before he
is restored to Julian and his own homeland.[31]

It is in this same text that we find a most moving passage on
the bond of love and gratitude that united Julian with the man

[27] For the influence of the παιδαγωγός on the formation of his pupils' ἦθος
see Plut. *Mor.* 439 f.
[28] IV. 241d and Hom. *Il.* Λ 401.
[29] See below, p. 70.
[30] IV. 252d and Hom. *Od.* ω 402.
[31] Hom. *Od.* κ 562.

to whom he owed the discovery of the Homeric world: 'When I put myself to trial to find out how I am and will be affected by your departure,' says Julian to Salutius, 'I felt the same anguish as when I first left my tutor at home' (IV. 241c). It must have been a cruel blow for him when in 342 the imperial order came that he was to be transferred to a castle in mountainous Cappadocia.[32] At the age of eleven Julian had to give up for the second time in his life all that was dear and familiar to him: Mardonius, his maternal grandmother, whom he was never to see again, and the charming villa this lady owned near the Bithynian coast, where the child spent many a summer holiday. 'In its profound calm one can lie down and read a book while from time to time resting one's eyes on the delightful spectacle of the ships and the sea. As a boy I used to think that this small estate was the most lovely summer place there is.'[33] The memory of this boyish happiness must have remained with the old lady: when she died she left her estate to Julian. But almost ten years had to pass before the prince could return to this enchanting place. For the time being the gentleness of Bithynia had to be exchanged for the harshness of Cappadocia. And the brutality with which he was taken away left a lasting impression on Julian:

Dragging me from the schools when I was still a mere boy and summoning my brother from his exile . . . they imprisoned us in a certain farm in Cappadocia; and they allowed no one to come near us. How shall I describe here the six years we spent in the estate of a stranger, being watched like those kept in the 'Persian castles', while no stranger came to see us and not one of our own friends was allowed to visit us; so that we lived shut off from every liberal study and from all free intercourse, in a glittering servitude, and sharing the exercises of our slaves as though they were comrades. For no companion of our own age was ever allowed to come near us. (V. 271b-d)

In the 'castle of oblivion',[34] where Julian spent all the period

---

[32] Macellum, described by Julian as ἀγρός τις (V. 271b). On the topography of Macellum, see A. Hadjinicolaou, 'Macellum, lieu d'exil de l'empereur Julien', *Byzantion* xxi (1951), 15-22.

[33] *ep.* 4. 427c.

[34] In the passage quoted above (V. 271c), Julian compares Macellum to the 'castles of oblivion' where the Persians kept their illustrious prisoners; cf. Procopius, *De Bello Persico* I. 5. 7.

of his adolescence absolutely cut off from any human company
except for that of his unsubtle brother,[35] the one thing that
really depressed him was the lack of intellectual stimulus,
aggravated by the total absence of even elementary freedom
and by the imposition on him of studies and practices fundamentally alien in spirit to those with which he had become
familiar in his reading of Homer.

In the opening page of the *Hymn to King Helios* we have a
glimpse of the state of mind of the solitary adolescent as he
struggled hard to find his identity. Deprived of friends, good
masters and books, and haunted by a very real fear for his life,
instead of abandoning himself to depression or developing a
cynical outlook on life, like his brother Gallus,[36] Julian simply
turned inwards and, with his intuitive gift, tried hard to discover
the norms of the good life.[37] He pursued knowledge through the
most oblique and even dangerous paths,[38] and the demon of the
absolute—for he was born a perfectionist—urged him to claim
from the surrounding cosmos, in the absence of anyone to
instruct him, the answer to the questions with which his unquiet
nature tormented him. Thus he came to perceive that there was
such a discipline as astrology, akin both to theology and to
philosophy, in whose principles one could indeed find some
explanation and even solution of the fundamental mysteries of
being (XI. 131a).[39] He felt that, incontestably, the immense and
apparently impersonal cosmos was a world both more friendly

[35] Julian felt genuine pity for his half-brother, who turned out a complete brute;
cf. Amm. XIV. 1. 10; XIV. 7; XIV. 11. 28. Significantly enough, the only
reason that Julian suggests for Gallus' criminal behaviour is his lack of an appropriate education (V. 271d–272a); cf. Libanius XII. 35.

[36] On Gallus' cynicism and cruelty, see Amm. locc. citt.

[37] V. 271d–272a.

[38] As, e.g., borrowing profane books from the library of George of Cappadocia,
later bishop of Alexandria; see *epp.* 106. 411c; 107. 378bc.

[39] As A. D. Nock has pointed out, 'Conversion and Adolescence', *Essays on
Religion and the Ancient World* (ed. Z. Stewart), Oxford 1972, 469–80, esp. p. 478,
the contemplation of nature was one of the ways leading to religious conversion
in antiquity. Cf. Lucretius, *De rer. nat.* V. 1204 ff. For the continuity of this
attitude, see the comments that Demetrius Ralles Kabakes, a fervent adept of
the Platonic School of Mistra in the fifteenth century, wrote in the margin of the
opening page of the *Hymn to King Helios*—in the copyist's picturesque spelling
and construction the scholium reads: μάρτυς μου ἐστιν ἥλιος ὅτι καὶ πρός
με τιούτος πόθος συνέβη οὔπο μὴ ιζʹ ἐτῶν ὄντα καὶ μηδὲ παρά τινος
ἀκείκωα τὸ τηχὸν πρὸς αὐτῷ τοῦτο, in J. Bidez, *La Tradition manuscrite et
les éditions des discours de l'empereur Julien*, Gand–Paris 1929, 78.

and more truthful than the one in which he had been brought up, and in which, with the single exception of a short interval due to Mardonius' consoling presence,[40] he had experienced only isolation, caused either by death or some less radical form of parting.

His need for love and communication and his thirst for knowledge were thus fused into that δεινὸς πόθος for the rays of the Sun of which he later writes:

From my childhood an extraordinary longing for the rays of the god penetrated deep into my soul; and from my earliest years my mind was so completely swayed by the light that illumines the heavens that not only did I desire to gaze intently at the sun, but whenever I walked abroad in the night season, when the firmament was clear and cloudless, I abandoned all else without exception and gave myself up to the beauties of the heavens; nor did I understand what anyone might say to me, nor heed what I was doing myself. (XI. 130cd)

But such moments of blissful forgetfulness, when a sense of a freedom greater than can be granted by man to man overwhelmed Julian, were comparatively few. During his stay at Macellum the prince was entrusted to the care of a new tutor, George of Cappadocia, later bishop of Alexandria, from whom he acquired the precise knowledge of Christianity that is reflected in his polemical treatise against the Galileans; yet nowhere in Julian's writings is George acknowledged as his master. Indeed one of the few references to him is due to the purely fortuitous circumstance that he possessed a considerable library which Julian wished to inherit after his death.[41] Otherwise, his cruel murder on 24 December 361 at the hands of the pagan mob of Alexandria[42] not only fails to bring a word of

---

[40] Julian never ceased to acknowledge his deep gratitude to Mardonius, and that not only verbally. We know from Libanius that 'the old man' was frequently the emperor's guest at dinner during Julian's residence in Constantinople: ἑνός γέ τινος γέροντος καὶ συνδειπνοῦντος καὶ τούτου γε τοῦ γέροντος ἀρετῆς τε ἐπιμελουμένου τῆς ἄλλης (LII. 21). Förster was the first to identify this γέρων with Mardonius (see the index of his edition of Libanius); this is indirectly confirmed by Julian himself, οὐδὲ γὰρ ἐπαιδοτριβήθης καλῶς οὐδὲ ἔτυχες καθηγεμόνος, ὁποίου περὶ τοὺς ποιητὰς ἐγὼ τουτουὶ τοῦ φιλοσόφου, since the pronoun οὑτοσί at VII. 235a (οὐδὲ . . . φιλοσόφου) must refer to Mardonius, who taught Julian the poets, and indicates that he was present at the lecture that his imperial pupil gave to answer the provocation of the Cynic Heracleius.

[41] *epp.* 106; 107; see above, p. 22 n. 38.

[42] Cf. the discussion of the identity of George's murderers by Sozomen, V. 7. 4 ff. On the possible motives for George's murder, see Epiphanius, *Pan. Haer.* 76. 1.

B

compassion to the lips of his old pupil, but inspires the following imaginary exchange between Julian and the bishop's murderers:

But now, by the gods, though I wish to praise you, I cannot, because you have broken the law. Your citizens dare to tear a human being into pieces as dogs tear a wolf, and then are not ashamed to lift to the gods those hands still dripping with blood! But, you will say, George deserved to be treated in this fashion.—Granted, and I might even admit that he deserved even worse and more cruel treatment.—Yes, you will say, and on your account.—To this too I agree; but if you say by your hands, I no longer agree. For you have laws which ought by all means to be honoured and cherished by you all individually (*ep*. 60. 379d–380b).[43]

If one reads Ammianus' account of the life and career of George of Cappadocia, one may understand Julian's feelings: George was an opportunist who profited from the ruin of many people. He made a career for himself under Constantius by embracing Arianism and, especially, by acting as an informer.[44] Such a man was certainly not the tutor to inspire Julian with confidence in, still less respect for, the teachings of Christianity. It is hardly surprising that, during the period of his sojourn at Macellum, Julian never faced Christianity otherwise than in a lukewarm manner. The antipathy he felt towards his teacher, and his resulting indifference to whatever George taught him or asked him to do, led Julian to seek and realize his moments of spiritual exaltation in a sphere from which all Christian notions were excluded.

It is not possible for us to say which were the elements in Christianity to which Julian objected at this age. From his later writings, and especially from the fragments of his *Contra Galilaeos*, it becomes apparent that he ultimately rejected the whole of the doctrinal foundation of Christianity, yet this happened only once he had formulated his own philosophical system. At this early period, it should be remembered, Julian had not yet even discovered that there was such a discipline as philosophy. Neither a fervent convert nor consciously anti-Christian, Julian was still only fumbling, and the confused way

---

[43] Here, exceptionally, I follow the text of W. C. Wright, to whom I also owe the translation.

[44] Amm. XXII. 11. 5 ff.; see also Gibbon, *The Decline and Fall of the Roman Empire* (ed. J. B. Bury), ii, London 1909, 498.

in which he conceived at that stage the as yet vague and unformulated notions that were subsequently incorporated into
his religious credo kept him quite unaware of the incompatibility
between the two religions, neither of which he had yet consciously embraced. He had only some indications, based on
some obscure intuition, which pointed out the way that he was
to follow; they were enough to prevent him from committing
himself to Christianity, but not clear enough to engender any
conflict in his soul. Even later, he was never to experience the
psychological tension to which men like Augustine and
Gregory of Nazianzos were continuously subject. He baldly
states the fact that till his twentieth year he walked in the road
of Christianity (*ep.* 111. 434d), but adds no expression of
contrition, guilt or repentance, as would have been the case
with a man of Julian's fanatical nature had he felt that he had
consciously erred.

The other two instances when Julian refers to his ignorance
of what he considered to be the right path strengthen the hypothesis that he had been only nominally a Christian. The first
appears at the end of the crucial passage where Julian speaks of
his spiritual anxieties at Macellum, and describes his pantheistic
exaltation (XI. 131a); when he says: 'let that darkness be
buried in oblivion', he refers, as is quite clear from the context,
to his ignorance at that period of the right path, rather than to
his attachment to the Christian faith. In the second passage,
also from a dogmatic writing, the *Hymn to the Mother of the Gods*,
Julian uses exactly the same phraseology when thanking Cybele
for not having disregarded him when he was wandering in the
darkness (VIII. 174c), and proceeds to clarify what he actually
means by the word 'darkness': far from indicating any conscious
rejection of the right way to salvation (as would have been the
case if Julian were at that stage 'der leidenschaftlich Christ'
that Schemmel and Bidez claim),[45] it refers to the existence of
some 'superfluous and vain elements in the irrational impulses
and motions of my soul' (VIII. 174c), of which the gods helped
him to purify himself.

If Julian's own writings suggest that he did not at any point
embrace Christianity fervently, it is necessary to examine our
other sources now, bearing in mind the problem of the prince's

[45] Schemmel, art. cit. 459–60; Bidez, *Vie*, 32–4.

alleged apostasy. Ammianus states bluntly that Julian 'quam-
quam a rudimentis pueritiae primis inclinatior erat erga
numinum cultum, *paulatimque adulescens, desiderio rei flagrabat*'
(XXII. 5. 1), while all Christian writers speak of his genuine
attachment to Christianity over the period of his adolescence.
Gregory of Nazianzos wonders how a man, who in his extreme
youth had been a reader in the Church, and who had honoured
the martyrs by the performance of pious works and the construction of altars, could have thus changed beyond all recognition.[46]
The notion that Julian was an apostate in the essential rather
than the formal sense of the word is an important theme in the
account of Socrates, who speaks of him as of one who at some
point in his early twenties exchanged his genuine fervour for
Christianity for an attitude of pretence[47]. Sozomen, following
Socrates, likewise declares that it was at a relatively mature age
that Julian abandoned the faith in which he had been brought
up in favour of the teachings of the Neoplatonists.[48] In illustration of this argument, Gregory and Sozomen both retail an
interesting anecdote from Julian's early life. Gallus and Julian,
they say, started building a small monument on the tomb of
St. Mamas in Cappadocia[49]; but, while Gallus' work progressed
satisfactorily, Julian's every attempt came to nothing. The
conclusion that both authors draw from this episode—in
apparent contradiction of their fundamental argument—is that
Julian, even at that stage, had no faith. Yet this is only a passing
note. The view that Julian was a sincere devotee of Christianity
during his adolescence appealed even to Libanius, who describes the prince's 'conversion' to Hellenism as a moment of
grace.[50] This romantic image of a Julian, counterpart of St
Paul experiencing illumination on the road to Damascus,[51] and
becoming a fervent adept of Hellenism after having been its
passionate persecutor, is exactly the kind of cliché to which
every religious propagandist has inevitable recourse. It is only

---

[46] Greg. Naz. *or.* IV. 97.

[47] Socrates, III. 1. 19.

[48] Soz. V. 2. 5.

[49] Greg. Naz. *or* IV. 24–6; Soz. V. 2. 12–14.

[50] Lib. XII. 34; XIII. 11: τὸ σφοδρὸν μῖσος κατὰ τῶν θεῶν ἐπέσχες ὑπὸ
τῶν μαντευμάτων ἡμερούμενος; id. XVIII. 18.

[51] For the parallel, see Bidez, *Vie,* 60; for a more realistic view, Browning,
Julian, 44–5.

curious that modern critics should fall into the trap and continue to see Julian's 'conversion' in such terms.[52]

It is not the problem of Julian's formal Christianity that is here at stake; whether he was baptized or not is not a question of essence.[53] What is important for the understanding of his subsequent development is to know if Julian had, over the years of his youth, undergone a religious conversion in the sense in which Justin the Martyr did, and a more intimate acquaintance with his writings rules out this possibility, suggesting instead that in the religious sphere Julian walked along a relatively straight, if ascending, path till, in his twentieth year, he was gratified with an at once essential and formal initiation in the mysteries of the spiritual life.

In 348 Gallus was suddenly ordered to leave Macellum and present himself at Court.[54] Julian, of whose fate the imperial order said nothing, seized the opportunity and, interpreting silence as consent, terminated his exile too, either at the same time as his brother or shortly afterwards.[55] He then moved to Constantinople.[56]

In the city of his birth, towards which he never missed an opportunity of expressing his emotional attachment,[57] Julian returned to study rhetoric. His main masters were the pagan Nicocles and the Christian Hecebolius, about both of whom we know a good deal.[58]

'A priest of justice, the prince of education, knowing, if any did, the innermost secrets of Homer's mind and of all the choir around Homer',[59] such was the man who succeeded Mardonius as Julian's spiritual guide. Nicocles could aspire to the title of τὸ τῶν Ἑλλήνων ὄφελος[60] in a double sense: not only as one of the most distinguished grammarians of the fourth century, but

---

[52] As, e.g., Nock, 'Conversion and Adolescence', *Essays*, 476.

[53] Gregory of Nazianzos for one seems to think that Julian was a baptized Christian, *or.* IV. 52.

[54] V. 271d–272a. For the chronology see W. Koch, 'Comment l'empereur Julien tâcha de fonder une église païenne', *RBPh* vi (1927), 140–1.

[55] Amm. XV. 2. 7.

[56] Baynes, art. cit. 251.

[57] See below, p. 108.

[58] Socr. III. 1. 10; Lib. XV. 27; XVIII. 12; etc.

[59] Lib. XV. 27.

[60] Lib. *ep.* 1211. 2.

also as a man of exemplary morality, a trait which could hardly
have failed to leave Julian untouched. A deeply learned man
and a gifted teacher,[61] a fervent and sincere follower of the
Hellenic faith,[62] Nicocles was also among those very few who,
after Julian's death, dared to mourn his loss publicly, in contrast
with Libanius who, congratulating him for the courage that he
displayed, feels the need to make an apology for the 'sensible'
attitude that he himself had adopted.[63]

If it was Nicocles who introduced Julian to the allegorical
interpretation of Homer, thus bringing him dangerously close
to the doctrines of the Neoplatonists, it was Hecebolius—a
character much ridiculed in our sources[64]—who taught him
rhetoric. Hecebolius' chameleon-like attitude to moral and
religious matters, fluctuating according to the several changes of
official religious policy in the mid-fourth century, is highly
characteristic of the general ideological climate of an era about
which we are accustomed to think, somewhat unsubtly, in
terms of mighty conflicts. Yet between fourth-century paganism
and Christianity there existed an extensive no-man's-land where
intellectuals could easily be trapped. Hecebolius does not provide the only example of such an attitude among Julian's
acquaintances. Pegasius' career as bishop of Ilion under
Constantius, and as a member of Julian's pagan clergy subsequently, is an analogous and far more interesting case, since he
managed to convince both parties of the genuineness of his
beliefs (*ep.* 79). Likewise, Synesius, bishop of Cyrene, Themistius, the official panegyrist of all the emperors between Constantius and Theodosius, and Palladas, the last pagan Greek poet,[65]
were all powerful and complex figures, who stood mid-way
between Hellenism and Christianity, and adopted elements from
both thought-worlds. Often their allegiance to either camp went

[61] Lib. *epp.* 810. 7; 1210; 1211; 1383. 5; 1487. 1.
[62] Lib. *epp.* 1196, 1211.
[63] Lib. *ep.* 1487. 2: ἔδειξας δὲ τὴν σαυτοῦ φιλοσοφίαν, εὖ τε φερόμενος καὶ
μεταπεσόντος τοῦ πνεύματος, οὔτε τότε ὁρμήσας ἐπὶ πλοῦτον οὐ καλόν,
τὸν χειμῶνά τε ἐνεγκὼν ἀνδρείως.
[64] See, e.g., Socr. III. 13. 5: τοῖς ἤθεσι τῶν βασιλέων ἑπόμενος, ἐπὶ μὲν
Κωνσταντίου διαπύρως χριστιανίζειν ὑπεκρίνατο· ἐπὶ δὲ Ἰουλιανοῦ γοργὸς
Ἕλλην ἐφαίνετο.
[65] On Palladas' 'Christianity', see C. M. Bowra, 'Palladas and the converted
Olympians', *ByzZ.* liii (1960), 1–7; also Alan Cameron, 'Palladas and Christian
Polemic', *JRS* lv (1965), 17–30.

only as far as the label that they had chosen for reasons of social convenience. Other less conspicuous personages, endowed with a lesser sense of diplomacy, failed to understand the importance of sticking to a label; and, realizing that they moved in a limbo-area, they felt that declaring themselves as pagans or Christians was a mere formality conditioned by the needs of the moment.

Both Hecebolius' ambivalent character and the shallowness of the discipline that he taught must have failed to appeal to Julian, who nowhere in his writings acknowledges the man who became a fervent adept of Hellenism as soon as his pupil was proclaimed emperor.[66] But we may perhaps detect a reference to him in the passage in which Julian deplores the manner of the utterly ignorant rhetors:

They, because they have nothing to say and cannot invent anything from the matter in hand, are always dragging in Delos and Leto with her children, and then 'swans singing their shrill song and the trees that echo them', and 'dewy meadows full of soft, deep grass', and the 'scent of flowers', and the 'season of spring', and other figures of the same sort. When did Isocrates ever do this in his panegyrics? Or when did anyone of those ancient writers who were genuine votaries of the Muses, and not like the writers of today?[67]

It is easy to grasp on what grounds Julian makes the antithesis. Just as in Homer he had perceived the essence of things below the harmonious rhythm of lines, so when he read the great orators with Nicocles and even Hecebolius,[68] he realized that Attic rhetoric was for ever associated with specific political and cultural circumstances, and was not to be fully appreciated unless one went mentally and emotionally through the conflicts to which it owed its immediate genesis and *raison d'être*. When, later, Julian promulgated a series of laws aimed at the restoration of the *curiae*,[69] his vision of an empire in which individual cities would more or less return to the ancient condition of city-states owed something to the deep impression that Attic rhetoric, linked for ever with the Athens of the fourth century BC, had exerted on his mind.

---

[66] *ep.* 194 (*ELF*, pp. 263–5), addressed to the sophist Hecebolius, is spurious; see F. Cumont, *Sur l'authenticité de quelques lettres de Julien*, 12 ff.

[67] VII. 236ab; cf. II. 126c ff.; III. 52cd, 78cd; *ep.* 61. 422a; etc. See also Themistius, 336c.

[68] Lib. XV. 28.

[69] See below, pp. 103 ff.

Yet, however exclusively Julian may have been devoted to his studies, his presence in the imperial capital, where, without his even realizing it, he was gaining much popularity, did not cease to be a major cause of suspicion.[70] 'How gladly I would retail the long story of the toil and terrors that friends and kinsmen hung over my head just as I was about to embark on the study of philosophy; but you know it all only too well' (VI. 259bc), Julian wrote to Themistius when all the dangers had faded into reminiscences. Like so many other highly sensitive beings, Julian seems to have derived a kind of morbid pleasure and even pride from recounting the story of his past miseries. His misfortune was that more often than not he chose the wrong audience for this kind of confidence.[71] But we should never forget that this heart, which now Julian opened with such extraordinary *sans-gêne* before an uncomprehending crowd, had over its most tender years been the lonely witness of impossible griefs and agonies.

It is only thanks to his belated confession to Themistius that we can form some faint idea of the close surveillance over Julian during his stay in Constantinople, until in 351 Diocletian's capital, where intellectual life was flourishing on a smaller scale than in the imperial city, but in a less controlled manner,[72] was chosen for a second time as the prince's residence.

Nicomedia marked the great turning-point in Julian's education, for there, at the age of twenty,[73] he first came into contact with Neoplatonism. Libanius himself was in Nicomedia at that time, and the fact that Julian had received strict orders not to follow his lectures, naturally induced him to try to find some 'oblique way'[74] of circumventing the prohibition that Hecebolius' professional jealousy had imposed on him. By tipping a student, he received copies of the notes taken at Libanius' lectures.[75] But that was the least of things forbidden in which Julian was to indulge during his stay in Nicomedia. From

---

[70] Lib. XVIII. 13; XIII. 10; Soz. V. 2. 15.

[71] The most unfortunate example of this tendency is the *Misopogon*, in which Julian reveals intimate secrets to an unsympathetic crowd.

[72] Lib. XIII. 11.

[73] *ep.* 111. 434d.

[74] Lib. XVIII. 15.

[75] Lib. XVIII. 13–15; Socr. III. 1. 15.

Libanius, who is careful to draw the distinction between rhetoric and philosophy,[76] we know that Julian, coming for the first time into close contact with the latter discipline in Nicomedia, was able at last to understand clearly where his salvation lay: Hellenism, that affluent and mysterious current, was to take him straight to the goal of his existence. 'A spark of divination (μαντική), which had escaped the attention of the impious, was still glimmering in Nicomedia' in the mid-fourth century.[77] This statement of Libanius is confirmed by Gregory of Nazianzos who, in his desire to discredit μαντική, uses the word γοητεία[78]—the term for common witchcraft, and even black magic.[79]

For the adepts of Iamblichan Neoplatonism μαντική was not simply an art or science which could be studied and mastered by any reasonably intelligent human being; it was a god-sent gift, an innate virtue of the prophetic soul.[80] Of this rare talent, which not only allowed man to foresee the future, but ultimately enabled him to achieve union with God,[81] Iamblichus speaks at length. The whole of Book III of the *De Mysteriis* is consecrated to the definition of μαντική and the description of its varieties and their characteristics, while a considerable part of Book X expounds and praises the benevolent effects of divination, which is closely linked and often identified with theurgy.[82]

Yet the divine Iamblichus did not succeed in infecting all his pupils with his own enthusiasm for the arcane disciplines that he taught and practised. There were those in his circle who, after pursuing their studies under the great master, went on expounding the sober system put forward by Plotinus. One of

---

[76] Lib. XII. 30.
[77] Lib. XIII. 11.
[78] Greg. Naz. *or.* IV. 31.
[79] To describe philosophers as γόητες was a common slander in late antiquity; cf. IX. 197d for Julian's recognition of the fact. On the distinction between γοητεία and μαντική, see Iambl. *Myst.* III. 25; Nicephorus Gregoras, *Explicatio in librum Synesii De Insomniis*: PG 149. 542: ἄλλο ἐστὶ γοητεία καὶ ἄλλο μαγεία καὶ ἄλλο φαρμακεία. Cf. Lewy, *Chaldaean Oracles*, 285–7.
[80] See XI. 131b; Iambl. *Myst.* III. 1: οὐδ' ὅλως ἀνθρωπικόν ἐστι τὸ ἔργον, θεῖον δὲ καὶ ὑπερφυὲς ἄνωθέν τε ἀπὸ τοῦ οὐρανοῦ καταπεμπόμενον, ἀγέννητόν τε καὶ ἀΐδιον αὐτοφυῶς προηγεῖται.
[81] *Myst.* X. 4: μόνη τοίνυν ἡ θεία μαντικὴ συναπτομένη τοῖς θεοῖς ὡς ἀληθῶς ἡμῖν τῆς θείας ζωῆς μεταδίδωσι, τῆς τε προγνώσεως καὶ τῶν θείων νοήσεων μετέχουσα καὶ ἡμᾶς θείους ὡς ἀληθῶς ἀπεργάζεται.
[82] *Myst.* X. 4, 8; cf. III. 31.

them was the Cappadocian Aedesius—the successor of Iamblichus as the head of the Neoplatonic School—whose lecture-
room in Pergamon was attended by pupils from Greece and all
western Asia Minor so that 'his fame touched the stars'.[83]
Aedesius' reputation duly reached Julian in Nicomedia, where
he had already mixed with the local circle of philosophers.[84]
'Following on the report of the wisdom of Aedesius, Julian
came to Pergamon',[85] and meeting the famous master, he was
so struck by his personality that he clung to him, 'longing to
drink down learning open-mouthed and at a gulp', and displaying so insatiable a thirst for knowledge that some thought
he had been bitten by a poisonous snake.[86]

This was the first proper contact Julian had with Neoplatonism. His response to it at once reveals his passionate and
fanatical nature, and helps us to evaluate the importance of
Neoplatonism in the formation of his character. Aedesius was
a very old man,[87] and the devotion of a pupil as *exalté* as Julian
naturally tired him. He tried to put this across to his enthusiastic student, but Julian refused to understand. So one day
Aedesius called him and told him plainly that it would be
better for both if Julian were to follow the lessons of 'his own
genuine sons' Eusebius of Myndos and Chrysanthius of Sardis.[88]
As Julian was soon to discover, the two men had complementary frames of mind. While Eusebius was an adept of dialectical
philosophy, believing in the power of λόγος, Chrysanthius was
a man cast in the Iamblichan mould with a passion for theurgy
and divination.[89] True to his beliefs, Eusebius never failed to
conclude his discourses with the same stereotyped sentence:
'Only dialectic discussion can lead to the discovery of true
being. As for the tricks which charm and delude the senses,
they are the work of miracle-mongers, insane men who have

---

[83] Aedesius: pupil of Iamblichus, Eunap. *V. Phil.* V. 1. 5; adept of discursive
Neoplatonism, ibid. VI. 1. 4: μικρὸν ἀποδέων ᾿Ιαμβλίχου, πλὴν ὅσα γε εἰς
θειασμὸν ᾿Ιαμβλίχου φέρει; settled in Pergamon in Mysia, ibid. VI. 4. 7; successor of Iamblichus, ibid. VI. 1. 1: ἐκδέχεται δὲ τὴν ᾿Ιαμβλίχου διατριβὴν καὶ
ὁμιλίαν ἐς τοὺς ἑταίρους Αἰδέσιος ὁ ἐκ Καππαδοκίας.

[84] Lib. XIII. 11.

[85] Eunap. *V. Phil.* VII. 1. 9.

[86] Ibid. VII. 1. 11.

[87] Ibid. VII. 1. 10: εἰς μακρόν τι γῆρας ἀφῖκτο, καὶ τὸ σῶμα ἔκαμνε.

[88] Ibid. VII. 1. 12–14.

[89] Ibid. VII. 2. 1.

been led astray by material powers' (Eunap. *V. Phil.* VII. 2. 3). Julian's curiosity was increased by these words, and he was quick to ask for an explanation of their meaning.

'Maximus', Eusebius replied, 'is one of the oldest and most learned students, who, on account of his exceptional intelligence and super-abundant eloquence, scorned all logical proof in these matters and impetuously resorted to the acts of a madman. Not long since, he invited us to the temple of Hecate and summoned many witnesses of his folly. When we had arrived there and had saluted the goddess, he said: "Be seated, my well-beloved friends, and observe what shall come to pass, and whether I differ in anything from common humanity." When he had said this, and we had all sat down, he burnt a grain of incense and recited to himself the whole of some hymn or other; then he reached such a point in showing off that the statue of the goddess first began to smile, then even seemed to laugh aloud. We were all much disturbed by this sight, but he said: "let none of you be terrified by these things, for presently even the torches which the goddess holds in her hands shall kindle into flame." And before he could finish speaking the torches burst into a blaze of light. Now for the moment we came away amazed by that histrionic miracle-worker. But you must not marvel at any of these things, even as I marvel not, but rather believe that the thing of the highest importance is that purification of the soul attained through reason.' (Eunap. *V. Phil.* VII. 2. 6–11)

Eusebius' words had the opposite effect to that intended. Deeply impressed by his description of Maximus, Julian declared, as Plotinus had of Ammonius Saccas,[90] that he had at last dis-covered the man for whom he had been searching, and, taking leave of Chrysanthius, he rushed to Ephesus to meet him.[91]

When later, in his attempt to organize the pagan clergy, Julian sought to express his ideal of the philosopher-priest, he envisaged a man of supernatural virtues, endowed with γνῶσις and invested with the δύναμις that flowed from it.[92] This ideal had its theoretical basis in Iamblichus' portrait of the ἐπιστήμων θεουργός,[93] so fully described in the *De Mysteriis* and exemplified

[90] Porph. *V. Plot.* 3.
[91] Eunap. *V. Phil.* VII. 2. 12.
[92] Iambl. *Myst.* VI. 6: δύναμιν διὰ τὴν πρὸς θεοὺς ἕνωσιν ἣν παρέσχηκεν αὐτῷ τῶν ἀπορρήτων συμβόλων ἡ γνῶσις. See below, p. 182.
[93] See Iambl. *Myst.* III. 18; VII. 4.

by the master of Apamea in his aretalogy of Pythagoras.[94] But the men whose example inspired Julian in his undertaking were primarily Maximus and Chrysanthius. The latter was to occupy one of the highest posts in his pagan *ecclesia*,[95] while Maximus was raised to the spiritual office of καθηγεμών.[96]

To Julian's mind Maximus was 'the most outstanding man [he] ever met' (VII. 235ab). Above all he was the healer of his soul, the spiritual physician who had extirpated folly and arrogance—τὸ μανιῶδες καὶ θρασύ (VII. 235b)—from the prince's intemperate heart, by injecting into it a potent dose of σωφροσύνη, a job all the more difficult, as Julian himself recognized, because the pupil had felt himself 'armed with all the external advantages that birth and society can confer' (VII. 235b).

Admiration, respect, gratitude and human tenderness were soon to be fused into the fervour of a love not unworthy of the name of ἔρως. And soon the pupil came to experience for the sake of Maximus all the poignant torments that are the lot of those who love; during his campaign against Constantius, Julian's thoughts will dwell constantly on Maximus: 'I call Zeus, great Helios, mighty Athene and all the gods and goddesses to witness how on my way down to Illyricum I trembled for you. And I kept enquiring of the gods—not that I ventured to do this myself, for I could not endure to see or hear anything so terrible as one might have supposed would be happening to you at that time, but I entrusted the task to others' (*ep.* 26. 415ab). Julian will also confess how once in Gaul his inner obsession with Maximus deluded him into mistaking for his master a traveller wearing the philosopher's cloak. But, though deprived of his presence, Julian had at least the consolation of a regular correspondence with his καθηγεμών during his years in Gaul.[97] When at last in 361 the period of uncertainty was over,

---

[94] See below, pp. 125–6.

[95] Eunap. *V. Phil.* XXIII. 2. 7: τὴν ἀρχιερωσύνην τοῦ παντὸς ἔθνους λαβών. For Julian's dependence on Chrysanthius, ibid. VII. 4. 4 ff.

[96] *ep.* 89b. 298b; on καθηγεμών as the divinely inspired spiritual guide of a person or community, and often as the god himself, see IX. 202d; also the entry καθηγεμών in H. G. Liddell–R. Scott, *A Greek–English Lexicon*, Oxford 1940⁹, suppl. 1968. For an interesting parallel, see Masai, *Pléthon*, 307: Cardinal Bessarion, in the letter of condolence he sent to the sons of Pletho, calls their father the common καθηγεμών of them all. See below, p. 185 n. 93.

[97] *ep.* 26. 414b.

and overnight Julian became the sole and incontestable ruler of the empire, he could no longer master his emotion as he wrote to Maximus: 'everything crowds into my mind at once and chokes my utterance, as one thought refuses to let another precede it—call this a disturbance of my soul or whatever you will' (*ep.* 26. 414a).

Yet Maximus did not rush into the open arms of his pupil upon receiving this letter; in an attempt to obtain favourable omens for his journey, he lingered for a time in Asia Minor,[98] thus disappointing Julian's expectations. How understandable then that when one day towards the beginning of 362 a messenger announced the sudden arrival of Maximus, the emperor interrupted a sitting of the Senate and, 'forgetting who he was', ran at full speed to kiss his master![99] The sober Ammianus may well have been shocked at such a breach of imperial etiquette, but Libanius was much more to the point when he compared Julian with the μανικός Chaerephon dashing to embrace Socrates on his return from Potidaea.[100] Master and pupil were now to stay together until the night in Mesopotamia when death separated them.

Maximus' complex and contradictory personality has much puzzled the biographers of his distinguished pupil. Modern scholars agree in seeing in him only a miracle-worker and a charlatan almost solely preoccupied with his own fame and material prosperity. Half the trouble is that we are for ever condemned to look at Maximus through Eunapius' distorting mirror. As with the rest of his philosophers, Eunapius entirely failed to grasp the quality of Maximus' inner life, and what he offers instead is an improbable collection of bizarre details. Thus our only hope of ever seizing something of the personality of the man who exerted such an enormous influence on Julian is to concentrate on our other sources and refrain from interpreting them in the light of our modern prejudices.[101]

Like most contemporary and subsequent Neoplatonists, Maximus was a man endowed with exceptional powers of

[98] Eunap. *V. Phil.* VII. 3. 12 ff.
[99] Amm. XXII. 7. 3.
[100] Lib. XVIII. 155 and Plato, *Charm.* 153b.
[101] For the fruitful results of such an approach, see Brown, *Religion*, 119–42.

reasoning,[102] well trained in classical philosophy[103] and with a pronounced mystical streak which, as was to be expected in a man of his time and education, caused him to fall easily under the spell of theurgy.[104] Once Maximus began to be worshipped like a god at Court, he also began to assume grand and arrogant airs which, to Eunapius' mind, were incompatible with the precepts of the philosophy he was preaching;[105] yet it is not impossible that this hieratical rather than arrogant attitude was approved, and even suggested, by Julian himself, whose own conception of priesthood was directly derived from Iamblichus.[106] Libanius compares Maximus to Achilles' tutor, the wise Phoenix,[107] and conveys the salutary impact of his influence on Julian by echoing Plato,[108] or by having recourse to one of the key-words of late-antique philosophical vocabulary: for the young prince Maximus was ὁ τῆς γνώμης ἰατρός, a judgement with which Julian himself did not disagree.[109] As for Ammianus, he describes Maximus, long after Julian's death, in the following terms: 'a famous philosopher, a man with an extraordinary reputation for learning, as a consequence of whose teaching Julian the emperor acquired immense learning' (XXIX. 1. 42). Eunapius, who had met Maximus, gives a detailed description of his highly impressive personality and his visionary and introspective glance—a portrait in fact of the typical late antique philosopher.[110]

[102] On the dialectical treatises that Maximus composed, see K. Praechter, 'Maximus 40', *RE* 14. 2567-69, and *ELF*, No. 158. Likewise, Proclus, who was well trained in dialectical philosophy, regarded theurgy as the highest form of truly divine wisdom that could be acquired by any human being (Marinus, *V. Procli* 28: οὐκ ἔτι μέχρι τῆς θεωρητικῆς ἔστατο), and did not refrain from performing miracles whenever he judged it necessary (ibid. 28-9).

[103] Lib. XVIII. 18; Amm. XXIX. 1. 42.

[104] On miracles performed by Maximus other than the one quoted above, see Eunap. *V. Phil.* VI. 9. 3-7. For an interesting Christian parallel to the miracle performed by Maximus on account of Sosipatra, see Brown, *Religion*, 137.

[105] Eunap. *V. Phil.* VII. 4. 2.

[106] See below, pp. 182 ff.

[107] Lib. *ep.* 694. 5.

[108] Lib. XIII. 12: ὁ δοκῶν καὶ ὢν σοφός.

[109] Lib. XII. 34; cf. *ep.* 694. 4. See above, p. 34.

[110] Eunap. *V. Phil.* VII. 1. 1. Cf. Amm. XV. 8. 16 (on Julian). On the type of the Greek philosopher in late antique art, see Garth Fowden, 'Pagan philosophers in late antique society: with special reference to Iamblichus and his followers', unpubl. diss., Oxford 1979, 252-97.

Such was the man who initiated Julian into the Neoplatonic Mysteries. To his contemporaries Julian was the man who 'had communicated with δαίμονες during innumerable ceremonies',[111] the one 'who came in contact with the bodiless while still himself inhabiting a body'.[112] The first such experience Julian had was clearly the initiation that Aedesius had anticipated when recommending the prince to his pupils.[113] Under the direction of Maximus, who thus became once and for all Julian's spiritual father, the prince was initiated in the Neoplatonic Mysteries in a cave at Ephesus in 351.[114]

That initiation must have been a profoundly moving experience for Julian. But any attempt at a reconstruction of the ceremony which marked him for life is bound to be unsatisfactory. Even if we knew the exact succession of δρώμενα and the meaning of their symbolism we would still find it impossible to participate emotionally in the τελετή. As unfeeling anthropologists we would at the best produce a dry factual report from which the spirit of the thing described would be totally absent.

But at least it is legitimate to ask: what did Julian seek in this initiation? In psychological terms 'a concrete living embodiment of his conversion at Macellum'[115] and the acquisition of a sense of *belonging* at last to a group. Most importantly though, Julian found in Neoplatonism the conclusive answer to the ultimate metaphysical question:

He who will not by a process of divinely inspired frenzy turn the plurality of this life into the unified essence of Dionysus—an essence which inhabits even the divisible in its totally indivisible, whole and everywhere unadulterated and pre-existing form—runs the risk of seeing his life flow into many channels and while flowing be torn to shreds and, thus torn, vanish away. And when I say 'flow' or 'torn to shreds', no one should consider the bare meaning of the words and suppose that I mean a mere trickle of water or a thread of linen, but he must understand these words in another sense, that used by Plato, Plotinus, Porphyry and the divine Iamblichus. One who does

---

[111] Lib. XXIV. 36.
[112] Eunap. *Hist.*, fr. 23: τοῖς ἀσωμάτοις ὁμιλήσας σῶμα ἔχων ἔτι. Cf. also Lib. XV. 30: καὶ μόνος σὺ τὰς ἐκείνων ἑώρακας μορφὰς εὐδαίμων εὐδαιμόνων θεωρός, καὶ μόνῳ σοι φωνῆς θεῶν ὑπῆρξεν ἀκοῦσαι.
[113] Eunap. *V. Phil.* VII. 1. 13.
[114] *ep.* 111. 434d.
[115] Browning, *Julian*, 58.

not interpret them thus will laugh at them no doubt, but let me
assure him that his will be a Sardonic laugh, since he will for ever
be deprived of that knowledge of the gods which I hold to be more
precious than dominion over the entire world, Roman and barbarian
put together, yea I swear it by my Lord Helios. (VII. 222a–c)

The spiritual teaching of the Platonic masters on the essential
unity of all life found in Julian an ardent believer, ready to
sacrifice on the altar of this mystical truth all the unreal, yet
irresistibly attractive, brilliance of the sensible world—its fatal
γοητεία. But, as with all the things of the spirit, this deeply in-
grained belief was to Julian an unproven proposition—the gift
of intuition rather than of experience; at the imperfect stage
where he still was when he wrote these enthusiastic lines he
needed above all symbols to sustain him in his struggle towards
ἁπλότης—that momentary flash which was to illuminate the
integral unity of the universe at the end of his ascent: and along
his lonely path, humanly enough, Julian longed to see a few
directing signs and some milestones recording his spiritual progress. Yet for this he would have to turn to an organized religion, for no philosophy, however well endowed with moral
code, or even ritual, could ever fulfil this need.

Such must have been the unconscious considerations which,
probably as early as 351, induced Julian to take the decisive
step of a first initiation in the Mithraic mysteries—a step that
was by no means incompatible with his allegiance to Platonism.[116] And, while many a concrete symbol used at the
initiatory ceremony must have struck Julian as a familiar echo
from his religious background, his encounter with the central
divinity of the mysteries surely produced on him the emotional
impact of a tragic ἀναγνώρισις. Rather like Electra suddenly
realizing that the kind stranger is Orestes himself, Julian had
the unexpected revelation that the mysterious and poignantly
distant royal star, towards which he had felt so passionately

[116] For the well-attested interest of the Platonists in Mithraism, see R. Turcan,
Mithras Platonicus: Recherches sur l'hellénisation philosophique de Mithra, Leiden 1975;
cf. R. L. Gordon's ingenious analysis of the *De antro nympharum* with reference to
the iconography of the Sette Sfere Mithraeum at Ostia, 'The sacred geography
of a *Mithraeum*: the example of Sette Sfere', *JMS* i. 2 (1976), 119–65. From
Porphyry onwards solar piety became an important feature of Neoplatonism.

drawn in his adolescent years,[117] was none other than the
guardian god Mithra, 'the cable and secure (ἀσφαλής) haven'
in which he could now take refuge from the storms of the open
sea (X. 336c).

In the excitement of his first initiation Julian thought that he
would be able to exchange the storms of his external existence
straight away for a permanent anchorage in the port of Mithra
—a false impression which his god was quick to dispel: 'do
bear in mind that thou must without fail return thither'
(VII. 231c) was the express command of Helios who, far from
being moved by the young man's tears, told him in no ambiguous terms that he still considered him to be uninitiated and that
the only road to security (ἀσφαλῶς) is the one that passes
through the tribulations of human society (VII. 231d).

In these two sayings of the god, which allude to the formal
structure of the mysteries, the initiate has also encapsulated the
ultimate spiritual message of his religion. The pursuit of moral
and spiritual perfection—which was the main preoccupation
and foremost priority in the life of the devotee—was intimately
linked with his duty as a member of human society. Yet this
worldly fulfilment of the Mithraist had its corollary in the
internal structure of the mysteries, where the notion of continuous progress was conveyed by the seven degrees of initiation. The transition from one grade to the next was symbolically
represented as the ascent of the individual up the planetary
ladder until the wholly passionless purified soul reached the
transcendental sphere of the fixed stars, having discarded like
garments on the way all its greedy passions and sensual
desires,[118] together with its intellectual pride, ambitious aspirations and idle tendencies.[119]

When at last, possessing the entire spectrum of knowledge
taught in the mysteries, the Mithraist reached the seventh grade
of initiation, he was considered to have left behind the sphere of
movement and change—the sphere of genesis—for the divine
realm which was free of the laws of time and space applicable
to the cosmic and human universe. There, in the final stage of

[117] See above, pp. 22–3.
[118] For the use of the word χιτών in this sense, see III. 96c; cf. Plot. *Enn.*
I. 6. 7. 6–7.
[119] F. Cumont, *Les Mystères de Mithra*, Paris 1913², 146.

apogenesis,[120] liberated from the cycle of birth and rebirth—fully saved in Mithraic terms—the *pater* was secure in eternity.

The term ἀσφαλής, which must have belonged to the secret vocabulary of the mysteries, clearly describes this state of blissful knowledge, as Julian's usage suggests: in both instances a god uses the word addressing an initiate, but, whereas the passage that refers to Julian's spiritual condition at the period when he was still a private citizen[121] makes it obvious that the prince had as yet a very crude knowledge of the Mithraic teaching, the tone of Hermes to Julian in 362 suggests that by that time the emperor was a fully saved Mithraist—one who had exhausted the springs of spiritual knowledge.[122]

Yet that stage was to be reached only in 362, in Julian's private Mithraeum in Constantinople, where the emperor also made a point of acting as an initiator for at least one of his close friends.[123] In the early 350s Julian had only just embarked on an unknown path, but one which widened dramatically and revealed to him quite unsuspected horizons. The consequences of this first initiation in the Mithraic mysteries were to be perceived and realized slowly even by such an easily impressionable devotee as Julian, for they were inner changes, the gradual discovery of suppressed vocations.

The man who had spent the greater part of his formative years in complete isolation, with Nature and his books as his only friends, certainly kept in later life a taste for seclusion and solitude away from the noise of cities.[124] But as a balanced human being, Julian bore within himself the seed of sociability. He longed for the company of kindred spirits and was endowed with a capacity for love and devotion which he never missed an opportunity to express. Yet both the peculiar circumstances of his early life and the education he had received seemed to conspire to turn him into the prototype of the intellectual snob, sympathetic only towards his equals, divorced from practical

---

[120] Porph. *Abst.* IV. 16. Except for the grade of *pater* the others were still subjected to metempsychosis.

[121] VII. 231d, see below, pp. 174-5.

[122] This is suggested by the verb ἐπιγνῶναι used by Hermes; cf. my article, 'A contribution to Mithraic Theology: the Emperor Julian's *Hymn to King Helios*', *JThS* N.s. xxviii (1977), 371.

[123] Ibid. 362.

[124] See *ep.* 4; cf. the idyllic description of Paris in XII. 340d-341a.

life and indifferent to the destinies of the large masses of his fellow-men. That, far from evolving in this way, Julian actively exploited his inner resources for human love and understanding, while at the same time developing a rare sense of worldly commitment, was one of the results of his devotion to Mithra. For Mithraism was a religion with a well-defined moral code, which consisted of a number of specific commandments inspired by the general principle of justice. In the case of Julian the god had prescribed that he should worship divinity, display loyalty to his friends, treat his subjects with *philanthropia* and on all occasions show himself above passions and desires.[125] In this incessant battle against evil within and evil without Julian had a vivid sense of being assisted by Mithra, the god who, unlike all the other youthful divinities of the East, had always been *invictus*, even by physical death. At a later stage of his development, Julian seems to have taken the daring step of coming to face his god not just as a commander and a protector but even as the model for his own career on earth; in the role of the restorer of order in the world and redeemer of the Roman empire Julian saw himself as a human replica of Mithra, one to whom 'a mortal frame was given that he might discharge these duties', before achieving divine status.[126]

On his return to Nicomedia Julian was no longer an angular adolescent. The fears for his own safety, the petty arrogance which had long served him as an intellectual shield, the resentment and opaque embitterment which had till then blunted his inner sight, all began to melt under the constant action of fervent spiritual belief. There in Bithynia, the young man took his first timid steps towards an act of reconciliation with the world:

Confident in Hermes, he advanced along a road smooth, untrodden and pure, full of fruits and of thousands of beautiful flowers of those which are dear to the gods, a road that was lined with ivy, laurel and myrtle trees. (VII. 230d)

And as his reputation spread afar, all the devotees of the Muses and of the other gods hastened by land or sea to see him and stay with him. Yet once they were there, they found it difficult to tear themselves away; for Siren-like Julian held them not only by his speeches, but also by his innate gift for inspiring love. Knowing very well how to love, he taught the others to do the same, so that, becoming genuinely attached to him, they found it painful to leave him.[127]

Poets, rhetors and philosophers of both Greek and Latin culture[128] flocked to Julian in his literary retreat in Bithynia.[129] They were all welcomed by the prince in Nicomedia, and many of them were invited to spend the summer months in the charming villa that he had in the meantime inherited from his grandmother.[130] There Julian showed himself delightfully informal: he would produce for his friends 'a fragrant, sweet wine, which did not depend on time for the gifts of Dionysus and the Graces', but as soon as it was made flowed from the jars like 'a rill of nectar'.[131] Duly tempered by the water of the Nymphs, the bowl of Dionysus[132] refreshed the evening discussions of the learned circle, and sometimes helped the transition from an erudite subject to something of more practical concern; those who were to be Julian's collaborators often suggested that he might one day become the lord of the empire; and with what decisiveness and ardour would he not then stop the process of decadence![133] Ailing humanity would get the only doctor capable of healing her.

Such ideas were not entirely displeasing to Julian.[134] The spectacle of diseased humanity caused great pain to him now that he had begun to be transformed from an unselfconfident youth, fumbling for his own salvation in the midst of a hostile world, into an articulate young man sure of his beliefs. In the cave of Mithra he had learned how, far from recoiling before responsibilities, he ought to take arms against the sea of troubles that surrounded him. Overwhelmed by a sublime feeling of pity for mankind and conquering the last peaks of self-resistance, he had broken down in a state of total submission before his god: 'dispose of me as ye will' (VII. 232cd). 'And if a god had

---

[127] Lib. XVIII. 20.
[128] Ibid. 21.
[129] Lib. *ep.* 13.
[130] See above, p. 21.
[131] *ep.* 4. 427d, cf. Hom. *Od.* ι 359.
[132] *ep.* 4. 428a.
[133] Lib. XVIII. 21: τὴν φθορὰν τῆς οἰκουμένης.
[134] See Lib. XIII. 13–14; cf. XIV. 42; cf. Socr. III. 1. 21.

promised him that order would be re-established on earth by the action of others, I think he would have been all too happy to decline the crown; for his main desire was not to rule but to benefit the cities.'[135] Libanius knew very well what was going on in the mind of Julian at that time, for at least one of the prince's intimate friends in Bithynia, Seleucus, served as a link between him and the sophist.[136]

Yet Julian's life in Bithynia was not simply one of study and leisure. It was also a life of action. During the three years he spent there he repeatedly showed how determined he was to stand by the side of his friends and coreligionists. Faithful to the principle of worldly commitment nascent in him he would not spare any trouble:

Did I not even go so far as to leave the country for the sake of my friends? Indeed, you know how I took the part of Carterius when I went unsolicited to our friend Araxius to plead for him. And on behalf of the property of that marvellous woman Arete, and the wrongs she had suffered from her neighbours, did I not journey to Phrygia twice within two months, though I was physically very weak from the illness that had been brought on me by former fatigues? (VI. 259cd)[137]

We can perhaps imagine something of the quality of the discussions Julian had in Phrygia with Arete, who had probably been a pupil of Iamblichus,[138] for it is not unlikely that the man who ten years later was to celebrate the festival of Attis and Cybele in Neoplatonic terms was inspired precisely by the conversations he had with this venerable lady to try and discover the real meaning behind the occult ritual of the Phrygian mysteries by becoming an initiate—a fully fledged μύστης. 'Through impious blood he washed away the waters of baptism':[139] the terms in which Gregory of Nazianzos chooses to describe Julian's apostasy—consummated, as he believed, in the early 350s—refer unequivocally to the baptismal rite of the cult of Magna Mater, the *taurobolium*. This information

---

[135] Lib. XVIII. 23.

[136] Lib. *ep.* 13.

[137] On Julian's illness, see Lib. *ep.* 13; on the favours that he distributed to pagan intellectuals, ibid. 35. 7.

[138] See J. Bidez, 'Le philosophe Jamblique et son école', *REG* xxxii (1919), 39.

[139] Greg. Naz. *or.* IV. 52.

fits in with Julian's always apparent desire to do things properly. The most appropriate place for people to be initiated into the mysteries of Cybele was Phrygia, and Julian did not visit this area again before the composition of the *Hymn to the Mother of the Gods* in March 362 when he was in Constantinople.[140]

Yet, however carefully concealed from the public eye, Julian's activities in Asia Minor soon attracted official attention. In order to allay any suspicion of a pagan conspiracy, Julian made a point of becoming a reader in the Church of Nicomedia,[141]

> where with loud voice and piously obedient
> many a Holy script he reads with emotion,
> while the populace admires all this Christian devotion.[142]

Had Aesop been there, says Libanius, he would have written a fable, not about an ass in lionskin, but about a lion concealed under the hide of an ass.[143] Daring joke, probably richer in meaning than one suspects: the usual pagan slander on Christianity as the religion of the crucified donkey acquires a strange contemporary relevance when associated with one who was probably at that time a Mithraic lion.[144] Yet, just as in Aesop's fable the ass betrayed his true nature, so too Julian's deception was not totally convincing. His long absence from Nicomedia in 351 and the strange company he kept in Bithynia disquieted the Caesar Gallus who, after the first reports on his brother's behaviour, dispatched to Bithynia Aetius, the founder of the most extreme of the Arian sects, the Anomoeans.

A cultured man and a fine dialectician, Aetius had express instructions to probe Julian's mind. The prince had long discussions with him on dogmatic matters, and the subtle mind of the Arian theologian made a deep impression on Julian. But the appreciation was mutual. The man who in his early years had known the degradation of manual labour, but spared no sacrifice in order to be able to afford the study of philosophy, must have felt a strange affinity with Julian. Here was somebody

---

[140] On the date of the composition of the *Hymn to the Mother of the gods*, see VIII. 178d and Lib. XVIII. 157; cf. *Julien* II(1). 102.

[141] Socr. III. 1. 20.

[142] C. Kavafy, 'Julian in Nicomedia'; transl. J. Phillipson, *Cavafy: Collected Poems—A Verse Translation with Scholia* (forthcoming).

[143] Lib. XVIII. 19.

[144] The fourth and most crucial grade of initiation.

animated by the same passion for knowledge as himself and
armed with the same determination to overcome external
obstacles. Why then, Aetius felt, should he give away the secret
of a mind so akin to his? He obtained permission from Gallus to
visit Julian frequently,[145] and used all the fire of his eloquence to
persuade the Caesar that his brother had not been shaken in the
least in his supposed Christian beliefs. As for Julian, he was
delighted to find such an ally. As soon as he became emperor,
he acknowledged officially in a letter to Aetius the pleasure he
had derived from his company, invited him to Court, and treated
him with the same generosity as his pagan friends.[146]

In the spring of 354 Constantius received disquieting reports
about Gallus and, before the year was out, he had summoned
his Caesar to the West and had him executed. The moment was
ripe for the sycophants around the suspicious emperor to
whisper in his ear what meagre information they had about
Julian's seemingly inoffensive activities in Bithynia. They
adroitly reminded Constantius that the prince had left Macellum without official permission, and added that on his way to
Italy the disgraced Caesar had stopped in Bithynia to see his
brother.[147] The evidence seemed sufficiently incriminating for
Julian to be summoned to Milan and kept under arrest at a
near-by village.

The exchange of almost complete freedom for solitary con-
finement was seen by Julian as a tribulation imposed on him
by his god: ἐγὼ τῷ στρατοπέδῳ παρέμενον—'I did not abandon
my post, at the moment when—as the [uninitiated] multitude
would put it—I was running the risk of death' (VI. 259–
260a), wrote Julian later in an attempt to convey something of
his state of mind during the six months of seclusion at Como.
Confident of divine protection, he performed his duty with a
brave spirit. He tried to prove his innocence, but without
resorting to 'anything mean or low or ignoble' (VI. 260a). He

---

[145] Philostorgius, III. 27: καὶ πολλάκις πρὸς Ἰουλιανὸν ἀπεστάλη [sc.
Aetius]. See esp. *ep.* 46 where Julian speaks in terms of an 'intimate friendship',
καὶ συνηθείας μεμνημένος.

[146] *ep.* 46; see also *Julien* I(2). 39; Philostorg. VI. 7; see below, p. 127.

[147] Amm. XV. 2. 7, who places the meeting of the two brothers in Constantinople.

put his case across to the philosopher Themistius—a coreligionist with great influence at court—in letters which were far
from containing complaints—μήποτε ὀδυρμῶν πλήρεις (VI.
260a); and generally he showed himself capable of a blend of
cautiousness and resolution[148] in the defence of his cause,
though at a deeper level he remained unshaken in his belief in
divine justice. And the course of events justified his expectations. A *dea ex machina* appeared in the person of the empress
Eusebia,[149] who interceded in his favour with Constantius. Full
of self-confidence, Julian presented himself at the interview with
the emperor arranged by Eusebia and obtained what he wanted
(II. 118b). No sooner had he acquitted himself than he set out
for Nicomedia. But the 'evil demon who had devised [his]
previous troubles' interfered again and his journey was cut
short (II. 118c).

This time Julian did not even have time to speculate on his
fate, for Eusebia had already concluded an excellent trans-
action on his behalf, 'the exchange of gold for bronze, of a
hecatomb for nine oxen',[150] and Julian sailed for Athens.

Having grown up in the painful awareness that his fate was
in the hands of a capricious despot who had by stages eliminated
all his kinsmen, Julian had never allowed himself the innocent
pleasure of making plans for the future. His instinctive reaction
to his situation was to convince himself that his destiny really
lay in the hands of divine Beings, who were more powerful,
equitable and loving than the lord of the *oikoumene*. Occasionally, as in the relatively relaxed atmosphere of Bithynia, he
would forget the porcelain-like fragility of his existence, and
dreams of power would pass before his eyes. But that was an
easy leap to make, for the dreams never acquired the more
concrete form of plans. So Julian had never dared to nurture
consciously the hope that one day he would arrive in Athens—
his 'true fatherland, the land he loved and for which he longed'
(II. 118d)—to complete his studies. And as was natural, he
was overcome with joy when the doubly unexpected order
came. Now he too would participate in the 'great festival'
(VI. 260a), would see the holy city of Hellenism and would

---

[148] As later in Gaul, cf. Amm. XVI. 2. 11: 'providus et cunctator'.
[149] Amm. XV. 2. 8: 'adspiratione superni numinis'; cf. V. 273a.
[150] VI. 260b and Hom. *Il.* Z 236.

drain the last drops from 'the cask of memory' in the place that was truly the focal point of Greek culture.[151]

With his head full of romantic prejudices the prince arrived in the famous university town in the summer of 355 and was fortunate enough not to experience the disappointment that more often than not awaits the man who approaches reality through the medium of legend.[152] And when a few months later he was summoned to leave Athens, Julian felt that to die there would have been a better lot:

What floods of tears I shed and what laments I uttered when I was summoned, stretching out my arms to your Acropolis and imploring Athene to save her suppliant and not to abandon me, many of you who were there can attest, and the goddess herself, above all others, is my witness that I even begged for death at her hands there in Athens rather than my journey to the emperor. (V. 275a)

These are words with the ring of truth. In Gaul, the mere memory of Athens was enough to turn Julian into a Corybant (II. 119d); and his nostalgia only grew with time and success: in the midst of all the pomp of royal state the emperor regretted those Attic days whose rhythm had so perfectly suited his heart (VI. 260bc).

The luxuriousness of the intellectual and spiritual life of Athens struck Julian all the more because it sprang out of modest surroundings; for the material decline into which Athens had long been subsiding provided her lovers with an additional cause of pride. What one sought there was not the enjoyment of τρυφή, but the acquisition of wisdom in holiness.[153] The sophist Iulianus and his successor the Armenian Prohaeresius both lived and taught in 'a small and cheap house; but the place exhaled the fragrance of Hermes and the Muses, thus differing in nothing from a temple.'[154]

During his stay in Athens Julian often went there to listen to 'the king of rhetoric'.[155] At the age of eighty-seven Prohaeresius' 'rhetorical power was still so great and he so sustained his worn body by the youthfulness of his soul' that to the young Eunapius

[151] Amm. XVI. 5. 8.
[152] Cf. Synesius' *ep.* 56 (Garzya), written at the moment when he actually decided to go to Athens, with *ep.* 136.
[153] Greg. Naz. *or.* XLIII. 21; cf. Lib. XVIII. 28.
[154] Eunap. *V. Phil.* IX. 1. 4.
[155] Ibid. X. 7. 4.

he appeared as 'an ageless and immortal being, a god who, unsummoned, had revealed himself to humanity.'[156] We can be sure that the impression Prohaeresius made upon Julian some eight years earlier was similar: the Christian teacher inspired in the heart of his pupil lasting respect and admiration for his learning and character alike.[157]

Yet the ties that were to bind Julian to Prohaeresius' chief rival in Athens, the Bithynian Himerius,[158] were of a different and stronger character. In Himerius the prince found a co-religionist. An initiate in the Eleusinian mysteries and soon—under Julian's personal auspices—a devotee of Mithra,[159] Himerius had developed over the years an intense private interest in Neoplatonism, probably under the influence of his father-in-law Nicagoras—the same Platonist philosopher and δαδοῦχος of the Eleusinian mysteries who in 326 had visited the Valley of the Kings in Egypt.[160] Nicagoras himself belonged to a dynasty of philosophers—the so-called family of Minucianus[161]—and was directly descended from Autoboulos, the father of Plutarch of Chaeronea. Ever since the second century AD the members of this outstanding family had displayed a persistent interest in philosophy, the Eleusinian mysteries and the affairs of the city.

Whether it was through the initiative of Nicagoras that the Eleusinian mysteries became closely connected with the teaching of the Platonists, or whether his own dual interest was symptomatic of a development that was already growing under its own momentum, we shall never know. Yet by the 350s this link had been firmly established and Julian's intense desire to be initiated in the rites of Demeter was the fruit of the frequent promptings of his Neoplatonic masters; when still at Ephesus, the prince had been advised by Maximus and Chrysanthius to go and see the hierophant of Eleusis, who was in a position to reveal to him even greater mysteries than the ones into which

---

[156] Eunap. *V. Phil.* X. 1. 3–4.
[157] See *ep.* 31: cf. below, p. 127. For Prohaeresius' fame, see Lib. *ep.* 275.
[158] Suda I. 348.
[159] Himerius XLI. 1; 8.
[160] Cf. J. Baillet, 'Constantin et le dadouque d'Éleusis', *CRAI* (1922), 289 ff.
[161] See O. Schissel, 'Die Familie des Minukianos. Ein Beitrag zur Personenkunde des neuplatonischen Athen', *Klio* xxi (1927), 361–73.

he had already been initiated.[162] Once in Athens, 'he began greedily to absorb the wisdom of the most holy of the hierophants',[163] and, after many a long discussion with the descendant of the Eumolpids,[164] Julian came to grasp the spiritual wealth that lay hidden beneath the apparently incongruous symbols and rites of Eleusis.[165]

Yet, if Athens appealed so much to Julian, it was not primarily for the talented rhetors she possessed nor even because she was the centre of age-old mysteries. Now, in her autumn season, the city of Pallas was slowly beginning to receive the profits from the rich harvest she had produced and sent abroad. Fully grown, the two major streams of Neoplatonism mounted towards their primordial source: 'Athens has many pure streams which spring from its own soil, while many too flow from without the city, no less precious than those that are native. And her people love and cherish them and desire to be rich in what alone makes wealth enviable' (II. 119cd).[166]

Both the adepts of the sober system of Theodore of Asine—the Θεοδώρειοι—and the enthusiasts of Iamblichan theurgy were expounding their views in Athens at this time. Of the first—who, as a result of the development of Neoplatonism, were to suffer a *damnationem memoriae*—tradition has not even preserved the names. To Julian at least they were the heretics of the Neoplatonist Church.[167] But the adepts of Iamblichus whom Julian met in Athens made a lasting impression on him. Distinguished among them was the Epirote Priscus, the pupil of Aedesius, of whom Julian had heard when still at Pergamon. That was a 'true philosopher',[168] endowed with both knowledge and wisdom, and possessed by religious awe for the δόγματα of Neoplatonism, which he jealously kept from any profane ear.

With the spontaneity that distinguished Julian whenever he

---

[162] Eunap. *V. Phil.* VII. 3. 1.
[163] Ibid. VII. 3. 6.
[164] Ibid. VII. 3. 1.
[165] VIII. 173ab. On his repeated discussions with the hierophant of Eleusis, who later, at Julian's bidding, went to Gaul, see Eunap. *V. Phil.* VII. 3. 6–7. The pattern of simultaneous interest in Neoplatonism and the mysteries, that Julian's career illustrates, is further supported by the example of Iamblichus 2, cf. Lib. *ep.* 801.
[166] Cf. Them. 336d.
[167] See *ep.* 12.
[168] Ibid.

felt himself on safe ground, he now started pursuing Priscus, as once he had pursued the old Aedesius.[169] The philosopher seems to have liked this enthusiastic adept of the spiritual life and, despite the dangers that a close association with him might involve for both parties, he encouraged Julian to become an *habitué* of his house. There the prince met Priscus' family, his wife and children, even his sister and brother-in-law, who was also a great admirer of Iamblichus and an adept of theurgy.[170]

In this at once learned and fervent atmosphere Julian spent many a happy hour, whose ambiance he sought to reproduce as soon as the external factors of his existence would allow it. At his repeated invitation,[171] Priscus set out for the West in 359 and stayed there for some time.[172] Later, when Julian became emperor, he summoned to Constantinople the man whose virtues he had already celebrated in verse.[173] Priscus accepted the imperial invitation and remained at Julian's side from the time he arrived at Court until the emperor's death in Persia.[174]

Yet a deeper understanding of the spiritual life was not the only profit Julian carried away with him from Athens. In the city of Pericles Julian encountered, especially among the intelligentsia, a rare feeling of civic patriotism. This long and unbroken tradition, thanks to which Athens had remained in a very real sense a capital city, was to persist well into the fifth century. Even as late as 484 the Minucianus clan could still provide Athens with its *archon*,[175] only a few years after the most brilliant representative of Athenian Neoplatonism, the *diadochos* Proclus, had had to go into exile as a result of his involvement in civic politics.[176] 'The maintenance over generations, sometimes over centuries, of a prominent position in the intellectual and political life of the city by families whose members could easily have sought Roman office, but who did not choose

---

[169] See above, p. 32.
[170] *ep.* 12.
[171] *epp.* 11, 12, 13.
[172] Lib. XII. 55–6.
[173] Ibid.; for the invitation of Priscus to Court, see Eunap. *V. Phil.* VII. 4. 3 and 7.
[174] Amm. XXV. 3. 23.
[175] Marin. *V. Procli* 36.
[176] Ibid. 15.

to do so',[177] was a characteristically Athenian tradition which did not leave Julian unmoved. What indeed made him treat Athens as a capital city when he became emperor[178] was not simply his antiquarianism and his religious enthusiasm. Julian the statesman perceived in Athens the continuing strength of the *polis*, which he later sought to make the foundation-stone of his administrative reform.

When leaving Athens, Julian wept publicly, but went away with the conviction that the patron goddess of the city had become his personal divine *comes*.[179] Later, the Roman emperor who never saw Rome conferred on the Athenians the title of the Greeks *par excellence*,[180] and acknowledged Athens as his true fatherland[181] and the capital of Hellas. At the moment of his election as Augustus, he waited for the sanction of the hierophant of Eleusis,[182] and on his death-bed he discussed the immortality of the soul with Priscus and Maximus, two representatives of the Iamblichan Neoplatonism which was now beginning to take root in Athens. Himerius, the sophist aristocrat, and Celsus, the gifted fellow student from Athens,[183] became friends and collaborators, and were nominated to posts from which they were able to expound the values they had acquired there. On his departure from the sacred city of Hellenism, Julian had stored up in his heart and mind much that was to fertilize in him both the man of the spirit and the statesman. Nor did the city itself forget him; to the representatives of the tradition at whose well-springs Julian had drunk during his stay there, the memory of his reign remained a powerful symbol. It was by no mere fanciful whim that the Neoplatonic *diadochos* Marinus should have found nothing more to say of his predecessor Proclus' death, than that it occurred 'in the year 124 from Julian's reign'.[184]

---

[177] F. Millar, *JRS* lix (1969), 21. On the son of Himerius 3, Iamblichus, and his activities in Athens, see A. E. Raubitschek, 'Iamblichos at Athens', *Hesperia* xxxiii (1964), 63–8. On this extensive topic, see also A. Frantz, 'From paganism to Christianity in the temples of Athens', *DOP* xix (1965), 187–205.

[178] V. 287d; cf. 270b.   [179] V. 275ab; Lib. XIII. 28.

[180] XII. 348bc; cf. VIII. 159a.   [181] II. 118d.

[182] Eunap. *V. Phil.* VII. 3. 7; cf. below, p. 74 n. 112.

[183] Amm. XXII. 9. 13; Lib. *ep.* 1581. 2. See also Seeck, 'Celsos 15', *RE* iii. 1883–1884.   [184] Marin. *V. Procli* 36.

II. MILES MITHRAE

Οἰκεῖόν ἐστιν ἄνθρωπος φύσει πράξει καὶ ἐπιστήμῃ. IX. 190a

In the autumn of 355 Julian was summoned from Athens to Milan. This time a mounting feeling of revolt overcame the young prince. He obeyed the imperial command, knowing there was no alternative, but it was in a state of great—if momentary—disillusion with life, which stirred in him a genuine wish for death, that he started on his journey. For the second time within a year Julian was to be held prisoner in a Milanese suburb, unsure of what the future held for him, while his fate was being deliberated at the palace.

The emperor's chief preoccupation at that moment was the fate of the western provinces; sacked by the barbarian,[1] and wracked by internal religious discords,[2] they had of late proved a fertile breeding-ground for usurpers, who had vainly sought to pacify them.[3] After so many unhappy experiments, it became clear that only the prestige of a legitimate representative of the imperial power could carry the day.[4] The empress Eusebia, an intelligent woman who both understood politics and knew how her husband's mind worked, pointed out the only satisfactory solution that could save her from having to set out for those barbarous lands: Julian should be made Caesar and sent to Gaul.[5] The first round of the game had been won and Julian was recalled from Athens.

But in her obstinate attempt to persuade her husband Eusebia was opposed by all the courtiers, who naturally feared the sudden elevation to power of one who was most unlikely to be well disposed towards them.[6] Day followed day and the

[1] Amm. XV. 8. 1. From the late third century onwards Gaul was constantly under attack from the Saxons, Franks and Alamanni; cf. Stein, *Bas-Empire* i. 143.
[2] See below, p. 54.
[3] On usurpers, see Amm. XV. 3. 7; XV. 5; Lib. XVIII. 31: τῶν δ' ἐκεῖσε πεμπομένων στρατηγῶν μείζονα ἢ ἐξῆν ζητούντων.
[4] Amm. XV. 8. 1–2; Lib. XII. 40: μάλιστα δὲ τὸ περὶ τὴν ἑσπέραν ἐπόνει, καὶ μικρὸν ἦν στρατηγὸς εἰς ἐπανόρθωσιν, ἀλλ' ἔδει βασιλέως ἐπισχήσοντος τὸ ῥεῦμα.
[5] Amm. XV. 8. 3.
[6] Amm. XV. 8. 2.

pressure on Constantius increased, till Eusebia's final assault proved decisive. Meanwhile, the news of what was happening in the palace filtered through to Julian (V. 275b). The state of excited indignation in which he had left Athens proved a more lasting disposition than philosophical indifference, and he soon fell prey to the deepest depression. The fear of death seized him and in his agony Julian turned away from the ungraspable sphere of divinity and sought comfort in the immediacy of human warmth. He wrote an imploring letter to Eusebia asking her to arrange a quick return home for him. But the hysterical tone of his text struck even Julian himself; he had hardly finished it when he began to wonder whether he ought to send such a compromising missive to the empress. As the night advanced, his hesitation changed into an intolerable agony. Summoning his remaining forces at last, Julian urgently addressed a fervent prayer to his protectors. And once more the voices of his gods were heard threatening the most ignominious of deaths, should Julian send the letter (V. 275c). During that night Julian had reached a *cas limite*: he had known the horror of excessive fear,[7] and had overcome it. After such an experience life took on a new aspect of utter simplicity: ἐξ ἐκείνης δέ μοι τῆς νυκτὸς λογισμὸς εἰσῆλθεν, οὗ καὶ ὑμᾶς ἴσως ἄξιον ἀκοῦσαι—'from that night a thought entered my head which perhaps it is worth your while to hear too: what is human wisdom when compared with divine omniscience? As the servant of the immortals one should submit to their will in the certainty that whatever they decide is in one's best interest.'[8] Εἶξα καὶ ὑπήκουσα—'I yielded and obeyed' (V. 277a), and the slavery of Caesarship began.[9]

Yet the realities of office were sadly remote from the dreams Julian and his friends had nurtured in Bithynia and, despite his brave assertion, that he would accept whatever the gods sent him with equanimity, Julian did not succeed in steeling himself to perfect resignation: inwardly he still reacted against the μοῖρα κραταιή—the mighty destiny—that had so unexpectedly seized him, and it was with an air of utter sullenness

[7] V. 276c: δέει τοῦ θανάτου.
[8] V. 275d–276d.
[9] See above, p. 17. Cf. XII. 352d.

that he stood before the army as it acclaimed him.[10] Receiving with the purple a royal bride, whose existence Julian hardly ever noticed, he set out for Gaul in December 355 escorted by 360 soldiers.

In the year 355 Gaul, once a rich province, was a devastated land.[11] Forty-five towns along the banks of the Rhine had been occupied by the Alamanni, while the tax-collector was competing with the barbarian in contriving the ruin of the rest of the province.[12] In urban centres and countryside alike the problem of depopulation was becoming acute,[13] while for those who saw themselves condemned to end their lives in the province the only alternative to complete resignation seemed to be adherence to 'the moral insurrection' led by Hilary of Poitiers.[14] The utter demoralization of these men, whom experience had taught that nothing could be more fallacious than the belief of the ancient world in the immortality of cities, is well conveyed by Rutilius Namatianus who, referring to the cities of Gaul, observed: 'Cernimus exemplis oppida posse mori' (*De reditu suo*, 414). In his Greek way, Libanius described with equal bitterness the state to which the cities of Gaul were reduced by the time Julian set out for the West: 'You were going to names of cities rather than cities, in order to create cities rather than to make use of ones that already existed' (XIII. 23). What indeed the young Caesar found on his arrival in Gaul was a place 'turned upside down'.[15]

If Julian did not know how to tackle the complex problems that confronted him, he was at least in a position to measure the full extent both of their magnitude and of his own incompetence. The sterile indignation that had overwhelmed him

[10] Amm. XV. 8. 11, and above, p. 17.
[11] Amm. XVI. 5. 14; XX. 8. 15; *Pan. Lat.* IV. 18. Cf. the dark picture of Gaul before Julian's arrival, painted by Mamertinus, 4. 1–2, and the complete transformation of the province on Julian's departure, 4. 3. See also C. Jullian, *Histoire de la Gaule* vii, Paris 1926, 170–6 and 181 ff.
[12] V. 279ab; Lib. XII. 48. Zosimus speaks of forty cities (III. 1. 1). On taxation, see Jullian, op. cit. viii (1926), 39–44; cf. Zos. II. 38.
[13] Jullian, op. cit. vii. 24–9; Jones, *LRE* ii. 1040–5; cf. Zos. loc. cit.
[14] Jullian, op. cit. vii. 176–86, cf. 20 ff.; A. Piganiol, *L'Empire chrétien*, Paris 1972², 105–7.
[15] V. 277d: τὸ τῶν Κελτῶν ἔθνος ἀνατετραμμένον; cf. Amm. XV. 5. 2; XVI. 2. 12.

at the moment of his elevation to the Caesarship[16] was now left well behind. During the winter that he spent in Vienne Julian became familiar with the distinctly Roman world of political power; he sweated under the daily discipline of military exercise, and acquired direct experience of provincial administration.[17] At the same time, as was to be expected of a man of Julian's character and upbringing, he chose to construct his empirical edifice on a firm theoretical foundation: a considerable amount of his time at Vienne was devoted to the study of Caesar's *Commentaries* and Plutarch's *Lives*.[18] From this reading Julian emerged with a considerable understanding of the military and diplomatic history of Rome[19] and with his self-confidence bolstered:

For many of those records of the experience of men of old, written as they are with the greatest skill, provide a vivid and brilliant picture of past exploits to those whom time has kept away from such spectacles. It is thanks to such readings that many a young man has acquired a greater intellectual and emotional maturity than a whole lot of old men put together, so that the only advantage that old age seems to confer on mankind, I mean experience, thanks to which an old man 'can talk more wisely than the young', even this the study of history can give to the diligent youth. (II. 124bc)

In this passage we have the magic key that unlocks one of those transitory moments in Julian's psychology when, almost unconsciously, he attempted to justify the peculiar circumstances of his life at a particular point in time by having recourse to his own unique thought-world. The at once more general and more specific question that such a passage provokes is to what extent Julian's entire outlook at this period was affected by the sudden changes in his life style or, conversely, how much of these changes were brought about by an inner—yet so far dormant—drive. Was Julian converted abruptly and full-heartedly in the winter of 356 from an adept of the *vita contemplativa* into a follower of the *vita activa* or

---

[16] A state of mind that persisted till Julian reached Vienne: 'He was often heard to mutter in complaining tones that he had gained nothing, save to die in the midst of heavier work' (Amm. XV. 8. 20).

[17] Amm. XVI. 5. 9–10.

[18] *Julien* I(1). 98 n. 3.

[19] Julian seems to have even composed a history of domestic and foreign affairs, Amm. XVI. 5. 7.

C

did he simply yield to the demand of circumstances? The second alternative seems to describe faithfully enough his state of mind at the moment he became Caesar;[20] yet this bona-fide resignation appears to have given way gradually to a genuine involvement with the fortunes of the empire, which nevertheless never supplanted, or even undermined, his deeply rooted conviction that the *vita contemplativa* is the highest possible form of human existence. After a few years spent in Gaul Julian could still write to two old fellow-students: 'If anyone has persuaded you that there is anything more delightful or more profitable for the human race than to pursue philosophy at one's leisure, without interruptions, he tries to delude you, being a deluded man himself' (*ep.* 8. 441a). In the *Epistle to Themistius*, written at the moment when Julian was about to start his career as sole ruler of the empire, he returned to the same point. Not without some sarcasm, he declined Themistius' offer to play an active role in politics and sent him back to his books on the grounds that θεωρία is superior to πρᾶξις.[21]

On this major problem of Greek philosophy Julian subscribed to Plato's view, from which the even stricter Neoplatonic position derived.[22] He did not regard earthly rule as an end in itself, or as a means by which the goal of an individual's existence was to be attained; he only saw it as the hard mission with which the gods had entrusted him, and he consented to fulfil it as best he could out of a sense of duty: 'he became a king not because he was enamoured of kingship, but because he saw that the human race needed to be ruled', writes Eunapius,[23] echoing a famous passage in the *Republic*, where the ruler is presented as the one who, having walked out of the Platonic cavern into the light, returns and imposes upon himself the thankless task (ἐπιταλαιπωροῦντας) of governing those who are still in the darkness.[24] The sage regards earthly

---

[20] Cf. XII. 352d.

[21] VI. 264bc; see below, p. 93.

[22] For a few characteristic passages see Plato, *Rep.* 520c ff.; Albinus, *Epitome* II. 3; Plot. *Enn.* I. 4. 7; III. 8 (*passim* and esp. 4. 39 ff.); Porph. *Abst.* I. 36 ff.; Marin. *V. Procli* 14.

[23] *Hist.*, fr. 23.

[24] *Rep.* 540b: τὸ μὲν πολὺ πρὸς φιλοσοφίᾳ διατρίβοντας, ὅταν δὲ τὸ μέρος ἥκῃ, πρὸς πολιτικοῖς ἐπιταλαιπωροῦντας καὶ ἄρχοντας ἑκάστους τῆς πόλεως ἕνεκα, οὐχ ὡς καλόν τι ἀλλ᾽ ὡς ἀναγκαῖον πράττοντας.

rule not as καλόν but as ἀναγκαῖον, and, while governing and educating the new generation of rulers, he yet dedicates the greater part of his time to philosophy. Julian was even more radical than the philosopher of the Platonic *Republic*: he hoped to be a latter-day Diocletian, retiring altogether when he had completed his work of social and religious reform.[25]

It was in this Platonic sense of mission that Julian faced his role as Caesar. He assumed, and even wore, the *vilis corona*, the cheap crown offered him by Constantius, which 'resembled that of the director of a gymnasium attired in purple'.[26] He accepted ungrudgingly the close surveillance inflicted on him by Constantius' generals in Gaul, and, within the limits of his well-defined ἐξουσία, he concentrated on doing his duty, while entrusting the outcome of his actions to the hands of the gods. His serene self-confidence stemmed henceforth from the conviction that the same divine power that had allotted to him certain tasks would also help him to achieve them.[27] At the same time he pushed his trust in providence to its logical conclusion and slowly let grow in himself a sense of dynastic pride, which strengthened his commitment to the cause of Rome: he felt that it was an additional token of divine favour that birth should have made of him a member of the imperial family.[28]

Armed with the minimum of knowledge that his task required, in the summer of 356 Julian began his attempt to 'gather up the broken fragments of the province'[29] by tackling the most pressing danger first. The story of the highly successful campaigns against the barbarians which he conducted during the years 356–9 is told in great detail by Ammianus,[30] who was

[25] See Julian's harangue in Amm. XXIV. 3. 7: 'certe discedam; nec enim ita vixi, ut non possim aliquando esse privatus.'

[26] Amm. XXI. 1. 4; cf. A. Piganiol, 'La couronne de Julien César', *Byzantion* xiii (1938), 243–8, esp. 246 ff., for his ingenious interpretation of J. V. 278.

[27] *ep.* 14. 385c: τοῦ θεοῦ συμμαχοῦντος ἡμῖν, ὅσπερ οὖν ἔταξεν. Bidez points out that ὁ θεός mentioned here cannot be other than Mithra (*Vie*, 219); ὁ πάντα ἐφορῶν Θεός of *ep.* 11 must also be Mithra; see Lib. XVIII. 39: τὸ πιστεύειν αὐτῷ συστρατεύειν τοὺς θεούς.

[28] See below, pp. 62, 64–5, 72, 76, 113, 171, 174 ff.

[29] Amm. XVI. 1. 1.

[30] Amm. XVI–XVIII. 2. The battle of Strasbourg is related in XVI. 12. Note Ammianus' surprised admiration, expressed in the introductory section of his account of Julian's exploits in Gaul in XV. 9. 1 and again in XVI. 1. 2. On his *fortitudo* and military genius, see Amm. XXV. 4. 10–14. Cf. V. 280cd.

an eye-witness until the eve of the battle of Strasbourg. This decisive victory, after which Julian was for the first time 'hailed as Augustus by the unanimous acclamation of the army',[31] inaugurates for him a period of outward tensions and inner conflicts which were to pave a steep path to the throne. It is true that the Caesar appeared to be horrified by the undue honour that his excited soldiers claimed for him; yet it is equally certain that over that triumphant moment the spark of ambition was kindled in Julian's heart. As if to mark this sudden realization, he dedicated to the battle of Strasbourg βιβλίδιον ὅλον, a whole little book, whose every page vibrated with an enthusiasm which, as even a sympathetic reader felt, was somewhat excessive.[32]

Military success followed military success. Once he had repelled the Alamanni from Roman territory, Julian attacked them on their own soil and then took care to secure the frontier by compelling them to build fortresses;[33] he also recruited élite corps among the barbarians and used them to defend Roman Gaul.[34] By 361 the Caesar had achieved what seemed impossible, 'and after he left the western regions, so long as he was on earth, all nations preserved perfect quiet, as if a kind of earthly wand of Mercury were pacifying them.'[35]

As impressive as his military achievement in Gaul was the victory that Julian won in the social field. Justice as the ruling principle of human society was his main preoccupation, as one would have expected from a man whose enthusiastic nature had been sealed by a Platonic education and the teachings of Mithraism.[36] 'Dividing his nights according to a threefold schedule—rest, affairs of state and the Muses'[37]—he devoted

---

[31] Amm. XVI. 12. 64.

[32] Eunap. *Hist.*, fr. 9; cf. Lib. *ep.* 35. 6.

[33] Amm. XVII. 1; 10. 9; XVIII. 2. 3–6; XX. 10. 3; Lib. XIII. 30: Γαλατῶν αἱ πόλεις ἀνίσταντο θεωρούντων μὲν ἡμῶν οἰκοδομούντων δὲ τῶν βαρβάρων; cf. ibid. XVIII. 77.

[34] Amm. XX. 4. 4; Zos. III. 7.

[35] Amm. XXV. 4. 14; a point generalized by Lib. XXIV. 37: βασιλεὺς δὲ Ῥωμαῖος ἐν γῇ Ῥωμαίων οὐκ ἦν, πάντα δὲ ἡσύχαζεν ἀντὶ τῆς παρουσίας ἀρκοῦντος τοῦ δέους; cf. Lib. XII. 51: τρόπαιον ἀκίνητον τὰς πόλεις ὤρθωσας. On the chronology of Julian's campaigns, see now G. W. Bowersock, *Julian the Apostate*, London 1978, 36–44.

[36] *ep.* 8. 441d; *ep.* 89a. 453a; *ep.* 89b. 299b.

[37] Amm. XVI. 5. 4. Julian never abandoned the regime he inaugurated in Gaul, Amm. XXV. 4. 5–6.

his superabundant energy during the three winters he spent in Paris (357–9) to the administrative restoration of the province.

After only a short stay in Gaul, Julian realized that the most serious evil to which the province was exposed—the corruption of the fiscal system—was exclusively the fault of the State. The barbarian invasions had only aggravated an evil which had been inherent in the administration of the empire since the time of the Antonines.[38] The poll-tax, which did enough harm to the social fabric even in periods of normality, became totally destructive whenever a province was hit by war or bad harvests:[39] for, amongst the effects such calamities entailed was, naturally enough, a deficit between the sum required by the *indictio*[40] and the amount levied from the province. Over such situations the State would normally impose a supplementary tax. In 358 the returns from Gaul were in deficit, but when the praetorian prefect Florentius, 'after having reviewed the whole matter (as he asserted), demanded that whatever was lacking in the poll-tax and land-tax accounts be supplied out of special levies, Julian, knowing about such measures, declared that he would rather lose his life than allow it to be done.'[41] He then staged one of those *coups de théâtre*, that Julian so much loved, and by an exact and accurate computation he showed that the amount of poll-tax and land-tax already collected sufficed to meet their financial needs.[42]

Strict economy was not the only measure that Julian adopted in order to deal with the situation in Gaul; he also tried to provide for a fair distribution of the tribute and was careful never to remit arrears, as he knew that only the rich would profit from it.[43] Even more importantly, he publicly exposed and often managed to curb the corruption of the highly placed, despite the considerable resistance he encountered.[44] The efficiency of this policy, which Julian followed on a larger scale

[38] Jones, *LRE* 767–823, 1053–5. On the system of taxation as it developed under the Tetrarchy, see Browning, *Julian*, 4–7.

[39] See Amm. XIX. 11. 3 on Illyricum.

[40] The special decree issued every fifteen years, which fixed *per caput* the sum that each province had to pay to the State. Cf. Jullian, op. cit. viii. 33 ff.

[41] Amm. XVII. 3. 2; cf. V. 282c.

[42] Amm. XVII. 3. 4: 'scrupulose computando et vere'.

[43] Amm. XVI. 5. 15.

[44] Cf. V. 282c; Mamertinus 4. 2: '[Urbes] iudicum nomine a nefariis latronibus obtinebantur'; Amm. XVIII. 1. 4.

as Augustus, is strikingly illustrated by the example of Gaul: 'When he first entered those parts, he found that twenty-five pieces of gold were demanded by way of tribute from everyone as a poll- and land-tax; but when he left, seven only for full satisfaction of all duties. And on account of this (as if clear sunshine had beamed upon them after ugly darkness), they expressed their joy in gaiety and dances.'[45] Thanks to Julian's administration, Gaul witnessed a brief renaissance again.[46]

It must have been a great relief for Julian that, in the midst of all the deceptions and insincerities forced upon him by his position, closely supervised as he was and even calumniated by Constantius' agents (V. 278c), he was still able to give full expression to the sense of justice and equity which was so vital a part of his genuine self. At the same time he had the additional satisfaction that a man prone to show off may derive from proving to others his competence in a field other than the primary area of his activity.

In his attitude at this period there appears clearly for the first time in Julian's life the pattern that underlies his most tragic work, the *Misopogon*: the urgent need for universal approval and praise for the (admittedly laudable) qualities he possessed and which he exploited, as he justifiably thought, for the general welfare. Yet in his Gallic days popularity was the effortless harvest of a chain of actions both conscientious and brilliant, and his juvenile enthusiasm soared on the wings of unabated success. It seemed indeed a long time, at least in terms of Julian's condensed existence, before the wings of Fortune shrank, affecting his inner balance and letting the symptoms of egocentricity shine out in all their mean and pathetic ugliness. But in these salad days, when strife was matched by reward, Julian was still too happy not to consent to sacrifice his outward dignity for a cause that he regarded as noble and worthy of himself. Being determined to accomplish his mission as best he could, he felt that deliberately to endanger his life would have been an act of desertion and even stupidity.[47] He even judged it necessary to go out of his way in order to demonstrate his

[45] Amm. XVI. 5. 14. On Julian's fiscal policy, see also Amm. XXV. 4. 15.

[46] Amm. XVI. 5. 14; Mamert. 4. 3; cf. Jullian, op. cit. vii. 226–7.

[47] *ep.* 14. 385c, note the verb ἔταξεν. Even Gregory of Nazianzos mentions Julian's belief that he had a worthy mission to accomplish, *or.* V. 8.

subjection to Constantius, not only by carrying out the emperor's orders and by mortifying his own pride whenever he judged it necessary, but also by undertaking to glorify the emperor's virtues. He composed two panegyrics on his cousin and one on Eusebia.

The first panegyric on Constantius was written during the winter of 356/7 and brought to the Court by the eunuch Eutherius, Julian's trustworthy chamberlain.[48] The oration in honour of Eusebia was composed at about the same date— certainly the last touches were not put to it earlier than June 357, as the concluding passage refers critically to the imperial visit to Rome[49]—and reached the Court at the same time as *Panegyric* I or shortly afterwards.

Rhetorical clichés abound in both orations, but Constantius' panegyric follows so faithfully the model of the βασιλικὸς λόγος established by Menander,[50] that it arouses the suspicion that its author saw in slavish imitation the only way of absolving himself from the charge of lying. By refusing to make intelligent use of the ready-made model before his eyes he proclaimed unambiguously that his true self—whether on the intellectual or the emotional level—was not participating in the composition of this disgraceful panegyric, in which Constantius appeared as the ideal king.

Within the rigid scheme of this over-conventional 'royal speech', Julian succeeded nevertheless in inserting a minimum of his own thoughts by way of extravagant praise, polite suggestions or peripheral remarks. Julian's own obsession with the improvement of the welfare of the *poleis* through the alleviation of their taxation is presented as the major concern of an emperor whose financial policy ruined the provinces,[51] while the autocratic ruler[52] is praised as 'a citizen obeying the laws

---

[48] See the portrait of Eutherius in Amm. XVI. 7. 4 ff.; also O. Seeck, *RE* vi. 1500.

[49] Amm. XVI. 10, and II. 129bc.

[50] Menander, Περὶ ἐπιδεικτικῶν, *Rhet. Gr.* iii. 368 ff.; also the indices of parallel themes in the panegyrics on Constantius, composed by Themistius, Libanius and Julian, drawn up by C. O. Gladis, *De Themistii Libanii Juliani in Constantium orationibus*, Diss., Breslau 1907.

[51] I. 21d, 42d–43a; cf. Amm. XXI. 16. 17.

[52] Next to his iconography, which conveys effectively Constantius' hieratic idea of imperial status (e.g. the bust of Constantius in the Palace of the Conservatori),

and not as a king who is above them' (I. 45cd)—a remark
which verges on the sarcastic.[53]

Yet Julian's artificial panegyric reveals its author's psychology in more than just the studied unoriginality of its composition. After all Julian applies this technique only in those
passages that deal with Constantius as a person. When he
comes to discuss the more abstract principle of dynastic legitimacy Menander's mask falls, and we are allowed a glimpse of
the writer's private thoughts. Unlike professional panegyrists,
Julian here speaks with the involvement of an insider, and
through many complementary passages we can follow stage by
stage his intellectual and emotional itinerary until the point
when he felt a fully fledged Flavian. The flashes of anger that
illuminate Julian's text whenever he speaks of usurpers are
personal outbursts, and the reference to Claudius Gothicus as
the founder of the second Flavian dynasty has the air of vested
interest about it.

The panegyric on Eusebia is an infinitely more straightforward text. In it Julian expresses his especial gratitude to
the empress: he dedicates a whole oration to his benefactress
(though Menander had stated that the encomium of a queen
should form part of the $\beta a\sigma\iota\lambda\iota\kappa\grave{o}s$ $\lambda\acute{o}\gamma os$),[54] and makes a point of
praising the things that are dearest to his heart, whose experi-
ence or possession he owes to Eusebia: Athens and philosophy,
and books.[55]

Towards the end of 357 Julian's position became singularly
precarious. On the day of the battle of Strasbourg he had
crossed a bridge, both in real and in psychological terms, and
he knew that there could be no return. The world had ap-
plauded him as a brilliant general, and the repercussions of this

---

we have the evidence of Ammianus (XXI. 16. 7; XVI. 10. 10) and of Eutropius:
Constantius was 'vir egregiae tranquillitatis' (X. 15). Cf. Warren Bonfante, *PP*
xix (1964), 414 ff.

[53] In his oration to Constantius Themistius had addressed the emperor in a
language more befitting Constantius' own theocratic conception of the ruler: he
identified him with the divine law and proclaimed him to be above all human
institutions (15b). As for Constantius himself he advanced one step further than
his panegyrist and, in his *Letter to the Senate*, he looked forward to a society that
would have no need of laws, for he regarded the very concept of law as a sign of
the perversion of human nature, and not as an absolute standard to which the
wise man should conform (*Dem. Const.* 20c).

[54] Menand. op. cit. 376.   [55] II. 118c–120b and 123d–124d.

applause set the chord of ambition moving in his heart. Not without good reason, Constantius' courtiers drew his attention to the changing situation in Gaul; and in their sarcastic criticisms of Julian all was not mere slander.[56] It was essential for the Caesar at this stage to produce a new guarantee of his loyalty to the emperor. Following on the precedents that he had already set for himself, he now composed a third panegyric, in appearance designed to commemorate Constantius' heroic deeds, but in reality to express what was in his own mind.

This lengthy oration opens ominously by recalling the quarrel of Agamemnon and Achilles. The parallel is obvious enough, but anger soon overcomes subtlety, and Julian cannot resist the temptation to tell Constantius—who had just proclaimed Strasbourg as his own victory—that 'Agamemnon did not behave to his general temperately and tactfully, but resorted to threats and even insolent acts, when he robbed Achilles of the reward of his valour' (50a). This elephantine hint is followed by a stern warning, but a warning combined with an implicit statement of Julian's ultimate loyalty to Constantius, that we need not doubt:

The moral is that kings ought never to behave insolently nor use their power without reserve nor be carried away by their anger like a spirited horse that runs away for lack of the bit and the driver; at the same time Homer is warning generals not to resent the insolence of kings but to endure their censure with self-control and serenely, so that their whole life may not be filled with remorse. (III. 50bc)

If momentarily the idea of a revolt against his cousin entered his mind, Julian had too strict a morality to succumb to such a temptation: he recalled that his Mithraic faith required from him respect for the social order and obedience to his superiors and he realized that any rash action, however outwardly successful, was bound to sow in him a sense of guilt and repentance. So he remained loyal to Constantius, but not slavishly so. For now Julian was a general, an administrator and a political thinker, while birth had made of him the second most powerful individual in the empire. He was going to tell his cousin all that.

Two incompatible themes (which Julian had not yet reconciled for himself) run through this oration: the one, proclaiming

[56] Amm. XVI. 12. 67 ff.

that dynastic legitimacy is the hallmark of kingship, had only recently taken root in Julian's mind; the other, asserting that ἀρετή and ἀνδρεία, and not birth, are the characteristics of the true king, owes its hold over Julian's mind to the Platonic education he had received.

The first theme is characteristically fourth-century, and Byzantium's respect for Julian certainly owes something to this particular facet of his political thinking, which he went on developing in the years to come. If the greatness of the Pelopids, who after all ruled only a part of Greece for barely three generations, was not unworthy of Homer's Muse, what praise could suffice to convey the power of a House that had ruled the *oikoumene* for four generations? (III. 51b ff.). In the way this rhetorical question is formulated two significant details catch the attention of the reader: Julian finds support for his theory of *Dei gratia* kingship in Homer's description of Zeus and Hermes investing the Pelopids with the symbol of royalty,[57] while he uses the first person plural of the personal pronoun when referring to the genealogy of Claudius Gothicus, the alleged founder of the dynasty of the Second Flavians.[58] Whereas in his first panegyric Julian had expressed his strong feeling of dynastic commitment always by way of addressing Constantius, in this new oration each passage dealing with the idea of lawful power has a definite auto-panegyrical flavour, which Constantius can hardly have failed to notice.[59]

Once he has established that the notion of βασιλεία applies to two individuals in this particular case, Julian launches on an exposition of the duties of the king, which must surely have angered Constantius. The Platonic ideas—often distilled through Dio Chrysostom—that Julian introduces in the central section of the speech (III. 81a–92b) were far from being popular in Constantius' circle. 'Law is the off-spring of Dike, the sacred and truly divine offering of the most mighty god' (III. 89a), while the king is but the guardian of the divine word (III. 88d), and not 'the law animate', as official imperial propaganda had it.[60] He does not derive his authority from

---

[57] Hom. *Il.* B 101 ff.
[58] III. 51c: τά γε μὴν τῆς ἡμετέρας ξυγγενείας ἤρξατο . . . ἀπὸ Κλαυδίου.
[59] III. 58a, 76d–78a.
[60] Them. 14d–15d; 64b; 118d; 127b; 212d; 228a.

birth, which is not a sufficient guarantee of ἀρετή, but from his own inherent virtues, as moulded by education.[61] Using transparent similes, Julian then accuses the majority of the representatives of the House of Constantine of having been born bastards, with souls unmarked by the distinctive sign of ἀρετή which would have led them to perform their royal duties conscientiously (III. 81cd). Ingeniously inserted in this context, the phrase 'when the fortunes of Greece had not yet fallen' strikes home a bitter truth: Constantine and his sons had let the process of decadence set in by neglecting the functions of a king.

These functions, according to Julian, are primarily those of the priest and the prophet (III. 68bc)—duties which within the context of Christianity, and according to the spirit of the new religion, Julian's uncle and cousin had indeed performed. Like him, they felt and expressed in all possible ways that 'the true ruler ought to have his gaze fixed on the king of the gods, whose prophet and servant he is'.[62] But which king of the gods? In this second panegyric Julian makes no secret of his religious beliefs. His supreme deity is Zeus (III. 83a) or Helios, and he already speaks with the authority of their appointed vice-gerent on earth: 'Often men have stolen the votive offerings of Helios and destroyed his temples and gone their way, and some have been punished, and others let alone as not worthy of the punishment that leads to amendment' (III. 80c). These are direct threats to Constantius, and they are followed by a profession of Julian's Neoplatonic faith: the popular religion, proclaiming the existence of visible gods in Helios or Lucifer (III. 82d) and of heroes born from them, and the current demonological beliefs (III. 90 ff.) are certainly truthful at the level of sensible perception; yet, adds Julian, these things ought to be regarded by the wise man as no more than a symbolical representation of spiritual truths.

This Neoplatonic defence of mythology leads Julian effortlessly back to his main theme and, drawing directly from Plato's *Statesman* this time, he enumerates the criteria on which the βασιλικὸς ἀνήρ must choose his collaborators;[63] as for the king

[61] III. 80a, 81bc, 83a.
[62] III. 90a; cf. the golden coins struck in 325, which represent Constantine with his eyes turned upwards, Eus. *V. Const.* IV. 15.
[63] III. 90c ff.; cf. below, p. 119.

himself, he is truly worthy of his mission when showing equal concern for the three main duties that have been entrusted to him: the defence of his country, the social and economic prosperity of his people and, above all, the administration of justice.[64] Thus Julian, drawing on his own experience as a ruler in Gaul, composed a panegyric of his own deeds and sent it to Constantius. Yet, predicting the emperor's inevitable outburst of wrath at such an extraordinary piece of propaganda for his own cause, he warned his cousin about the evils that would befall him if he continued listening to calumnies. Harking back to his original theme, Julian invokes Zeus, the protector of friendship, and talks about λοιδορία: 'What a terrible thing is slander! How truly does it devour the heart and wound the soul as iron cannot wound the body!' (III. 96a). Sooner or later, it arouses in the heart of the suspicious man a conflict which will tear him apart.[65] In this connection Julian does not neglect to warn his cousin against ὕβρις. He uses now flattery, now concealed threats to frighten the superstitious emperor and, as if by the way, he recalls the foolishness of those who trusted in Fortune, forgetting how capricious a deity she is.[66]

Yet all had not been said. In 358 Julian was an infinitely more complex being than his panegyric suggests. His increasing involvement with the fortunes of the empire had gradually become obsessive, yet without stifling in him more private vocations whose cultivation demanded both time and emotional energy. The few letters that survive from this transitional phase in Julian's life show that, by enlarging the circle of his often conflicting commitments, the Caesar had become a more passionate and self-demanding being. His attachment to the philosophical life, his taste for occasional solitude and his need for intellectual stimulus were heightened by the adverse circumstances of his new career. In nostalgic letters to friends, with whom he had once shared the cultivated existence of a gentleman, he complained about the barbarity of his surroundings in Gaul and implored them to come and relieve the burden of intellectual

[64] On Julian's activities as a judge, see Amm. XVI. 5. 12–13; XVIII. 1. 4; XXII. 10; XXV. 4. 7; XXX. 4. 1; Lib. XVIII. 151; Greg. Naz. *or.* IV. 75; V. 21; see also below, p. 118.

[65] Julian will return to this point: what ruined Constantius was ἡ πρὸς τοὺς φίλους ἀπιστία (VII. 233c); cf. Mamert. 3.

[66] III. 96b ff.; cf. Hom. *Od.* θ 209–10.

isolation.[67] Shyly, he told them of the commentaries he had composed on Aristotelian texts[68] and, with an irritated passion bred of intellectual starvation, he asked for rare works of Neoplatonic scholarship to be sent to him.[69] At the same time, isolated from the fervent spiritual atmosphere of Pergamon and Athens and constrained to keep his religious convictions strictly to himself, Julian saw his faith becoming more intense and established a more effortless communication with the divine. The supreme deity in its solar manifestation had now become his personal guide, protector and saviour, and to his coreligionists Julian would never tire of acknowledging this allegiance which he regarded as the sole source of his success.[70] Then, confusing the voice of piety and duty with the ever quickening impulse of political ambition, Julian tells his friends how his only motive in life is to be of some use to them 'and when I say "you", I mean the real philosophers' (*ep.* 13); he is already dreaming of the moment when, as sole ruler, he will re-establish the ancestral rituals and will call the ἀληθινοὶ φιλόσοφοι to a share in the empire. By 359 this dream is expressed in unambiguous terms: in a letter to his close friend Oribasius Julian confesses his feeling that it will not be long before he is left sole Augustus. This presentiment has its root in a prophetic dream which, characteristically, came over a moment of great depression, when Julian had to steer his way through the adverse current of intrigue. Irritated by his inability to advance along the path he had himself chosen, Julian lets all the indignation that overwhelms his proud nature burst out in a letter to a friend who knows the situation in Gaul well: 'Often enough,' he says, 'I kept silence at the expense of my own dignity.'[71] Julian goes through the humiliations that he suffered, alludes to his quarrels with the praetorian prefect and finally comes up with the poignant question: 'Should one then keep silent or engage in battle?'—ἆρα σιωπᾶν ἢ μάχεσθαι ; 'the first course is idiotic, servile and odious to the gods; the latter is just, manly and liberal.'[72] Becoming more and more worked up while telling

[67] Lib. *ep.* 35; cf. J. *epp.* 8; 9; 13.
[68] *ep.* 12.
[69] Ibid.; see also above, p. 56.
[70] *epp.* 11; 26; 28.
[71] *ep.* 14. 384d.
[72] Ibid. 385a.

the story of all the concessions he had made—concessions
a less proud man would hardly have noticed—in this intensely
private letter Julian strikes a tone halfway between self-praise
and self-pity; yet, the reader instinctively recognizes the voice
of the self-assured man, the man confident in his genius and his
star, who can afford indignation and boasting while anticipating the final triumph.

'God who has posted me here is fighting on my side.'[73] Such
was the sentiment that finally prevailed after each crisis of
depression that assaulted Julian in that difficult year of 359,
when a systematic war of nerves was declared on him, cul-
minating in the recall of his mentor Salutius, in whom Julian
had found a substitute for Mardonius and even Maximus.

Salutius was a native of Gaul.[74] He was a man of great culture
versed in Greek philosophy and rhetoric,[75] but also an able
administrator with a rigorous sense of duty and a passion for
justice.[76] Having for many years held key administrative offices
in his homeland, he had acquired a deep knowledge of all the
problems that the province was facing and had worked out in
his mind the possible solutions.[77] When Julian arrived in Gaul,
Salutius, now a quaestor, was attached to the prince as his
counsellor. Soon Julian acquired a blind confidence in a man
whom he came to admire and respect as much for his culture
as for his integrity.[78] He listened to his advice and followed his
suggestions so closely that the rumour that was once spread
about Scipio and Laelius now acquired new life, and Salutius
was whispered to be the real author of Julian's achievements
(IV. 244cd). Libanius, however, preferred to see the relationship in Homeric terms, Salutius playing Phoenix to Julian's
Achilles.[79]

[73] *ep.* 14. 385c.
[74] IV. 252a. For Salutius' career, see *PLRE* s.v. 'Saturninius Secundus Salutius
3'; however, as A. D. Nock, *Sallustius, Concerning the Gods and the Universe*, Cambridge 1926, p. CI n. 14, and G. Rochefort, *Saloustios, Des dieux et du monde*, Paris
1960, pp. XI–XII, maintain, against *PLRE* s.v. 'Sallustius 1', he was also the
author of *De diis et mundo*. I follow them in accepting that Salutius—who had a
philosophical training, was a close collaborator of Julian and the dedicatee of
the *Caesars* and the *Hymn to King Helios*—was also the author of the Περὶ Θεῶν.
[75] IV. 247d; 252ab.
[76] Ibid.; 241d, cf. Lib. *epp.* 668. 2; 1298.
[77] On the general respect that Salutius enjoyed, see Amm. XXV. 5. 3.
[78] Greg. Naz. *or.* IV. 91; Socr. III. 19. 4; Soz. V. 20. 1.
[79] Lib. XII. 43.

But Florentius, the spokesman of Constantius' policy in Gaul,[80] disapproved of this situation. In the winter of 359[81] the longed-for opportunity occurred and Salutius was asked to leave Gaul. This event proved to be yet another step for Julian on his way to the throne, taking place as it did at a moment when he was acutely conscious of all the risks and humiliations imposed on him by his 'glittering servitude'.[82]

Yielding to his impulsive nature, Julian brooded over his grief. In the oration he composed he brushed aside the clichés proper to a προπεμπτικὸς or a παραμυθητικὸς λόγος, and let tears of grief and wrath flow abundantly: 'It is natural that grief should be biting my heart. Who is the kindly friend to whom I can turn in the future? With whose guileless and pure frankness shall I now brace myself? Who now will give me prudent counsel, reprove me with affection, lend me strength for good deeds without arrogance and conceit and use frankness after extracting the bitterness from the words?' (IV. 243c). The great mission entrusted to him at a crucial moment in human history, when decadence has begun to invade all quarters of life,[83] cannot be fulfilled, Julian feels, without the aid of gifted and faithful collaborators.[84] But instead he is surrounded by thieves and sycophants, whose baseness he takes immense pleasure in denouncing: all they have to offer is a certain wicked skill in doing down the honest man.[85] Yet Julian is determined not to let their insidious influence erode his morale (IV. 247b). The tears of rage that he has shed bring him merciful relief and, turning his back on an unsatisfactory reality, which has almost stopped mattering, Julian adopts the attitude of a Roman Stoic. Pericles, whom he admired so much, now comes to console him with a sermon drawn straight from M. Aurelius:[86] in the midst of adverse circumstances, advises the Athenian statesman, Julian ought to withdraw momentarily from his surroundings and, relying exclusively on his own moral

[80] See above, p. 59.
[81] V. 282c; Lib. XVIII. 84 ff.; for the date of Salutius' recall to the Court, see Zosimus, *Histoire nouvelle* (F. Paschoud) ii(1), Paris 1979, pp. 75–6 n. 14.
[82] V. 271c; see his bitter complaints in this connection in *ep.* 14.
[83] IV. 248bc.
[84] IV. 242d ff.
[85] IV. 242a, 248b–d.
[86] IV. 246a ff.

and emotional capacities, go on performing the duties the State
has assigned to him. Yet this line of thought and feeling, perfectly in tune with the mentality of the pragmatic Salutius, can
comfort Julian at only one level. His optimism, which he finds
hard to express in rational terms, springs from a mystical
source. In the depths of his heart the Caesar is convinced that
the god 'invoked or uninvoked', cannot abandon him to carry
on his mission alone.[87] The Homeric quotations that Julian
uses throughout his text, if read in the light of this conclusion,
help to make clear what he wishes to convey: he has recourse to
Odysseus, the Neoplatonic hero *par excellence*, who combats the
sensible world with the assistance of Athene,[88] and, identifying
with him in misfortune, desperation and perseverance alike,
Julian feels confident that ultimately his patient endurance of
all tribulations will be rewarded by Providence. Once Salutius
is recalled, he is, like Odysseus, left to wage the battle against
evil alone;[89] lonely, weak and unhappy, he spends his days
weeping and imploring the god to assist him,[90] for, like the
Homeric hero, he has only one aim in life, and an aim which is
bound to be accomplished, since Providence—personified in
both cases by Athene—is on his side.[91]

The recall of Salutius in the year 359 was but one indication of
the direction in which Constantius' behaviour towards Julian
was to evolve. Tortured by envy and incessantly urged to dis-
trust his cousin, Constantius had given credit to the rumour that
made Salutius responsible for Julian's brilliant social policy in
Gaul.[92] Yet that was not the only field in which Julian had
proved successful, and his military renown which, translated
into practical terms, meant an army well trained and devoted
to its leader, excited Constantius' naturally suspicious mind
even more. A plan had to be devised urgently whereby the
victorious Caesar would be effectively stripped of any means of

[87] IV. 250a–c; cf. Thucydides I. 118.
[88] F. Buffière, *Les Mythes d'Homère et la pensée grecque*, Paris 1956, 413–18.
[89] IV. 241d; cf. Hom. *Il.* Λ 401.
[90] IV. 250a ff.; cf. Hom. *Od.* ε 82–4, 151–8.
[91] IV. 250b ff.; cf. Hom. *Od.* ν 332. On Athene as Julian's special protectress,
see also Lib. XVIII. 32; cf. below, pp. 174, 176.
[92] IV. 244c–d; cf. above, p. 68.

increasing his power and fame further.[93] An excellent opportunity soon presented itself.

In 359 Constantius entrusted the defence of the eastern frontier to the incapable Sabinianus.[94] For most of the summer in the small city of Amida near the Persian border 120,000 souls fought desperately on a double front: against the Persian soldiers outside the walls, and hunger, heat and plague within, till on the seventy-third day the town was taken. Upon receiving this news, Constantius left Sirmium and moved slowly towards the East. Any reinforcements from Gaul were at least welcome, if not absolutely essential, at so critical a moment.

It was probably at the instigation of Florentius that, in January 360, Constantius sent the military tribune Decentius to Gaul with an order to deprive Julian of his auxiliaries—the legions of the Aeruli, the Batavi, the Celts and the Petulantes— as well as 300 select men from each of the other divisions (that is, Julian's personal guard), in all more than half of the Caesar's total forces.[95] More to the point, the tribune had strict orders not to contact the Caesar himself, but to arrange the matter with his aides Lupicinus and Sintula.[96] Julian, who had recruited the natives on the condition that he would not send them away from their homes, and realizing that he was faced with a conflict of duties, tried to behave with impartiality.[97] He did not protest against the injustice done to his own person, but he could not help firmly opposing the one point that affected both his dignity and the fate of those who had trusted him as a leader.[98] Indeed there was something wild in Julian, which the education of a gentleman had not quite stifled and which made his heart go out to the Germans. A few years later, in the midst of the smooth Antiochenes, he was to recall with nostalgia τὸ φιλελεύθερόν τε καὶ ἀνυπότακτον τῶν Γερμανῶν—'the

---

[93] See Amm. XX. 4. 1 ('Constantium ... urebant Iuliani virtutes, quas per ora gentium diversarum fama celebrior effunderat'); XVI. 12. 67–70; XVII. 11. 1–2. Cf. V. 282c; Mamert. 4. 4–5. 1; Lib. XVIII. 90 ff. and Zos. III. 8. 3.
[94] Amm. XVIII. 5. 5.
[95] Amm. XX. 4. 2.
[96] Ibid. 3.
[97] Ibid. 4.
[98] Ibid.: 'illud tamen nec dissimulare potuit nec silere: ut illi nullas paterentur molestias, qui, relictis laribus transrhenanis, sub hoc venerant pacto, ne ducerentur ad partes umquam transalpinas.'

freedom-loving and independent character of the Germans'.[99] He was certainly going to stand up for these brave soldiers and find a way of not breaking his oath either to Constantius or to them. He thus sought to reach an honest compromise and, using his personal credit, he tried to quieten down the troops, who were already in revolt.[100] Since Florentius and Lupicinus now washed their hands of the situation,[101] Julian realized that it was up to him to take any initiative, and only ask for Decentius' ratification *ex post facto*. Yet his decisions were not made without a good deal of vacillation, at least according to Ammianus' account of these events.[102]

It was not only a clash of duties that tormented Julian at this moment. His half-articulated claims to absolute power, and all the hopes and ambitions that he had confided to Oribasius only a few months before (*ep.* 14), also played a considerable part in his psychological conflict. His increasing sense of mission, stirred by the general decay of the empire, and his awareness—based partly on experience and partly on intuition—that he was able to remedy the situation, his hurt pride and his bitter yet long-suppressed indignation at his treatment by Constantius, all these feelings, to which he gave clear expression in his valedictory speech to Salutius, pointed in only one direction: but a few days later, and all these latent yet converging themes melt into a clear vision, that of the Genius Publicus, appearing to the hesitating Caesar in his sleep and urging him in unmistakable terms to seize power.[103] Yet the same sense of pride that made Julian so sensitive to Constantius' behaviour towards him, also prevented him from acting disloyally towards his cousin; while his Mithraic faith, with its ideal of absolute justice and respect for the social hierarchy, strengthened him in his decision to safeguard Constantius' interests. He had made up his mind: he would do everything in his power to avert an open mutiny of the troops.

[99] *C.G.* 138b; see below, pp. 209–11.
[100] Amm. loc. cit. 12.
[101] Amm. XX. 4. 6 ff.; 8. 20–2.
[102] Amm. XX. 4. 9.
[103] Amm. XX. 5. 10: 'olim, Iuliane, vestibulum aedium tuarum observo *latenter*, augere tuam gestiens dignitatem, et aliquotiens tamquam repudiatus abscessi: si ne nunc quidem recipior, *sententia concordante multorum*, ibo demissus et maestus. Id tamen retineto imo corde, quod tecum non diutius habitabo.'

Posing as the advocate of his cousin's cause, he presented Constantius' decree to the soldiers in the most favourable light he could, promising that they would be accompanied to the East by their families, and painting in attractive colours the emperor's 'potestas . . . ample patens et larga', in which they were to share with the prospect of high moral and material rewards.[104] It is improbable that this act of Julian's was deliberately intended to produce the opposite effect; if it had been, Christian writers would undoubtedly have denounced it as a provocation, and certainly Ammianus would have hinted at it. Given Julian's sense of dignity, it should be seen as an act of good faith, as a flamboyant, yet genuine, gesture by which the prince sought as much as anything else to convince himself of the illegitimacy of his semi-conscious ambitions. He could repeat to himself that he had tried to avoid having to address his soldiers altogether, and had suggested to Decentius that the troops should not pass through Paris on their way to the East.[105] Decentius had not agreed, and as the situation had now evolved, it had escaped from the control of both the Caesar and the tribune.

Julian's soldiers were animated by a double resentment: they saw themselves condemned to leave both family and fatherland in order to embark on fresh dangers under a new leader in a far and strange country,[106] while they felt as a personal humiliation the offence done to their general's honour. Unable to understand the complicated hierarchy of Roman values resting on hereditary rank rather than personal merit, they revolted on the spot and proclaimed Julian Augustus.[107] Julian's attitude to the mutiny was one of firm opposition.[108] Using all his powers of persuasion, he first sought to convince the soldiers of the absurdity of their action, promising that he would obtain from his cousin permission for them to stay in their home country.[109] He argued in vain, however, and, 'in the face of extreme necessity',[110] Julian consented to accept the

[104] Amm. XX. 4. 12.
[105] Amm. XX. 4. 11; Lib. XVIII. 96.
[106] Cf. Amm. XX. 4. 10.
[107] Ibid. 14 ff.
[108] Ibid. 15: 'ille mente fundata, universis resistebat et singulis.'
[109] Ibid. 15–16.
[110] Ibid. 18.

redoubtable honour that his soldiers claimed for him. Thus it was that, at the beginning of spring 360, in the course of a most tumultuous night, Julian was proclaimed emperor in Paris according to the barbarian ritual.[111] Over this critical point in his career, the pious Julian turned instinctively to the gods and sought their guidance, feeling that his human reason was not adequate to make the right decision;[112] but in order to convey effectively his state of mind and the supernatural happenings that persuaded him to yield to the will of the troops, he had recourse once more to Homer. Overcome by his own helplessness, he turned to Zeus for aid: 'And when the shouting grew still louder and all was in a tumult in the palace, I entreated the god to give me a sign; and thereupon he showed me a sign and bade me yield and not oppose myself to the will of the army.'[113] We know from Ammianus that the sign to which Julian refers was the appearance of the Genius Publicus itself: now it was Julian and not Constantius who was the elect.

The gods who guarded the empire had recourse even to cunning in order to assure its prosperity, presenting his mission to Julian as a duty imposed upon him by necessity, but also arousing in him the desire to fulfil this mission to the best of his abilities.[114] The appearance of the Genius Publicus symbolizes the moment of Julian's 'conversion' to a theocratical

---

[111] Amm XX. 4. 17: 'impositus scuto pedestri et sublatius eminens, nullo silente, Augustus renuntiatus [est].' On the mode of election, see also Lib. XIII. 34; Zos. III. 9. 2. It must have been early spring because Julian was still in winter quarters: cf. Amm. XX. 8. 2.

[112] Eunap. *V. Phil.* VII. 3. 7: τὸν ἱεροφάντην μετακαλέσας ἐκ τῆς Ἑλλάδος καὶ σὺν ἐκείνῳ τινὰ μόνοις ἐκείνοις γνώριμα διαπραξάμενος, ἐπὶ τὴν καθαίρεσιν ἠγέρθη τῆς Κωνσταντίου τυραννίδος. Lib. XII. 59: ὁ δὲ ἔβλεπε πρὸς οὐρανόν, καὶ ἦν ὁμοίως ἥ τε δόσις ἥ τε λῆψις ἄμφω βουλὴ δαιμόνων. XVIII. 103–4: θεοὺς μόνους ἀξιόχρεως ἐν τοῖς τηλικούτοις ἡγησάμενος συμβούλους ἐρόμενος ἤκουσεν, ὡς ἐμμενετέον οἷς εἶχεν. Λαβὼν δὲ ψῆφον τὴν ἐξ οὐρανοῦ . . .

[113] V. 284c and Hom. *Od.* γ 173; cf. Lib. XII. 59, and J. *ep.* 26. 415b.

[114] V. 284d: οἵ τε τοῦτο βουλόμενοι γενέσθαι θεοὶ . . . ἐμοὶ . . . ἔθελγον τὴν γνώμην. 285a: χρῆν δήπουθεν πιστεύοντα τῷ φήναντι θεῷ τὸ τέρας θαρρεῖν. 286d: ταῦτα ἔπεισε μέ, ταῦτα ἐφάνη μοι δίκαια. Καὶ πρῶτον μὲν ταὐτὰ τοῖς πάντα ὁρῶσι καὶ ἀκούουσιν ἀνεθέμην θεοῖς. 287a: Julian assumes action ὑπὲρ τῆς τῶν κοινῶν εὐπραγίας καὶ τῆς ἁπάντων τῶν ἀνθρώπων ἐλευθερίας. Cf. the wish expressed at the end of the epistle: 287d: θεοὶ δὲ οἱ πάντων κύριοι συμμαχίαν ἡμῖν τὴν ἑαυτῶν ὥσπερ ὑπέστησαν, εἰς τέλος δοῖεν. Cf. Lib. XII. 59–60.

conception of kingship, for which he was the first emperor to provide an articulate justification.

After his election Julian did his best to avoid a break with his cousin. He planned all his movements with great caution, trying all the while to find a compromise between the two conflicting duties he acknowledged: the firm conviction that the gods had chosen him to save the collapsing empire, and his careful respect for the social hierarchy.[115] After much hesitation, he decided to send a letter to Constantius explaining how things had happened, and why he had to recognize the *pronunciamento* of Paris, and asking for a peaceful settlement of the matter.[116] He signed his epistle as Caesar, asking only that his office should henceforth cease to be a nominal one, and claiming the power to rule over Gaul, in the province's interest (V. 285d). In a fit of rage, Constantius rejected Julian's proposals, and in a haughty letter, which was read before the assembled legions in Paris, he ordered his cousin to keep within the bounds of his former power.[117]

Once again, the reaction of the soldiers proved decisive.[118] Once again, Julian went through a stage of profound self-questioning,[119] which in large part was resolved by the will of the gods communicated to him through 'presagia multa . . . et somnia'.[120] A whole year had elapsed since the negotiations between the two colleagues had begun. Meanwhile Constantius celebrated his third marriage in Antioch, while inciting the Alamannic leader Vadomarius to make life difficult for his Caesar.[121] Julian crossed the Rhine for the last time and, having settled as best he could the affairs of Gaul, he left Paris and moved southwards to take up quarters in Vienne. The last moral and emotional bond between the two cousins had been providentially broken by the almost simultaneous death of their

---

[115] V. 285a: ἀλλ' ἠσχυνόμην δεινῶς καὶ κατεδυόμην, εἰ δόξαιμι μὴ πιστῶς ἄχρι τέλους ὑπακοῦσαι Κωνσταντίῳ.

[116] For his hesitation, Amm. XX. 8. 2–3; on the content of the letter, ibid. XX. 8. 5–17.

[117] Amm. XX. 9. 2, 4, 6; cf. Lib. XVIII. 106.

[118] Amm. XX. 9. 6–7: 'exclamabatur undique vocum terribilium sonu: "Auguste Iuliane", *ut provincialis et miles, et rei publicae decrevit auctoritas recreatae quidem*, sed adhuc metuendis redivivos barbarorum excursus.'

[119] Ibid. XXI. 1.

[120] Ibid. XXI. 1. 6; cf. XXI. 14.

[121] Ibid. XXI. 3. 4–5.

wives, Helena and Eusebia, who both, in different senses, represented a link between the two Augusti.[122]

In the city where at the beginning of his public career he had been greeted by the population as 'imperator clemens et faustus',[123] where the blind old woman had prophesied at his approach that the man was coming who would restore the temples of the gods,[124] Julian returned to celebrate his *quinquennalia*. For the occasion he wore a splendid diadem—'too ambitious' in Ammianus' view—studded with precious stones.[125] The days were gone for ever when he could still be happy with the *vilis corona* thrust upon him by his senior colleague. As from November 360 the mints of Lyon and Arles issued a special commemorative series, in which Julian acknowledged his gratitude to the Gallic army for his election; on the reverse of the golden coins the legend read: VIRTUS EXERC GALL; while the obverse represented Julian and a royal eagle. The symbolism, which so shocked the Christian writers,[126] is clear enough: Julian was emperor *Dei gratia*, and the army of Gaul had acted as the agent of divine will.[127]

Yet when it came to politics, Julian knew how to be deliberately ambiguous in order not to offend or estrange anybody. While his coinage proclaimed his secret religious sympathies with those who were willing to recognize in the new Augustus a fellow-pagan, on 6 January 361 the rebellious Caesar was seen at church offering public prayer to the Christian God.[128]

If in religious matters Julian opted for caution, in military affairs he judged that what was required was daring and speed.[129] His ability to detect and grasp the right moment for action—in Greek terms, his feeling for the καιρός[130]—enabled

---

[122] On Helena's death, Amm. XXI. 1. 5; on Eusebia's death, ibid. XXI. 6. 4.

[123] Amm. XV. 8. 21.

[124] Ibid. 22; cf. Socr. III. 1. 29.

[125] Amm. XXI. 1. 4.

[126] Soz. V. 17. 3; see also below, p. 190.

[127] Cf. E. D. Gilliard, 'Notes on the coinage of Julian the Apostate', *JRS* liv (1964), 137–8. *Pace* Gilliard, the issue of Arles does not post-date 361, for Julian seems to have had a beard at least from 357: Amm. XVII. 11. 1; cf. Mamert. 6. 4.

[128] Amm. XXI. 2. 4–5.

[129] Amm. XXI. 5. 1: 'nihil tam convenire conatibus subitis, quam celeritatem sagaci previdens mente, professa palam defectione, se tutiorem fore existimavit.'

[130] On Julian's awareness of how crucial a factor in politics is the concept of καιρός, see fr. 165a; also II. 124d; III. 101ab; V. 285a; X. 325b; cf. below, p. 176 n. 58.

him to realize that no more time should be spent on delibera-
tion, now that he had pacified Gaul and assured himself both
of the assistance of the gods and the support of his soldiers,
whose feelings he had carefully probed by a timely harangue.[131]
This decisive speech opened with the words 'magni commili-
tones', an expression conveying better than any wordy assur-
ance the democratic attitude that Julian always retained
towards his soldiers.[132] He inflamed their ardour to fight by
praising their valour while recalling the deeds they had accomplished together when liberating Gaul. Confirming in this way
both their mutual solidarity and the soldiers' confidence in him
as an efficient leader, and mentioning in passing that he had
been raised to the rank of Augustus only in deference to the
will of his followers[133] and to necessity, he announced his plan
of action and, while asking for the troops' support and trust,[134]
he confided the issue to Fortune. His brief harangue closed with
advice to the soldiers on how to behave during the campaign
against Constantius. Characteristically, Julian laid particular
stress on the 'indemnitas provinciarum et salus', thus reminding
his provincial audience of his administrative achievement in
Gaul and seeking to arouse their resentment against Constantius.[135]

Once he had laid down the main lines of his plan, and taken
the decision that the army of Gaul should march against Constantius, Julian, 'who knew by experience the value of anticipating and outstripping an adversary in troubled times . . .
unhesitatingly committed himself to whatever Fortune might
offer',[136] and embarked on a course of feverish action. He
decided to march on Constantinople with his Gallic troops

---

[131] Amm. XXI. 5. 2–8; V. 286d–287a.

[132] V. 287c: τοῖς . . . συστρατιώταις τοῖς ἐμοῖς (referring to the same
occasion); Cf. Lib. XII. 67 (the soldiers following Julian) νόμῳ μὲν γὰρ μεθ᾽
ἑτέρων ἦσαν, φίλτρῳ δὲ μετὰ σοῦ πυνθανόμενοι γνώμῃ μὲν εἶναι βασιλέα,
πόνοις δὲ συστρατιώτην. As will be argued later, Julian was a contradictory
personality, who managed to reconcile a democratic attitude towards his subjects
with an increasingly theocratic conception of kingship. The incompatibility between the two was largely responsible for the situation at Antioch getting out
of control, as will be shown in chapter 6 below.

[133] Amm. XXI. 5. 5.

[134] Ibid. 6–7.

[135] Ibid. 8.

[136] Ibid. 13.

while Constantius was detained in Syria by the Persian war.
Yet, as he was not sure of the feelings of the people of Italy and
Illyricum,[137] he devised an ingenious plan whose inspiration he
drew from his model, Alexander the Great: his relatively small
army was to be divided into three parts, each of which would
follow a different route so that, 'being spread over various parts
of the country, they might give the impression of a huge force
and fill everything (*cuncta*) with alarm.'[138] The bulk of the army
was to be divided into two parts, one commanded by the experienced and trustworthy Nevitta, and the other by Jovinus,
and to proceed through Rhaetia and northern Italy respectively, towards Constantinople, while Julian himself, escorted
by a corps of 3,000 select soldiers, was to set out for the
Danube.[139]

The first two detachments of the army never found a historian to record their deeds, for all eyes concentrated on Julian,
who, 'like a meteor or a blazing dart, hastened with winged
speed to his goal.'[140] In his own words, he 'travelled over the
earth with the inconceivable speed and unwearied energy of
one who flies through the air' (V. 269d). The phenomenal
rapidity of this march was remarked upon by historian and
panegyrist alike. Here was an emperor who wanted to convey
to the public the idea that Providence guided him; the touch
of divine grace had filled him with the kind of superhuman
energy before which all obstacles disappear: 'As if advancing
along some carefully constructed public road in a city, Julian
traversed his pathless, steep and precipitous way. Perhaps
Apollo was his guide, smoothing the impassable ways, as of old
around the ditch of the Achaeans.'[141] Something of this general
feeling filtered through even to Gregory of Nazianzos, who thus
unwillingly fostered the legend that Julian was a demonic being.
With Ammianus, Libanius and Zosimus, he talked of the prodigious speed that brought his anti-hero from Gaul into the
heart of Illyricum in no time at all.[142]

[137] Amm. XXI. 8. 2: 'inter subita vehementer incertus'.
[138] Ibid. 3.
[139] Loc. cit.
[140] Amm. XXI. 9. 6.
[141] Lib. XII. 62. In XVIII. 111 ff. Libanius presents Julian as having conquered the towns along the route by persuasion, force or deceit.
[142] Amm. XXII. 2. 5: 'ab urbe in urbem inopina velocitate transgressum';

Once Julian had crossed the Rhaetian Alps and embarked on the Danube, the success of his operation lay entirely with secrecy and speed. He stole down the river like a thief,[143] but this was not the story he wanted the world to believe. A few months later, the eye-witness Mamertinus was to describe before Julian his progress along the Danube as a triumphant parade along a river either bank of which was lined with Roman provincials and barbarians. The prince, standing on the prow of his boat, covered in dust and sweat, yet his eyes shining like stars, passed like a vision, having no time to spare for those who longed to entertain him.[144] If inaccurate historically, this panegyrical description faithfully conveys the emperor's own idea of how his public image ought to be painted. Instead of the hieratic figure his predecessors had coined, bearing immobile the weight of gold and precious stones, its imperturbable gaze for ever fixed on one spot, we see a monarch who wants to win his subjects' hearts by reminding them that he too is a man, yet a man endowed with exceptional powers which he never tires of putting at their disposal. Mardonius' triumph is complete. The old tutor—who was soon to be admitted to the royal table[145] —had infused his pupil with the heroic and classical conception of life, to the point that some contemporaries thought the emperor incapable of behaving with royal dignity.[146]

On 10 October 361, in the quiet of a dark night,[147] Julian landed unexpectedly at Bononea. On the spot, he dispatched to Sirmium his general Dagalaifus with an order to seize the count Lucillianus, commander of a cavalry force guarding the entrance to the capital of Illyricum.[148] All happened as planned and when, a few days later, Julian himself appeared in Sirmium,

---

Lib. XVIII. 111: ὥσπερ χειμάρρους ἐφέρετο; Zos. III. 10. 3; Mamert. 6. 2: 'calcata regum capita supervolans, in medio Illyrici sinu improvisus apparuit'; Greg. Naz. *or.* IV. 47, cannot help marvelling at the ὁρμή and the τάχος πολύ of his mortal enemy in this situation.

[143] Amm. XXI. 9. 2: 'Occulte, ideo latens'; Greg. Naz. loc. cit.: καὶ τῷ λαθεῖν μᾶλλον ἢ τῷ κρατῆσαι τὴν πάροδον ἁρπάσας.

[144] Mamert. 6–7.

[145] See above, p. 23 n. 40.

[146] See above, pp. 16–17.

[147] Amm. XXI. 9. 6: 'senescente luna ideoque obscurante noctis maximam partem'.

[148] Ibid.

the inhabitants, overcome by amazement, thought that they
were faced with an apparition.[149] They feasted his 'adventus' as
the coming of a superhuman being and, politically, Julian
responded to their best expectations by spending one of the two
days he stayed in Sirmium in giving chariot races.[150] On the
third day at dawn, he pressed on to the south, encouraged by
the manner he had been received at the first major city on his
way. The feeling that elsewhere too he would be greeted as a
'health-giving star'[151] grew on Julian. He certainly liked this
role and, if the expression had become customary in panegyrical
language in connection with a ruler's 'adventus',[152] Julian
would see to it that in his case it was uttered again with the
spontaneity of discovery.[153]

Hellenism had always laid particular stress on the idea of
health. The goal of all Greek education was the attainment of
an ideal of sanity at once physical, social and spiritual, reflecting the unity of Hellenic culture itself. Any deviation from
normality either in the sphere of social and political life or in
the area of spiritual activity was unanimously recognized as
νόσος—disease.

In the second century the Christian apologists proclaimed
that out of the set of religious and cultural values that made up
the apolitical Hellenism of their day they chose to retain only
the cultural part, substituting for its religious core their own
revelatory religion.[154] To the mind of a contemporary conservative thinker, such as Celsus, who could not even conceive
of the possibility of a distinction between culture and religion
within Hellenism, the attitude of those men of Greek *paideia*
who had opted for Christianity was a clear symptom of intellectual disease. To him Christianity was a spiritual affliction
affecting man's inner sight and rendering him incapable of
perceiving the unity of his life on earth. Yet, despite Celsus'

[149] Zos. III. 10. 3: ἐν ἐκπλήξει πάντες ἦσαν, φάσματι τὸ συμβὰν
ἀπεικάζοντες.

[150] Amm. XXI. 10. 2.

[151] Ibid.: 'sidus salutare'.

[152] Cf. S. MacCormack, 'Change and continuity in late antiquity: the ceremony
of *Adventus*', *Historia* xxi (1972), 721–52.

[153] See Lib. XIII. 41–2. Upon his entry into Antioch Julian is again greeted as
a 'salutare sidus' (Amm. XXII. 9. 14).

[154] See Introduction, pp. 3 ff.

therapeutic efforts the 'disease' spread over ever wider social strata. Porphyry's dedicated attempt to arrest its course came to nothing, and in the next generation winds of defeatism started blowing over the pagan camp as a result of the changing social and political trends of the age. Men of Hellenic culture now spoke of their world as being sick.[155] Yet this feeling was accompanied by a belief in a messianic healer who would appear like a second Asclepios to heal diseased humanity.[156] Hermes Trismegistus' gloomy eschatological prophecies[157] were taken seriously in the gravely endangered society of the fourth century AD, in a world which had indeed 'grown decrepit' and 'opted for darkness instead of light and for death instead of life'.[158]

Such was the state of mind of not a few pagan conservatives in the 350s. Julian appeared and was greeted as 'the new god . . . the sweet and philanthropic',[159] the 'health-giving star', the healer, who had come in the person of the youthful ruler of the *oikoumene*, to save humanity from moral death.[160] By a reciprocal process of suggestion and acceptance, this idea came to dominate both Julian himself and his panegyrists. The theme of healing, in the sense of the improvement of humanity's moral and spiritual welfare, grows steadily on Julian, who in his writings links it with his sense of political mission.[161]

For about four months Julian had been exclusively a man of action, conducting a campaign whose outcome was to determine the fate of the empire and of his own life. At Sirmium he

[155] E.g. Lib. XVIII. 21.
[156] See below, p. 168.
[157] *Asclepius* 24 ff.
[158] *Ascl.* 26: 'haec et talis senectus veniet mundi: inreligio, inordinatio, inrationabilitas bonorum omnium'. Ibid. 25: 'et capitale periculum constituetur in eum, qui se mentis religioni dederit.' The description of paganism as 'mentis religio' coincides with Julian's view of Hellenism (*C.G.* 229c–e).
[159] Greg. Naz. *or.* IV. 94; cf. the comments of the Anonymous scholiast, *PG* 36. 1229.
[160] On this theme, see Him. XLI. 8: τὰ δὲ σύμπαντα ἰώμενος οὐ κατὰ μικρόν, ὥσπερ οἱ ταῖς ἀνθρωπίναις τέχναις τοὺς ἀρρωστοῦντας, ἀλλ' ἀθρόαις εὐθὺς τῆς ὑγείας ταῖς χάρισι. Cf. Lib. XVIII. 21, 122; XIII. 42; XV. 69; XVII. 27, 36; etc. See also below, p. 168.
[161] Cf. *ep.* 89b. 305b; VIII. 161b to be compared with Plato, *Rep.* 519a on the meaning of true *paideia*. See also the famous allegory from the invective against Heracleius, and esp. VII. 229c, where the word νόσος is used to describe Christianity. In this connection, see *ep.* 61. 424ab, where the Christians are compared to the φρενετίζοντες. On the latter theme, *inter alia, ep.* 114. 438b.

realized that he had reached a critical point. It was one of those moments in his career when he could not afford the slightest strategical mistake. Before the winter set in he hastened towards Thrace, occupied the pass of Succi and, entrusting the defence of this crucial position to Nevitta, returned to take up winter quarters at Naissos. His instinct warned him that he should not imperil what he had already achieved by endeavouring to march on the capital. While one after another the plains of Illyricum would be covered in snow, Julian, safely ensconced in Naissos, would prepare on all fronts for the decisive confrontation with Constantius. His subtle mind and passionate nature yielded to a tempting vision, not only of an enterprise crowned with success in diplomatic terms, but also of his own gratification with the pleasure of revenge. There, in the birth-place of Constantine, Julian would see that, before spring set in, the memory of his uncle faded away before a sense of gratefulness for his own achievement.

Yet Naissos was not only a place rich with Constantinian associations and, as such, important for Julian on the symbolic level. It also possessed more substantial virtues in its geographical position and great material wealth, which must have weighed heavily in his choice. Upon his arrival there Julian immediately proceeded to the recruitment of fresh forces from all over the territories in his control,[162] and used the *fabricae* of the city[163] to supply his swelling army with all its necessities.[164] But his main activity was in the field of diplomacy. It is just possible that, while descending the Danube, Julian had found time to satisfy the demands of the adjacent towns by granting 'immunitates, privilegia, pecunias',[165] and it is not unlikely that, in his attempt to win over their populations, he made public the contents of Constantius' letters inciting the barbarians to attack Julian.[166] This policy of civic benefaction and the public discrediting of his colleague was now to be pursued from Naissos on the grand scale. The Dalmatians and the Epirots were immediately granted the alleviation of a tax in kind they payed to the government, while many of the cities of Illyricum benefited

[162] Amm. XXI. 12. 2; 13. 6.
[163] *Not. Dign. or.* XI. 37.
[164] Mamert. 14. 1.
[165] Mamert. 8. 3.
[166] Lib. XVIII. 113; Socr. III. 1. 38.

from Julian's attempts to encourage the renaissance of provincial towns. Nicopolis, Athens and Eleusis were a few of those once important civic centres which 'were brought back to life by imperial action'.[167] The empty places on their municipal councils were filled and key administrative posts all over the western part of the empire were confided to personalities who had distinguished themselves in the field of letters.[168] As the count of sacred largesses, Mamertinus was well placed to observe the about-turn in the financial policy of the State: rather than enriching the imperial treasury, the provinces now started receiving money as a result of imperial munificence.[169] A striking illustration of this policy (which, in propaganda terms, of course paid immediate and substantial dividends), is provided by Rome, which at that moment was suffering from a food shortage. By swift personal intervention Julian solved the problem,[170] and, seizing the opportunity, he attempted to win the Roman élite over to his cause. In a letter to the Senate he bitterly criticized Constantine's policy, 'specifically charged Constantius with disgraceful acts and faults' and announced his own programme of reforms,[171] of which they had already seen an example. The *patres* were not amused. Greatly shocked at the irreverent remarks Julian made about Constantius, of whose personal dignity they had retained a deep impression,[172] the representatives of this august and notoriously conservative body reserved their contempt for the ungrateful rebel. Julian had clearly made a *faux pas* of which the *levitas*, which was so prominent a feature of his character,[173] was not the only cause. An easterner by birth and education, at home in the informal company of men of letters and soldiers, he had yet to encounter the glacial snobbery of these men, who prided themselves exclusively on their birth and wealth.

[167] Mamert. 9. 4.
[168] Lib. XVIII. 104; Amm. XXI. 10. 6, XXII. 7. 6; Zos. IV. 3. 3.
[169] Mamert. 10. 2.
[170] Mamert. 14. 2.
[171] This letter was described by Ammianus as 'oratio acris et invectiva' (XXI. 10. 7); cf. I. 8ab on Constantine's prodigality.
[172] Amm. XVI. 10. 9 ff.
[173] Amm. XVI. 7. 6: Eutherius sometimes criticized Julian 'Asiaticis coalitum moribus, ideoque levem'. *Levitas* is the first and, presumably, most serious fault that Ammianus attributes to Julian when drawing up the list of his negative qualities: he was 'levioris ingenii', XXV. 4. 16.

It is the motivation behind Julian's action, though, rather than the manner in which he carried it out, that is important. It was typical of Julian's conservatism that, rather than turning to Constantinople and seeking to obtain her alliance, he addressed himself to the Senate of Rome. Indeed Rome, with its thousand-year-old tradition, and not Constantinople, was to his mind the true capital of the empire. In his first panegyric on Constantius, Julian had already proclaimed the superiority of Rome over all other cities in no uncertain terms. 'The queen of cities'[174] was the symbol to which he invariably turned whenever he wished to convey the idea of the empire as a political and spiritual unity.[175] For obvious strategical reasons, Julian had to advance on Constantinople once he had taken the decision to confront Constantius openly. Having included Rome in the part of the empire under his control, he pushed on towards the city which 'surpassed all other cities in the same degree that she herself was inferior to Rome' (I. 8c), a striking statement in view of the contemporary iconographical and literary evidence for the idea of Rome and Constantinople as twins.[176] For Julian tended to think in terms of a different pair, that of Rome and Athens (I. 8c), as the respective symbols of the political and cultural principles on which the Roman empire stood:[177]

Has not Apollo, the co-regent of Helios, set up oracles in every part of the earth, and given to men inspired wisdom and introduced order into their cities by means of sacred and civil institutions? He Himself has civilized by means of the Greek colonies the greater part of the *oikoumene* and thus made it easier for it to obey the Romans who not only belong to the Greek race, but also have established and maintained sacred institutions and pious belief in the gods, which are things from beginning to end Greek. Moreover, the Romans have established a constitution not inferior to that of any one of the best governed states, if indeed it be not superior to all others that

[174] ἡ βασιλεύουσα τῶν ἁπάντων πόλις, I. 5c; cf. XI. 131d.

[175] I. 6b ff., 10b, 29c ff.; Rome is not just κρατίστη, but also θεοφιλής (VIII. 161b); cf. VIII. 180b.

[176] For the iconography of Rome and Constantinople in the fourth century, see J. M. C. Toynbee, 'Roma and Constantinopolis in late antique art from 312 to 365', *JRS* xxxvii (1947), 135–44. Cf. H. Stern, *Le Calendrier de 354: Étude sur son texte et ses illustrations*, Paris 1953, 124–44, for the symbolism of Rome, Constantinople and Trèves on the Calendar of 354.

[177] See Lib. XV. 36.

have ever been put into practice. For which reason, I too recognize
that the City is Greek, both in descent and in its constitution.
(XI. 152d–153a)

This statement of faith, proclaiming the spiritual, cultural and
political unity of the Roman empire in historical terms, must
have sounded somewhat forced in the mid-fourth century. For
it was a personal ideal and not a widely spread belief as it had
been in the second century; it was the vision of one man, which
grew in him despite, and even in contradiction to, the realities
of fourth-century politics, whereas in the Antonine era it had
been an attitude inspired in men, and almost thrust upon them,
by the circumstances around them.

Acting according to this ideal, in 361 Julian ignored the
claims of Constantinople and, instead, addressed epistles to
Rome and Athens, expecting to be judged by the Roman
Senate on political grounds, and by the Senate and people of
Athens on his own merits as an individual.

The letter that Julian sent to the Athenians survives in its
entirety. In accents reminiscent of Pericles' funeral oration
Julian describes Athens as the last stronghold and refuge of
justice in the midst of a now collapsing world (V. 269b), for
whose restoration he is fighting with all his forces (V. 286d).
The Athenians, who had once arbitrated in disputes between
the gods,[178] and produced citizens whose sense of justice became
proverbial, are now called to listen to Julian's apology and
pronounce their verdict. Before his favourite public the emperor
allows himself to indulge in self-pity and self-praise; he tells the
Athenians the story of his miseries and humiliations and of all
the wrongs done to him since the moment of his father's murder;
this bitter—and long-suppressed—reminiscence, long ensconced
in the prince's memory, at last explodes in a fit of rage. In sacred
wrath he denounces Constantius for the φονεύς, the murderer,
he is. How right the δήμιος—the assassin—was to laugh at the
stupidity and lack of dignity of one who faithfully served the
executioner of his entire family! (V. 281b). Yet 'I thought I
ought not to fight against my yoke' (V. 278c) and, overlook-
ing many a humiliation, 'I honoured myself by keeping silent'
(V. 278d). Julian tells the Athenians of the complete lack of

[178] Lib. XVIII. 115.

tenderness and the ever present fear that hung over his first years, and he further fires their righteous indignation by the narration of his exploits in Gaul. In a concise military style he tells his judges of the rare feats of strategy and heroism he performed for five years against all odds. Ἐμαχεσάμην οὐκ ἀκλεῶς, 'I fought not ingloriously' (V. 279b), is his final pronouncement on his military career in Gaul. This admirable verbal restraint alternates with pages of uncontrolled excitement, in which Julian re-lives the events of the night of his election. Then comes the detailed account of all the psychological upheavals and moral scruples experienced during the period when Julian step by step allowed his sense of divine mission to become the dominant theme of his life. Personal involvement and an incontestable—if erratic—literary talent allowed Julian to attain to the level of great oratory in these pages, which symbolize his own tribute to a city which was both the spiritual capital of Hellenism and the author's *alma mater*.

Other cities were also honoured with imperial letters.[179] During the years of his travels, Corinth had received Julian's father who, 'like Odysseus . . . was delivered from his long-protracted wanderings'.[180] Reminding the Corinthians of their ancient bond, Julian must have asked for their present support; Corinth, like Sparta, which also shared in the privilege of receiving a letter, was a flourishing centre of philosophical studies (II. 119bc) and this, combined with the prestige these two cities once enjoyed, was enough of a reason for Julian to treat them with exceptional reverence.

Yet, while preparing his defence on all fronts, Julian could not help being a prey to dark thoughts. He was well aware that Constantius with the bulk of the Roman army was advancing on Constantinople, and realized that there was a distinct possibility that some of the cities of the western and Balkan provinces, weighing up the possible outcome of the civil strife, might opt for loyalty to Constantius,[181] who was not only the legitimate emperor, but also one who had been able so far to crush every usurper who had challenged his throne.

---

[179] Lib. XII. 64; XVIII. 113; Zos. III. 10. 4; Mamert. 9. 4.
[180] *ELF* 20.   [181] Cf. the example of Aquileia, Amm. XXI. 11-12.

It is indicative of Julian's unease that at Naissos he never stopped consulting the gods about the future, accepting only reluctantly the favourable omens that the soothsayers of his circle announced to him, and questioning even what seemed most certain.[182] Doubt had now beset him, and for some time he suspected, if not that the gods had laid a trap for him, then at least his own competence as the inspired interpreter of their will.[183]

This situation was suddenly resolved when one day, towards the end of November or even the beginning of December,[184] messengers arrived at Naissos with the news of the emperor's death. On 5 November, the forty-four-year-old Constantius, who had set forth in great haste with his army to meet his cousin, died at Mopsycrenae, a small town in Cilicia near the Cappadocian border, after the long agony the oracles had foretold.[185] Julian was now the incontestable heir to the throne by his cousin's last wish,[186] the will of the army and by the general feeling for dynastic legitimacy so strongly rooted in the fourth-century mind.[187] The news of Constantius' death was received by Julian as the will of the gods.[188] Without the least delay, the new emperor set out for Constantinople, finding time during his march only to send a series of invitations to join him to those whom he wanted as spiritual masters and future collaborators. The bulk of these letters have been lost, and the few that remain contain gaps doubtless due to Christian copyists.[189] Yet even these few letters are enough to help us reconstruct Julian's state of mind at that moment. The epistles addressed to Maximus, to Julian's maternal uncle and namesake and to Eutherius, his faithful chamberlain, were perhaps written the very night that Julian heard of Constantius' death,[190] and betray a deep

[182] Amm. XXII. 1; Zos. III. 11. 1.
[183] Amm. loc. cit.
[184] Amm. XXII. 2. 1. For the chronology, see G. Schwartz, *De vita et scriptis Iuliani imperatoris* (diss.), Bonn 1888, 9.
[185] Amm. XXI. 15. 2–3 (with Seeck's correction of the date). See also Amm. XXI. 2. 2; XXI. 14; XXII. 1. 2; Zos. III. 9. 5.
[186] Amm. XXI. 15. 2; XXII. 2. 1; Zos. III. 11. 2.
[187] On this, see Calderone, *Entretiens Hardt* xix. 256 ff.
[188] On Julian's feelings at the announcement of Constantius' death, see Lib. XVIII. 119–20; J. *ep.* 28; cf. XII. 357c.
[189] Cf. *ELF*, introductory notes and *testimonia* to Nos. 26–46; also *Julien* I(2), 30 ff.
[190] See *ELF*, introductory notes to Nos. 26, 28, 29.

D

emotion. They are all pervaded by a feeling of relief at the miraculous resolution of the situation, without either bloodshed or the persecution of Julian's friends in the East:

We are alive by the will of the gods, freed from the necessity of suffering or inflicting the irreparable. I witness Helios—whom of all the gods I besought most earnestly to assist me—and King Zeus: I have never wished to kill Constantius; rather I have wished the contrary. Then why have I come? Because the gods expressly ordered me, promising safety if I obeyed, while, if I stayed, what I pray no god may do to me. (*ep.* 28)

Here Julian has expressed spontaneously and with clarity the preoccupations that were in the forefront of his mind during the months of his march against Constantius. At the same time he allows us to see the way in which the main forces that had worked on him during two distinct phases of his life had become fused. The desire to be a socially useful person, which Mithraism had kindled in him, was transformed by his experiences in Gaul into an all-pervading sense of worldly mission. Now— since the Genius Publicus had appeared before him—Julian believed that his primary duty in life was to restore a collapsing *oikoumene*, and in his attempt to fulfil this mission he had taken as his model and guide the god who had first encouraged in him a sense of worldly belonging: Helios-Mithra, supreme deity at once of the Neoplatonists and of the Roman state, was henceforth to inspire Julian in all his doings. To proclaim this belief as unequivocally as he could, upon his entrance into the capital, the emperor erected a Mithraeum within his own palace[191]— a thank-offering to the god who, having ensured the success of his revolt,[192] was now to help him save the empire from dissolution.

---

[191] Lib. XVIII. 127; cf. XII. 80; see also Him. XLI. 8: τεμένη μὲν ἐγείρων θεοῖς, τελετὰς δὲ θείας καθιδρύων τῇ πόλει ξένας.
[192] See *JThS* N.S. xxviii, 362 n. 1.

III. IULIANUS AUGUSTUS

The ritual invites us, who by nature belong to the heavens, but have fallen to earth, to reap virtue and piety in the field of our earthly conduct, and then hasten upwards to join the goddess of our forefathers and the principle of all life. (VIII. 169b)

Julian's zeal did not flag when he received the news of Constantius' death. Anxious to keep up his reputation as a superhumanly energetic leader, whose every action was inspired by the will of the gods, he left Naissos at once; 'and, as rumour is wont to exaggerate all novelties, he seemed raised even higher, as if borne on Triptolemus' chariot, which antiquity fond of myths represents as drawn through the air by winged dragons.'[1] On 11 December the emperor entered his native city warmly acclaimed by senate and people, whose relief was tempered by awe at the knowledge that imperial power had been bestowed upon Julian *nutu caelesti*—by divine grace.[2]

Julian emphasized his divine right by asserting his link with the Constantinian dynasty in symbolical fashion. As the funerary cortège with Constantius' remains sailed into the Bosphorus, the emperor stood waiting, bareheaded and weeping, ready to escort his predecessor to his last home, the Church of the Holy Apostles.[3] There he rendered in person the last honours according to the ritual dear to the deceased and saw that the rites of apotheosis were performed for the man whose lawful heir he now was.[4] A few weeks later, in a letter to a coreligionist, who seems to have been on Constantius' 'black list' during Julian's march on Constantinople, the new emperor will not hesitate to call Constantius a 'brother' and formulate the traditional wish that 'earth may lie light upon him'.[5]

It would not have been in Julian's character to be the narrow-minded persecutor of those who had associated innocently with

---

[1] Amm. XXII. 2. 3.
[2] Ibid. 5.   [3] Lib. XVIII. 120.
[4] Mamert. 27. 5; cf. 3. 2. Julian's behaviour made a lasting impression on Byzantium; see Psellus, *Accusation of the Patriarch M. Cerularius* xxxix, *REG* xvii (1904), 42.
[5] *ep.* 33; cf. *ep.* 60. 379a: τὸν μακαριώτατον Κωνστάντιον.

the previous regime. Doubtless it was with this thought in his mind that, as soon as the news that Julian was now the sole legitimate emperor reached him, the court-philosopher Themistius immediately dispatched a congratulatory letter to him, offering his services and flattering him extravagantly.[6] To this letter, which has not been preserved, Julian answered with a long epistle wholly devoted to questions of political philosophy, which constitutes in fact an attempt to define the ideal statesman.[7]

When writing the *Letter to Themistius* Julian's mind was full of the notions and precepts that Plato develops in his *Statesman* and *Laws*, and Aristotle in his *Politics*. They had both defined the βασιλικὸς ἀνήρ as a man who, through perfect knowledge, had raised himself far above the average of humanity; an enlightened being who directs human affairs by using the ἐπιστήμη he has acquired by contemplation of the ideal world. Plato even goes so far as to make an ἔνθεος of the statesman, by talking of the μοῦσα τῆς βασιλικῆς who inspires him in all his actions.[8] Measuring the magnitude of the task allotted to him, the student of the philosophers confesses that there is nothing exceptional in his nature to enable him to perform his mission adequately (VI. 254b, 267a). He talks of his love of philosophy, which he was not allowed to pursue as a full-time occupation, and, while admitting that even his incomplete philosophical training is an asset in the situation, he confesses that he can only face his present lot with trepidation. And, as a child of his age, Julian assigns Fortune the leading role in politics, which he knows to be a field where virtue and a wise policy can often prove of no avail (VI. 255d). Ἡ τύχη καὶ τὸ αὐτόματον—fortune and chance—form the one great theme of this text. In this

---

[6] VI. 253ab. In VI. 254b Julian points out that it is unworthy of a philosopher to flatter or deceive.

[7] Both Bidez and Rochefort maintain that the *Letter to Themistius* was written some time between the announcement of Constantius' death and Julian's arrival in Constantinople on 11 Dec. 361 (Bidez, *Tradition manuscrite*, Appendix I; Rochefort, *Julien* II(1), 10). Yet if the short period of time between these two dates is considered, it becomes apparent that it was hardly possible for Julian to have received a letter from Themistius and to have written an answer during his progress towards the capital. It would appear more probable that the *Letter to Themistius* was composed shortly after Julian entered Constantinople, at the very moment when he found himself faced with the problem of how to govern the empire. The content and the tone of the letter both support this assumption.

[8] Plato, *Pol.* 309d.

respect Julian's attitude is also the attitude of the classical man
who attempts to placate Fortune and the gods lest they should
be roused to wrath by his blind confidence in his rising star
(VI. 256c ff.): if the philosopher's felicity does not depend on
Fortune, the king's success does in a very real sense.[9] The great
classical theme of ὕβρις and its pernicious effects on human
existence find their natural place in this context. Abundant
evidence drawn from Greek and Roman history illustrates the
foolishness of mankind, before Julian concludes with a pessimistic remark (genuinely Thucydidean in spirit and expression)
about the inevitability of such behaviour.[10] He then proceeds to
link his major point—the omnipotence of τύχη in politics—with
Plato's own teaching (VI. 257d). Julian takes as axiomatic
Plato's classification of the factors that rule human affairs as
Θεός-τύχη and καιρός-τέχνη.[11] All that the statesman can
aspire to is τέχνη, the special training which can enable a
highly gifted nature to perceive and grasp on all occasions the
καιρός.[12] Yet to master this is beyond human ability, as Plato
himself had admitted. Julian quotes *in extenso* a lengthy passage
from the *Laws* which provides the key to his argument; it is
the myth about the golden age of Kronos who, knowing that
imperfection is inherent in human nature, entrusted the
guidance of human societies to demons. To Julian, with his
Neoplatonic training, the hidden meaning behind the Platonic
allegory is that the ruler should endeavour to govern and
legislate according to the divine part of his nature, banishing
any mortal and bestial element from his soul and aspiring to
the disposition of a demon.[13]

With reference to Aristotle, *Pol.* 1287a, Julian rejects the idea
of hereditary monarchy and the principle of *Dei gratia* despotism
(VI. 261), and even goes so far as to maintain that it is un-
natural for a man to be a king: 'it is not just that one man

---

[9] VI. 256cd; cf. Plato, *ep.* VII. 326a.

[10] VI. 257a–c; cf. Thuc. III. 82. 2.

[11] *Leg.* 709b; cf. *ep.* VII. 326a.

[12] The statesman's art consists in applying τὸ μέτριον καὶ τὸ πρέπον καὶ τὸν
καιρὸν καὶ τὸ δέον (*Pol.* 284e) in the field of politics.

[13] VI. 259ab and Plato, *Leg.* 713c–714a. Doubtless Julian also had in mind at
this point *Pol.* 309c–e, where one finds, next to the idea developed by Julian, all
the crucial words of which he makes use; cf. also the condemnation of Themi-
stocles, Cimon and Pericles as statesmen (*Gorgias* 519a).

should rule over many who are his equals, human nature being
by no means worthy of such an excess of fortune ... since the
reason that is in men, however good they may be, is entangled
with passion and desire, those most ferocious monsters.'[14]

After this direct attack on Themistius' view of kingship,[15]
Julian analyses the concept of law, quoting a passage in which
Aristotle summarizes Plato's views on this subject. Law is the
very conscience of the βασιλικὸς ἀνήρ, the pure λόγος in him
exempt from desire.[16] He who has contemplated τὸ μέγιστον
μάθημα—the Idea of τὸ ἀγαθόν[17]—occasionally has the right to
trespass on the boundaries of the written law by virtue of the
superior criterion which he now carries within himself, and
which coincides with the very Idea of justice on which alone the
ideal state should be founded.[18] But Julian is extremely reluctant to recognize this figure in himself. Indeed he faces himself
as a mediocre ruler, while at the same time pointing out that
the manifold problems that arise out of the government of a
world-empire make a ruler's task even harder than in classical
times.[19] Following Plato, he holds that in this imperfect state
what is required is absolute obedience to the law,[20] and in
defining the spirit in which the laws should be drawn up,
Julian again shows his allegiance to Plato by stating that the
legislator,

after purifying his mind and soul ... will enact his laws without any
consideration of the crimes of the moment or of immediate con-
tingencies. But, having reached a profound understanding of the
nature of government, and contemplated the Idea of justice, and
studied the essential nature of injustice, he will then transpose, so
far as this is possible, the absolute into the realm of the relative,
instituting laws which have general application to all the citizens

---

[14] VI. 261cd. For the popularity of this idea in certain circles in late antiquity,
see Lib., *Decl.* V. 84; Synesius, *De regno* 15.

[15] For a good analysis of Themistius' political philosophy, see Dagron, *T&MByz*
iii (1968), 1–242.

[16] VI. 261bc and Ar. *Pol.* 1287a; cf. *Nic. Eth.* 1180a, 21 ff.: ὁ δὲ νόμος
ἀναγκαστικὴν ἔχει δύναμιν, λόγος ὢν ἀπό τινος φρονήσεως καὶ νοῦ. See K.
Tsatsos, Ἡ κοινωνικὴ φιλοσοφία τῶν ἀρχαίων Ἑλλήνων, Athens 1962,
139.

[17] *Rep.* 505a.

[18] Loc. cit.; id. *Pol.* 294b; cf. 293ab.

[19] Julian was well aware that in order to rule the Roman empire one needed
ποικίλων ἠθῶν ἐμπειρίας, I. 13a; cf. 13d–14a.

[20] VI. 261a; cf. Plato, *Pol.* 300d–301a.

without regard to friend or foe, neighbour or kinsman. Indeed, it would be better if such a legislator promulgated laws not for his own contemporaries, but for posterity or for strangers, with whom he neither has nor hopes to have any private dealings. (VI. 262a–c)

This idealistic conception of the law as an emanation of the eternal Idea of justice recalls Plotinus' description of Minos, the intimate friend of Zeus,[21] as the ideal law-giver who framed his laws as an inevitably pale reflection of the divine truth and beauty he had once contemplated.[22] Such a view was totally alien to Themistius—a philosopher with an Aristotelian frame of mind, who spent a lifetime advocating a political philosophy applicable to the realm of the practical—τοῖς κοινοῖς ὠφελιμωτέραν.[23]

With conscious polemical intent Julian stresses the incontestable superiority of the contemplative mode of existence over the practical one, a theme to which he devotes the rest of the letter, proving that the same view had been held by all leading Greek philosophers, and pointing out to Themistius *en passant* that he does not even understand his Aristotle.[24] Then, as an appendix to his treatment of θεωρία and πρᾶξις, he declines with subtle irony Themistius' offer of collaboration('it is in your power by producing many philosophers or even three or four, to confer more benefit on the lives of men than many kings put together' (VI. 266a)). In other words, ἔρδοι δ' ἕκαστος ἥντιν' εἰδείη τέχνην: the Aristophanic maxim, quoted earlier in the letter,[25] must have already conveyed Julian's message to Themistius. As for himself, Julian continues, he has been called to perform a duty. He cannot escape, though he longs to, not because of his idleness, but on account of the acute awareness of his own limitations and inadequacy to perform his role satisfactorily (VI. 266c). He thus lays all his hopes of success in the hands of God, and exhorts his subjects to feel grateful to Him, if ultimately his reign is successful (VI. 267ab).

---

[21] ὀαριστὴς Διός, Hom. *Od.* τ 179.

[22] *Enn.* VI. 9. 7; cf. Iambl. *V. Pyth.* 27, and Proclus *In Remp.* I. 156. 12 ff.

[23] Them. 352c, 108ab and *or.* XXXIV. 3. See also n. 15 above, p. 92.

[24] VI. 263c–264a, 265a. In 256bc Julian had also attacked Themistius in the same manner, using *Nic. Eth.* 1100a. 33 ff. to address a biting remark to Themistius concerning the ideal of ῥᾳστώνη, so actively championed by him (cf. Them. 174d and below, p. 210 n. 69).

[25] VI. 260c and *Wasps* 1431: 'let every man practise the craft that he knows'.

The *Letter to Themistius* is a puzzling text. In it Julian categori-
cally rejects absolute monarchy and hereditary kingship, two
principles he actively championed during the rest of his brief
reign. Indeed these two ideas, which are developed in the
Contra Heracleium, the *Contra Galilaeos* and the *Caesars*, have deep
roots in Julian's past, for their history began on the night when
the Genius Publicus appeared to him in his sleep.[26] The celebra-
tion of Julian's *quinquennalia* in Vienne should be regarded as
another landmark in his intellectual development in this connection: he wore for the occasion 'too ambitious a diadem, set
with gleaming gems'. Ammianus, who reports this, contrasts
Julian's attitude with that he showed at the beginning of his
Caesarship.[27]

In the light of what precedes and follows, the *Letter to Themistius* appears as a momentary aberration. What the biographer
of Julian must do is to seek to explain what caused this sudden
and ephemeral change in attitude, which can neither be disregarded nor considered in isolation. To read the *Letter to
Themistius* independently of the rest of Julian's writings is to
fall into the same trap as all those who have come to the conclusion that Julian's conception of imperial power was 'reactionary'.[28]

With its 'classical' outlook on politics, the *Letter to Themistius*
appears very much as the product of Julian's particular education. After the long inner struggle in Gaul, and all the uncertain-
ties that had beset him during the march to Constantinople,
Julian arrived at the capital as sole emperor, and at last found
that there was no longer any external force that could prevent
him from beginning to fulfil his mission. He knew that both his
power and responsibility were unlimited. Alone, free and responsible, this sudden realization of his position momentarily
frightened him;[29] it was only natural that he should seek to
reassert his identity by invoking his only inalienable possession

[26] See above, pp. 72 and 74.
[27] Amm. XXI. 1. 4; cf. above, p. 76.
[28] See below, p. 113 n. 132.
[29] Cf. VI. 259b, where Julian confesses that he is frightened; VI. 253b, for
Julian's nostalgic remembrance of his ἀττικὰ διαιτήματα; VI. 260b; 255b, for
his adoption even of the Epicurean maxim λάθε βιώσας; see also VI. 267b,
where the emperor tries to shake off from his shoulders the responsibility of his
position.

—his education and cultural background. In the midst of despair and loneliness he was thus enabled to feel a strong bond of solidarity with the endless generations of men who, like himself, had had recourse to Homer and Plato in order to express their own emotions more fully, and to acquire a deeper consciousness of the conditions of their actual lives. Themistius, who was very much a man of his times, stated in clear terms that what constituted his only fortune—his πατρῷος κλῆρος— was his culture.[30] In the light of late antique conditions, in a society where so many immense fortunes collapsed within the space of a generation, such an affirmation can have been no mere figure of speech. Themistius, like all his contemporaries, felt and believed that in a world whose material condition was so exclusively governed by fortune, the only sure possessions that anyone could lay claim to were of either a spiritual or an intellectual order. Julian does not explicitly make this confession anywhere, but it is implicit in all his writings and deeds.

At the moment when all the magnitude of his task was suddenly revealed to him, he measured his own capacities and realized that they were not enough to meet it adequately. 'Seeing the vast amount of things that my present life involves, I blame it' (VI. 260b). The spectre of Tyche—the omnipotent ambiguous force which ruled supreme in the Hellenistic world —then appeared before his eyes and increased his sense of helplessness. In one sense, the *Letter to Themistius*, with its frequent references to Tyche, was an attempt to exorcise this blind force, while at a deeper level, it reflects the author's momentary refusal to accept the present in all its implications. At the moment when Julian sensed that the ground on which he stood was slippery, he forgot all the contemporary political theories that, subsequently, he so effectively put into action, and had recourse to the great masters of his early youth.

Yet, if Julian's rejection of παμβασιλεία—the idea of hereditary and absolute monarchy, which comes straight from Aristotle and is supported by the quotation of a passage from his *Politics*[31]—contrasts sharply with the conception of *Dei gratia* monarchy as well as with the whole metaphysical theory justifying the concept of dynasty which we owe to Julian himself,[32]

---

[30] Them. 233d; cf. Greg. Naz. *or*. IV. 104.
[31] 1286b, 1287a; and J. VI. 261b.   [32] See below, pp. 176 ff.

his view of the law as of divine origin was an idea that always remained with him. Indeed, Julian's manner of expounding this dogma in the *Letter to Themistius* can also give us a clue to the confused state of mind in which he was writing: as if not trusting himself, he quotes in support of his view a lengthy passage from Plato and comments on it; later he will reformulate the same idea, but using Neoplatonic vocabulary without finding it necessary to specify, far less quote, his source.[33]

In his *Letter to Themistius* Julian gave expression to a momentary disposition which, on the evidence of his actions and surviving writings, seems not to have returned to him for at least another year. As he entered Constantinople his mind was full of plans for the reorganization of the empire. His sense of its decadence was acute, and his most ardent desire was to re-establish a shaken order. Καὶ περικέκμηκα τὸ κλῖνον ἀναλήμψασθαι—'I have devoted gigantic efforts to restore what is declining':[34] thus Julian summarizes his policy during the first months of his reign. He saw to it that inscriptions greeting him as the man 'born for the good of the State', come 'to extirpate the vices of the past',[35] proclaimed his work of restoration throughout the empire. Only a few days after the emperor's entry into the capital the consul for 362 gave emphatic official expression to the spirit animating Julian's reforms. The new emperor had returned to the *respublica* its ancient freedom,[36] and the liberty born to the Romans in 509 BC had at last in 362 been restored in all its glory.[37]

What Julian's panegyrists described as 'liberty' was the suppression of some of the more striking innovations of the recent past, and a partial return to the traditions of Hellenism and *Romanitas*,[38] which to his mind were inextricable ideals, so that

[33] See below, p. 175.

[34] *ELF* 72, p. 86.

[35] *CIL* 10648 (from Pannonia Inferior): 'ob deleta vitia temporum pr[a]eteritorum'.

[36] Mamert. 30. 3.

[37] Ibid. 4; cf. Livy I. 60.

[38] The term *Romanitas*, which we shall use in the rest of this book to denote Julian's love for the old-fashioned Roman values, is perhaps best defined in the words of E. Démougeot: 'Devant les dangers, intérieurs et extérieurs, la conscience collective assimile les institutions du passé à la gloire de Rome et à l'amour de son œuvre... Le mot nouveau de "romanité" traduit bien ce patriotisme confus,

he often referred to them collectively as τὰ πάτρια.[39] The main objects of the reform Julian undertook in the administrative field were the restoration of the cities, the reorganization of public justice and the post, the settlement of the tax question and the reshaping of the army. The inspiration of the reform was Julian's spirit of traditionalism, while the principles followed in its execution were those of integrity and economy.[40] Yet, just as Julian was a genuine child of his age and, more importantly, a typical representative of the Constantinian dynasty, so his reforms in their overall conception and execution are recognizably Byzantine rather than reminiscent of the Antonine past.

To 'heal' the state, as fourth-century AD vocabulary would have it, Julian first applied his purgative policy on a small scale. As soon as he entered the palace in Constantinople, with its chaotic organization and dissolute morals,[41] he dismissed all the imperial eunuchs, most of the secret police (*agentes in rebus*) and most of the secretarial service (*notarii*).[42] Later he reduced to just fifty the number of household guards who benefited from allowances and were permitted to stay by the emperor.[43] As Socrates put it (while deploring Julian's policy), the only justification for the existence of these swarms of sinecurists was ἡ ἐκ τοῦ βασιλικοῦ πλούτου τοῖς πολλοῖς ἐγγιγνομένη κατάπληξις— the stupefaction caused by imperial splendour.[44]

---

déterminé surtout par ce qui le menace et recouvrant à la fois un idéal, un genre et un niveau de vie', *De l'unité à la division de l'empire romain, 395–410. Essai sur le gouvernement impérial* (diss.), Paris 1951, 34.

[39] For a selection of passages from Julian's works and from those of fourth-century Christians, where the phrase τὰ πάτρια occurs in connection with Julian's restoration of Hellenism, see K. J. Neumann, 'Ein neues Bruchstück aus Kaiser Julians Büchern gegen die Christen', *Theologische Literaturzeitung* xxiv (1899), 303. A phrase of Symmachus, which renders perfectly that attitude of the pagan élite in late antiquity, also sums up the spirit of Julian's reform: 'Instituta maiorum . . . patriae iura et fata defendimus', *Rel.* III. 2.

[40] The main accusation that Julian brought against Constantine was his utter lack of any sense of economy, which had resulted in his inability to administer the state entrusted to him (I. 8b, 43b; III. 97b; VII. 227cd; Amm. XXIV. 3. 4 (on Constantius)). The theme was adopted by Julian's panegyrists, Mamert. 11. 1, and cf. ibid. 10. 3: 'maximum tibi praebet parsimonia tua, Auguste, vectigal.'

[41] Amm. XXII. 4. 2–5; Lib. II. 58; XVIII. 135.

[42] Amm. XXII. 4. 1–2 and 9–10; Lib. XVIII. 130 ff.; cf. Rostovtzeff, *SEHRE* i. 513.

[43] *C.Th.* VI. 24. 1.

[44] Socr. III. 1. 53.

Yet this drastic reduction of the palatine staff was not directed merely by the principle of economy. It was also an expression of the more general tendency of Julian's policy towards decentralization. Reducing the bureaucratic machinery was one aspect only of a well co-ordinated plan, which also aimed at restoring the city councils to their previous importance within the framework of the imperial administration. The purge of the palace thus represents an attempt to strike at the roots of the bureaucratic aristocracy that had arisen from, and at the expense of, the provincial bourgeoisie.[45] Of course in their practical application these basically just and politically sound measures proved unfair in many individual cases.[46] Indeed the summary manner in which Julian carried out his purge illustrates the two traits of his impatient nature which were most pronounced over this period of his life: zeal exalted to the point of fanaticism, and an over-enthusiastic belief in his personal mission. Yet these two elements are indispensable ingredients in the psychology of a reformer, and those who criticized Julian for his indiscriminate winnowing of wheat and chaff alike forgot that the statesman must above all have the gift of abstract thought: when a ruler undertakes to change a social system, he cannot stop to consider the merits of individuals.[47]

The most ambitious part of Julian's programme was his restoration of the municipalities, a project closely related to the revival of Hellenic culture and religion. The city, which as an autonomous political, cultural and religious unit had been the very soul of classical Greek civilization, continued to be a living institution after Alexander's conquests. The Hellenistic states and, to a greater extent, the Roman empire itself, continued to be based on an agglomeration of cities,[48] which, while integrated within the empire, retained their autonomy to the extent that they had a governing body of their own—the municipal council—which both looked after the town's material needs

---

[45] See S. Mazzarino, *Aspetti sociali del IV. secolo*, Rome 1951, 186–7; J. H. W. G. Liebeschuetz, *Antioch: City and Imperial Administration in the Later Roman Empire*, Oxford 1972, 12; cf. Lib. II. 58 and XVIII. 135, who in the first passage clearly states the curial origin of the palatine servants expelled by Julian.

[46] See Ammianus' criticisms XXII. 4. 1–2.

[47] Cf. Browning, *Julian*, 126.

[48] In Roman times the term *polis* denoted a town and the surrounding rural area with its villages.

and, on a higher level, administered its social, cultural, artistic and religious life.[49]

Under the Flavians and the first Antonines there was a considerable flourishing of civic life: thanks to imperial munificence, the cities of Asia Minor in particular witnessed a splendid cultural renaissance, while, next to the prosperous older towns, the fringes of the empire too were urbanized, and old tribal centres were transformed into *poleis*.[50] But winds of change began to blow after the death of Marcus Aurelius which, in the words of Dio Cassius, marked the end of an era of gold and the beginning of one of iron.[51] During the third century the city life of the empire began to decline rapidly, chiefly on account of increasing inflation, continuous wars, which were both expensive and destructive for the provinces, and the general tendency of the imperial government towards a policy of centralization and military absolutism.[52] This decline should be understood as at once an economic and a cultural process, since the extent of the material prosperity of the towns was reflected in their cultural achievements. In a letter written to Julian in 358 Libanius summarized this conception of a prosperous city: 'you would wish that the cities had all the other advantages by which they prosper and, above all, that they were rich in literary production; for you are well aware that if this is wiped out, we differ in nothing from the barbarians.'[53]

[49] Jones, *LRE* 724–5; Rostovtzeff, *SEHRE* i. 130 ff.

[50] See D. Magie, *Roman Rule in Asia Minor to the End of the Third Century after Christ* i–ii, Princeton 1950, 639; A. H. M. Jones, *The Greek City from Alexander to Justinian*, Oxford 1940, 66 ff.; also Rostovtzeff, *SEHRE* i. 135 and ii. 592.

[51] Dio Cassius LXXII. 36. 4.

[52] On inflation (price of gold), see Magie, *Roman Rule*, 701, 719. On increasing centralization as an expression of absolutism, see H. Stuart-Jones, 'Administration', *The Legacy of Rome* (ed. C. Bailey), Oxford 1923, 134 ff. Rostovtzeff (*SEHRE*, 502–41) argues that in the third century the rural classes, from which the troops were mostly recruited, favoured the accession to the throne of a series of Illyrian peasants who did not appreciate the achievement of the cities and the importance of flourishing urban life for the prosperity of the empire, and that in doing so the peasantry took its revenge on the bourgeoisie. This view has been strongly criticized by N. H. Baynes, 'The Peasantry and the Army in the third century', *Byzantine Studies and Other Essays*, London 1955, 307–9, and by A. Momigliano, 'M. I. Rostovtzeff', *Studies in Historiography*, London 1966, 91–104, who attempts to trace the personal motives that induced Rostovtzeff to formulate his theory.

[53] *ep.* 369. 9; cf. Lib. *ep.* 1200. 2: ἐγὼ πόλεως κάλλος ἡγοῦμαι τὴν τῶν ἐνοικούντων ἀρετήν, οὐ μῆκος στοῶν οὐδὲ ὕψος θεάτρων οὐδὲ πλῆθος οἰκιῶν.

For the Graeco-Roman world culture was a double concept consisting of a purely intellectual aspect—*paideia* in its strictest sense—and a religious one which found concrete expression in literature and in the temples with all the works of art that adorned them. All these aspects of culture had a common driving force, Hellenism, as Libanius points out again and again,[54] and as Julian bluntly states in his law on education. These two inextricably connected notions—λόγοι and ἱερά— were closely associated with the *polis* as an autonomous institution, and it was not coincidental that the three declined and collapsed together.[55] Significantly enough, those emperors who neglected the cities in favour of an increasingly centralized bureaucracy also failed to appreciate that the πεπαιδευμένοι were an asset to the State, and, from Constantius onwards, attacked Hellenism both as a religious and an intellectual force.[56] Yet, obscurely sensing that civilization was dependent upon cities, they did not pursue their policies without some reluctance. This inconsistency is reflected in the laws concerning municipalities and paganism that were issued throughout the fourth century. On the one hand the emperors displayed indifference to the decline of the municipal councils and systematically undermined civic life by attacking the religious beliefs on which it was founded (while carefully distinguishing

[54] Lib. XVIII. 157 and LXII. 8, where λόγοι and ἱερά are described as ἀδελφά, οἰκεῖα and συγγενῆ. Cf. XVIII. 163.

[55] See Lib. *ep.* 664. 2: τὰς γὰρ πόλεις οὐχ οἱ πλουτοῦντες μόνοι ποιοῦσι λαμπράς, ἀλλὰ ὅσοι πόνους ὑπὲρ παιδείας ὑπήνεγκαν, cf. id. XXX. 42: the ἱερά are the eyes of the cities; XVIII. 147: the municipal councils are their souls. In his *Antiochene Oration* Libanius describes the βουλή as the ῥίζα, on which τὸ πᾶν σχῆμα τῆς πόλεως . . . ἕστηκε (XI. 133). Cf. XVIII. 163, a passage where cities, municipal councils and temples appear as an indissoluble whole. Festugière fundamentally misconceives the relationship of ἱερά and λόγοι in the classical tradition when he writes: 'D'une part les empereurs "chrétiens" d'autre part les moines ont attaqué tout ensemble et les temples et la culture grecque. C'est cette commune attaque qui a fait de ces deux un tout apparemment indissoluble' (*Antioche*, 235). 'Libanius lie ensemble ἱερά et λόγοι parce que les circonstances les ont effectivement liés: les empereurs chrétiens, qui se sont attaqués au culte païen, ont méprisé ou négligé les lettres grecques; la commune décadence de deux, qui, somme toute, eut pu être fortuite, apparaît ainsi comme un phénomène où se laisse voir un lien de cause à effet' (ibid. 239).

[56] See Lib. XVII. 7; XXX. 38; LXII. 8, 11; *ep*, 728. 3 etc. After Julian's death the situation reverted to what it had been before his accession, and stenographers (ταχυγράφοι) took the place of intellectuals in the administration, cf. Lib. *ep.* 1224. 6.

these beliefs from their aesthetic expression[57]); on the other hand, they formulated the wish that the *curiae*, stripped of all autonomy and sense of local responsibility, should still serve the imperial administration in a subsidiary capacity.

The steady decline of the municipal councils in the fourth century was the result of many factors. Modern historians speak of 'an alteration of the whole scale of values' expressed in, or caused by, the enormous growth of the central bureaucracy.[58] The spirit of civic patriotism was gradually superseded by the desire to acquire the honours and material advantages that an increasingly impersonal central administration could offer, without demanding the assumption of any responsibilities in return. The State was thus swallowing the City by encouraging the natural human tendency towards intellectual and moral laziness. At the same time the growth of the imperial bureaucracy entailed a shift of values in the social hierarchy—a municipal councillor who still wished and could afford to be a civic εὐεργέτης would always remain socially inferior to any member of the new bureaucratic aristocracy.

The sapping of curial morale by the State was effected not only by the encouragement offered to the emergence of a class of 'novi homines', to the eventual detriment of the bourgeoisie, but also by the reverse process: many of the responsibilities, which, by requiring a certain amount of initiative on the part of the *curiales*, were a proof of municipal self-government, were taken away by the State. The decurions virtually became civil servants, burdened with duties, but without powers. Coming to see themselves with the State's eyes, they gradually both lost self-respect and became less attached to their town.[59]

The economic factor also played a decisive part in what Petit calls 'the political resignation of city councils'. The bankruptcy of individual *curiales*, combined with recurrent exactions for military purposes, insidiously sapped the strength of the *curiae*.[60] Thus, as a result of combined internal and external factors of a

[57] *C. Th.* XVI. 10. 8.

[58] Jones, *City*, 207; P. Petit, *Libanius et la vie municipale à Antioche au IVe siècle après J.-C.*, Paris 1955, 294.

[59] See Petit, *Libanius*, 284–94; also J. H. W. G. Liebeschuetz, 'The finances of Antioch in the fourth century A.D.', *ByzZ* lii (1959), 356; cf. Lib. *ep.* 731 and XLVIII. 35, who makes an appeal to the patriotism of decurions.

[60] Jones, *City*, 204; cf. Lib. XLIX. 2 on extraordinary levies for war purposes.

moral, psychological, social and economic order, the institution of municipal councils was drastically shaken during the fourth century.

The richer decurions, responding to the spirit of the new age, left their towns and through bribery sought to secure a post in the Senate of Constantinople or the palatine service, to obtain codicils of rank which entailed exemption from curial responsibilities, or to go to the bar. Those who could not afford such expensive careers had recourse to lesser *officia*, the lower ranks of central administration or the army, or even sought refuge from responsibilities under the protection of professional hereditary guilds.[61] The Church was perhaps the widest avenue of escape, and the exodus of decurions *en masse* into the ranks of the priesthood, to whom Constantine had been quick to offer immunity from civic duties,[62] attained such dimensions that Constantine himself had to reconsider his decision and eventually forbid this escape-route to the members of municipal councils.[63]

It was only natural that the embittered and demoralized men who remained in the impoverished provincial councils (and for whom the initially honorary office had become a compulsory hereditary one[64]) displayed complete indifference to a decaying institution which they could not help facing as the very symbol of their own degraded status. That the councils themselves showed 'criminal negligence' in asserting their rights[65] by not summoning back the fugitives whenever they were legally entitled to do so, is not surprising: this negligence was both the sign of weariness and the effect of corruption, of which Libanius for one accused the *curiales*, and which is confirmed by the laws.[66]

By abundant but ineffective legislation the emperors sought

[61] On the flight of decurions, see Jones, *City*, 192 ff. with references. *C.Th.* XII. 1. 6 (AD 319) points out that many decurions preferred to lead a slave's existence rather than perform their onerous duties. On the absorption of provincial aristocracies by the Senate of Constantinople, see T. Kotula, *Les Curies municipales en Afrique romaine*, Breslau 1968, 133.

[62] *C.Th.* XVI. 2. 2.

[63] *C.Th.* XVI. 2. 6, and Jones, *City*, 198.

[64] *C.Th.* XII. 1. 14 (AD 326); cf. *CIG* 4411a–b, and 4412, where there is to be found the expression τάγμα βουλευτικόν. Cf. Kunkel, *An Introduction to Roman Legal and Constitutional History*, Oxford 1973², 136.

[65] Jones, *City*, 203.

[66] Ibid. 202–3, 347 n. 93.

to stop the decline of the *curiae*. In three laws we find a clear indication of the problems that this decline caused for the State;[67] yet, not a single one of the surviving forty-nine edicts on the municipalities promulgated by Constantine and his sons represents a serious attempt to remedy the situation. On the contrary, most of the laws contain loop-holes,[68] suggest total indifference to the fate of municipalities and seem to be motivated solely by the self-interest of a State bent on centralization and, consequently, in direct conflict with the interests of the cities.[69]

Such was the situation that confronted Julian. His *paideia* made him well aware of the key-position of the city in the Greek and Roman way of life, while his increasing confidence in his own capacities as a statesman[70] convinced him that he knew exactly how to reinvigorate the ailing *polis*. Finally, his personal experience as an administrator appeared to him to guarantee the achievement of his purpose: in Gaul, despite the strong opposition of Constantius' agents and all the manifold restrictions to which he was subject, he had to a large extent succeeded in solving the problem by concentrating on its financial aspect. This was how he was to begin now on the wider canvas of the empire as a whole.

Julian had hardly spent three months in his capital when his first series of edicts on municipalities was issued. The six laws of 13 March 362 show that the emperor had grasped in all their complexity the reasons for the decline of the city councils. Accordingly he decreed that lands usurped by the Church or the State should be restored to the cities[71] together with their revenues, which seem to have constituted a considerable source

---

[67] General laws attempting to stop the flight of decurions: *C.Th.* XII. 1. 6; 10; 11; 12; 13; 22; 29; 31; 37; 40; 43; 45; 48. For Carthage and the province of Africa: XII. 1. 7; 27. Sons of veterans bound to serve as decurions: XII. 1. 15; 18; 32; 35. Note esp. XII. 1. 13 (AD 326): 'Quoniam curias desolari cognovimus his qui per originem obnoxii sunt'; XII. 1. 25 (AD 338): 'Quoniam emptae dignitatis obtentu curias vacuefactas esse non dubium est'; XII. 1. 32 (AD 341): 'Nam rei publicae incommodum est curias hominum paucitate languescere'.

[68] e.g. *C.Th.* XII. 1. 29.

[69] For a good analysis (based on the texts of Libanius) of the opposition between the interests of State and City, see Petit, *Libanius*, 283 ff.; cf. Lib. XVIII. 147, on Constantius.

[70] Amm. XXII. 9. 1.

[71] *C.Th.* X. 3. 1; Amm. XXV. 4. 15; Lib. XIII. 45; *ep.* 828; Soz. V. 3. 2–3; *C. Just.* XI. 70. 2 (specifically on the cities of Pamphylia).

of wealth for the municipalities.[72] Julian was careful to compensate the cities both at a material and at a moral level by returning to them landholdings that had either been absorbed into the *Res Privata* or had passed to the State in an indirect way, through their new owners who were members of the bureaucratic aristocracy.[73] He also exempted the *curiales* from the tax payable in gold and silver (the *chrysargyron* or *collatio lustralis*) unless they were rich merchants.[74] This too was a doubly reassuring law; for it not only meant liberation from an odious tax for a large part of the population, but it also showed through its careful planning that the new emperor had both a pragmatic outlook and a strict sense of justice, neither disregarding his subjects' interest nor wishing to acquire popularity through extravagant demagogy, as would have been the case had he abolished the imposition altogether. The same sense of justice characterizes the other provisions of the same law, which summoned all Christian priests back to their curial seats, and fined those who sought to escape from their municipal duties through patronage, together with their protectors.[75]

Equally undemagogic is *C.Th.* XI. 23. 2 on tax collectors; Julian removes this burden from the senators and lays it on decurions as a lower order. The style is laconic, the tone almost arrogant: there is a world of difference between the brief, clipped wording that we find in Julian's legislation and the flowery style of Constantius' laws.

Last in this series of laws comes *C.Th.* XI. 16. 10, requiring that all administrative duties incumbent upon decurions should actually be performed by them; this obvious statement aims at reinforcing the morale of the *curiales*, for by reminding them of their public responsibilities the legislator emphasizes their importance in the functioning of the State machinery. A few months later Julian will express even more explicitly this major theme of his political thinking, by stating that the construction of roads is the private business of those living near them, for 'they must care for the places assigned to them, *iuxta morem*

[72] Mazzarino, *Aspetti*, 325 ff.
[73] Among the special privileges that Antioch received from Julian was a donation of land from the *Res Privata* (XII. 367d, 370d).
[74] *C.Th.* XII. 1. 50; XIII. 1. 4.
[75] Cf. *ep.* 54, a proof that Julian saw that his laws were enforced.

priscum'[76]—according to the old Republican habits. In April 362 Julian passed a law which practically abolished the imposition known as *aurum coronarium*,[77] which by then had become a regular tax levied upon all decurions. Julian made it once more a voluntary contribution, fixing its maximum at 70 staters of gold.[78] At the same time he cancelled municipal debts made great by long standing,[79] and a few months later he remitted all overdue taxes with the exception of the *chrysargyron*.[80]

For many more months, till the end of his brief career, Julian continued to legislate on the municipalities in an attempt to cover all aspects of this complex field. Thus he took care to relieve the cities of the considerable financial burden of maintaining the *cursus publicus*. By several laws of an extraordinary precision Julian reduced considerably the number of persons entitled to travel freely on the public post, leaving no room for the abuses that proliferated under his predecessors. He did not, as is often thought, actually make the *cursus publicus fiscalis* (that is, transfer its running from the municipal to the State budget), but he did lighten the financial burden on the cities through minute legislation.[81]

Lastly, Julian turned his attention to more specific matters; no detail was unimportant enough for him as he minutely occupied himself with the lesser problems that arose in the course of his summary legislation.[82] Bearing in mind how real a problem for the empire depopulation had become,[83] he exempted from all curial charges fathers of thirteen children, unless they chose themselves to remain members of the councils, in which case he decreed on their behalf an 'honoratissima quies'.[84] Another class that was accorded privileges was the *archiatri*,[85] whose profession Julian regarded as just as high and

---

[76] *C.Th.* XV. 3. 2.

[77] *C.Th.* XII. 13. 1; Lib. XVI. 19; Amm. XXV. 4. 15. See also *ELF*, pp. 84–7.

[78] Cf. Lib. XVIII. 193–4.

[79] *C.Th.* XI. 12. 2; Amm. XXV. 4. 15; Lib. XVIII. 163 (for the cities of Syria).

[80] *C.Th.* XI. 28. 1; cf. XII. 367d.

[81] *C.Th.* VIII. 5. 12–16. See Jones, *City*, 141 and 328–9; and W. Seston, 'Notes critiques sur l'"Histoire Auguste"', *REA* xlv (1943), 52–62.

[82] See *C.Th.* XII. 1. 52; 53; 54; 56. On the clarity of Julian's laws, cf. Amm. XXV. 4. 20: 'Namque et iura condidit non molesta, *absolute* quaedam iubentia fieri vel arcentia.'

[83] Jones, *LRE*, 1040–5.

[84] *C.Th.* XII. 1. 55.

[85] *C.Th.* XIII. 3. 4.

venerable an occupation as philosophy.[86] Conversely, the duty
of membership of municipal councils was extended to all those
who were rich enough to bear the expense.[87] This last measure
is important for our understanding of Julian; it shows that,
despite all his traditionalism, he did not face the Roman empire
simply as a body consisting of a certain number of clearly defined and mutually isolated social and professional classes. By
his attempt to break through the rigid boundaries that separated
the castes, he proved himself a radical and not a 'reactionary',
one who was prepared to put into practice the bold sentiments
of his youth, that the man in the street who achieves distinction
is better than the aristocrat who inherits a sense of honour.[88]

And yet Julian's legislation on municipalities was not wholly
just; it did not, for instance, take into consideration the case of
individuals who had gained their exemption by long service in
the army.[89] More to the point, it did not prove entirely effective
either: many of those who were chosen to be *curiales* were
totally unfitted for the office,[90] while others—and they were
many, as both Ammianus and Libanius assure us—still succeeded in buying immunity through heavy bribery.[91] Indeed
Julian's legislation on municipalities is closely analogous to his
reform of the palace. In both cases he acted too impatiently and
without adequate thought for the nuances of the matter, guided
solely by an abstract principle. In behaving thus Julian confirmed what was already a prominent trait in his character: an
unbending determination to push through his plans, whatever
the sacrifices involved, once he was convinced that their end
was right. Yet, more often than not he saw these ends, ideal in
themselves, in isolation from their historical or social context.
It was typical of Julian that he conceived of the legislator as
one who had no contact whatever with the society in whose
interest he promulgated his laws. Otherwise, he argued, with
sound Platonic logic, the legislator might be carried away by

[86] *ep.* 75b; cf. *ep.* 58.
[87] *C.Th.* XII. 1. 53. Specifically for Antioch Julian also extended membership
of the municipalities to the offsprings of curial families through the maternal line,
C.Th. XII. 1. 51; cf. Lib. XLVIII. 15; Zos. III. 11. 5; *C.Just.* X. 32. 61.
[88] II. 108c–109.
[89] Cf. *C.Th.* XII. 1. 56; also Amm. XXII. 9. 12; XXV. 4. 21; cf. XXII. 9. 8.
[90] Amm. XXII. 9. 8.
[91] Amm. XXII. 9. 12 and Lib. XLVIII. 17.

personal feelings, and favour his kinsmen and friends, or at any
rate a particular social group.[92] Fearing lest he himself should
fall into this trap in his legislation on the cities, Julian chose to
ignore particular cases—especially those class-interests which
clashed with what he conceived to be *raison d'état*—and apply
indiscriminately his all-too-rigid conception of what was just;[93]
while at the same time his optimistic confidence in the essential
goodness of human nature prevented this incorrigible Platonist
from suspecting that many would find a way of breaking his
law.

But the evidence drawn from the Codes illustrates one aspect
only of Julian's attempt to regenerate urban life[94]—an attempt
which was wholly based on political considerations and which
reflects his philosophy as a statesman. Of his emotional attitude
to cities there is little sign in the Codes. Julian the scholar and
antiquarian regarded cities as beings endowed with a soul[95]
and a distinct personality, capable of arousing in a monarch's
heart feelings of affection, scorn, sadness or hatred.[96] It was
indeed a bitter feeling of betrayal, which in time took the even
more unphilosophical form of aversion, that Antioch inspired
in him, as it was anger that the Christian cities of Cappadocian
Caesarea and Constantia stirred in his heart; incapable of controlling himself, he resorted in both cases to revenge.[97] But
Julian's capacity for love was as strong as his capacity for
hatred: before the ruins of Nicomedia, for ever linked with the
memory of Mardonius and the years of philosophical *otium* he

[92] VI. 262a–c; cf. III. 88d and above, pp. 92–3.

[93] Julian's over-rigid sense of justice is also attested by Cyril of Alexandria:
C.G. fr. 11, p. 236 (Neumann): ἐπιπλήττει εἰκῇ [sc. Ἰουλιανὸς] τοῖς ὑπέρ γε
τῶν ἐν ἀδικίαις παρακαλοῦσι θεὸν καὶ ἀφαμαρτάνειν τοῦ εἰκότος ᾠήθη
καὶ λέγει τοὺς ἐποικτείροντας τοὺς κακούργους κακούς.

[94] See *C.Th.* X. 3. 1, where Julian speaks of the 'reparatio cunctarum civitatum'.

[95] Cf. Lib. XVIII. 147.

[96] It was common for Roman emperors to address the citizens of a town collectively (cf. F. Millar, *The Emperor in the Roman World (31 BC–AD 337)*, London
1977, 410–20) almost as if they wished to exorcise their responsibility for the
decline of the *polis*. Julian, however, brought alive once more what had become a
mere convention. Nor did this escape the notice of his contemporaries: see Lib.
XIII. 45; XVIII. 129, 146 ff.; XLVIII. 17; XLIX. 3; Soz. V. 3. 4. It is significant also that Julian founded a city called Basilinoupolis, in memory of his
mother, cf. Jones, *City*, 92–3; see also *ELF* Nos. 20–1, *epp.* 54, 59, 60, 114, 115,
[Julian], 198 and Lib. XVIII. 187–8.

[97] *ep.* 78; Soz. II. 5. 7–9; V. 3. 4–8; A. M. H. Jones, *The Cities of the Eastern
Roman Provinces*, Oxford 1971², 280.

had enjoyed in his youth, the emperor burst into tears which, translated into real terms, became a most generous financial subsidy.[98] Though for Julian Constantinople lacked the symbolic significance of both Rome and Athens,[99] he displayed towards her all the uncritical affection and veneration that one reserves for one's parents: 'I love her as a mother; for I was born and raised there and I cannot be ungrateful towards her.'[100] Had he reigned longer, Julian could have been a great builder; for he made a definite effort to adorn his native city with monuments bearing the distinct mark of his personality:[101] a triangular obelisk was brought from Egypt, in exchange for a colossal statue of the emperor,[102] and work was begun on a big new port, which was to be connected with the centre of the town by a crescent-shaped portico. Typically enough, Julian gave the capital a public library in which he deposited many of his personal books;[103] this library, which was particularly strong in law, was at any moment at the disposal of lawyers and judges who wished to consult it.[104] This significant detail throws considerable light on Julian's idea of public justice: he regarded its officers as men who should be in direct contact with the sources of the law they administered, and desired that they should be continuously preoccupied with what to his mind was not a mere profession, but a high office and public duty which he himself did not disdain to perform regularly.[105]

If in his personal contact with cities Julian sometimes found himself the victim of irrational urges, he was nevertheless able to pursue with consistency a definite line of policy towards them. Once he decided as a matter of principle to afford the cities of the empire his moral support, he made a point of regarding

[98] Amm. XXII. 9. 4–5; Lib. *ep.* 35. 2.

[99] See G. Dagron, *Naissance d'une capitale: Constantinople et ses institutions de 330 à 451*, Paris 1974, 194–5. Cf. above, pp. 84 ff.

[100] *ep.* 59. 443bc; Mamert. 14. 6; Them. 59a.

[101] Him. XLI. 8.

[102] *ep.* 59.

[103] Zos. III. 11. 3; Lib. XIX. 19.

[104] On the location, contents and fate of Julian's public library, which was not a simple extension of the one founded by Constantius, see K. Manafis, Αἱ ἐν Κωνσταντινουπόλει βιβλιοθῆκαι αὐτοκρατορικαὶ καὶ πατριαρχικὴ καὶ περὶ τῶν ἐν αὐταῖς χειρογράφων μέχρι τῆς Ἁλώσεως (*1453*), Athens 1972, 24–5, 32–3. The Suda I. 401, reports the improbable detail that Jovian βιβλιοθήκην . . . κατέφλεξε σὺν πᾶσιν οἷς εἶχε βιβλίοις.

[105] See above, p. 66 n. 64.

their 'souls'—the municipal councils—as more respectable even than the sacred person of the emperor. Wishing to make senators and councillors fully conscious of the splendour and importance of their office, Julian stopped summoning them to his palace.[106] He genuinely regarded the senatorial order as the one 'in quo nos quoque ipsos esse numeramus',[107] and he proclaimed this belief in symbolic but unambiguous terms, by sitting with senators and councillors whether in Constantinople, Antioch or even the least important provincial town.[108]

In its motivation Julian's policy on municipalities was reactionary; for both in his legislation on the cities and in the explicitly democratic attitude that he adopted towards them he was inspired by his old-fashioned intellectual formation in the schools of Hellenism and *Romanitas*. Yet this behaviour corresponded only at one level to Julian's conception of the empire. His idea of the empire as an agglomeration of semi-autonomous cities, each of which was free to cultivate and expand its own local traditions, appears, when considered at a deeper level, to be far removed from classical or even Antonine standards. In fact the cities' freedom was very relative, being firmly conditioned by respect for tradition. For Julian, cities existed only for the sake of the empire, and were allowed to survive only if their activities harmonized with what he conceived to be the universal political and religious principles on which the Roman state was founded.[109] Thus the Christian city of Caesarea in Cappadocia was struck out of the catalogue of imperial towns,[110] and the capital of the East 'was entrusted' by Julian 'to the care of Adrasteia'[111] because of the irreverence that she showed towards the gods and their vice-gerent on earth. Julian's conception of the empire was essentially Byzantine, and his 'Hellenic' conception of municipalities makes sense only if we relate it to his theory of 'Ethnic Gods', according to which all political and religious traditions within the empire are allowed to flourish at a local level, providing those practising them recognize the

[106] Cf. Lib. XVIII. 154.

[107] *C. Th.* IX. 2. I.

[108] *ep.* 98. 399d; XII. 362b ff.; Amm. XXII. 7. 3; Socr. III. 1. 54; Mamert. 24. 5.

[109] Libanius grasped this point, see XVIII. 129.

[110] See above, p. 107 n. 97; *ep.* 78.

[111] XII. 370b; see also pp. 214–15.

universal rule of King Helios and that of his representative on
earth.[112]

Yet it was important to Julian that his theocratic state should
be founded on Hellenic and Roman values—τὰ πάτρια. Thus he
encouraged cities to take full consciousness of their unique individual character as tradition had moulded it. But to his mind
this 'tradition' was to be defined exclusively in religious and
cultural terms.

A happy city [Julian proclaimed] is the one that abounds in temples
and secret rites, and contains within its walls countless holy priests
who dwell in the sacred enclosures and who, in order to keep everything that is within their gates pure, have expelled all that is superfluous and sordid and vicious from the city—public baths and
brothels and retail shops and everything of the sort without exception. (IX. 186d)

It is by no means coincidental that the only towns to which
Julian took an aversion were those whose population was
chiefly Christian; nor is it surprising that his sense of justice
was not strongly offended when the Alexandrian mob murdered
the bishop George.[113]

Julian's plan to restore the pagan cults to the cities was put
into effect as soon as he entered Constantinople through
decrees ordering that 'the temples be opened, victims brought
to the altars and the worship of the gods restored'.[114] Yet popular response to these decrees was so unenthusiastic that Julian
had first to complain about the poor progress of Hellenism in
Asia Minor;[115] then to take action personally by ordering the
reconstruction of specific temples[116] under the supervision of

[112] Lib. XII. 83.

[113] See ep. 83: χρὴ τιμᾶν τοὺς . . . θεοσεβεῖς ἄνδρας τε καὶ πόλεις. On the
bishop George see above, pp. 23–4. The revival of the municipal councils and of
paganism are sometimes acknowledged as complementary aspects of Julian's
reform: Année Épigraphique 1969–70, No. 631: 'templorum [re]stauratori, cur[ia]rum
et rei publicae recreatori . . .'; L. Jalabert, 'Inscriptions grecques et latines de
Syrie', Mélanges de la Fac. Orientale de l'univ. St. Joseph ii (1907), 265–9: '[repara]tori
[orbis romani et] . . . [re]creatori [sacrorum . . .'; Dessau ILS n. 152: 'res|titutori
li|be[r]t[at]is et Ro|manae re|ligio[nis . . .'; cf. Mamert. 9.

[114] Amm. XXII. 5. 2; cf. Lib. XVIII. 126.

[115] ep. 84. 429c and ep. 78 (on Cappadocia); cf. also XII. 344b.

[116] See E. Littmann et al., Publications of the Princeton Univ. Arch. Expedition to
Syria iii, Greek and Latin Inscriptions A,2 (1910), 108, No. 186. See Zonar. XIII. 12
(Dindorf) iii. 212, and Lib. XVIII. 126 ff. for the temple of Asclepius at Aegae
in Cilicia, Amm. XXIII. 1. 2–3 for the reconstruction of the temple in Jerusalem,
and Soz. V. 20. 7 on the demolition of churches at Didyma.

close and trustworthy collaborators;[117] then, in June 362, to take a more drastic line by promulgating a law according to which the restoration of temples was to take priority over all other building schemes already undertaken by municipalities and by provincial governors.[118] Finally, towards the end of his reign, seeing that the work was progressing very slowly, the impatient Julian began to retaliate against the Christians.[119]

Emesa, Gaza, Hierapolis, Arethusa, Heliopolis, Apamea, Seleuceia,[120] possibly one or two other Syrian cities, certainly Athens,[121] greeted with enthusiasm Julian's attempt to revive paganism at the *polis* level. But almost everywhere else in the Greek East his dream met with little spontaneous response. Faithfully echoing this situation, contemporary inscriptions hail Julian as the restorer of the *curiae* and of the empire in general, without mentioning anything about his religious policy;[122] his twin attempt to regenerate urban life and paganism passed unnoticed by those who did not share his particular preoccupations. In the seventh century John of Antioch will still see in Julian *the only* emperor who ruled the Roman empire well.[123] While recognizing that Hellenism was as important a factor as *Romanitas* in Julian's policy, the tradition that John of Antioch echoes deplores its effects and deliberately ignores the con-

---

[117] Cf. *ep.* 80, instructing his uncle Julian to reconstruct the temple of Apollo at Daphne. Amm. loc. cit.: Alypius supervises the rebuilding of the temple at Jerusalem.

[118] *C.Th.* XV. 1. 3 (29 June 362).

[119] See *ep.* 115 and Amm. XXII. 13. 2.

[120] On Emesa, see XII. 357cd, 361a. Theodoret, *H.E.* III. 7. 5, reports that a church at Emesa was turned into a temple of Dionysos. On Gaza, see above, p. 107 n. 97. On Hierapolis, *ep.* 98. 401b ff.; on Apamea, Lib. *ep.* 1351. 3; 1391. 1; XLVIII. 14; on Seleuceia, Lib. *ep.* 1361. 3.

[121] It is clear from Lib. XVIII. 114 that the Athenians responded enthusiastically to Julian's pagan restoration; yet it is unlikely that the emperor undertook construction works in Athens. J. Travlos's seductive hypothesis, that Julian was responsible for the restoration of the Parthenon after its destruction by the Herulians in 267 (Ἀρχαιολογικὴ Ἐφημερίς (1973), 218–36) has now been challenged on the strength of archaeological data by A. Frantz, 'Did Julian the Apostate rebuild the Parthenon?', *AJA* lxxxiii (1979), 395–401.

[122] e.g. *CIL* ix. 417 (Italy) 'Reparatori orbis'; Dessau *ILS* 751: propagato[r]i libertatis et rei publ[ic]ae; cf. ibid. No. 755.

[123] *Hist. Chron.*, fr. 180 (*FHG* iv): μόνος τὸ Ῥωμαϊκὸν καλῶς διῴκησεν, ἀνώρθωσέ τε αὐτό, εἰ μὴ ἐς ἐναντίωσιν τὰ ἐκ τοῦ δαιμονίου κατέστη ... ἐβέβλαπτο δὲ μόνον περὶ τὴν τοῦ σωτῆρος Χριστοῦ δόξαν ἐναντίως ἔχων καὶ ἐνιστάμενος τοῖς τὰ Χριστιανῶν μετιοῦσι δόγματα, οὐ μὴν ὥστε ὠμὸν ἢ φονικόν τι ἐργάσασθαι πώποτε.

nection between the revival of the pagan cults and the regeneration of cities. It was indeed a western Christian, Prudentius, who crystallized this motif into what became the traditional Byzantine judgement of Julian the statesman:

> Principibus tamen e cunctis non defuit unus
> Me puero, ut memini, ductor fortissimus armis,
> Conditor et legum, celeberrimus ore manuque,
> Consultor patriae, sed non consultor habendae
> Religionis, amans ter centum milia divum.
> Perfidus ille Deo, quamvis non perfidus orbi/Urbi.
>
> (*Apotheosis* 449 ff.)

Prudentius was careful to record among Julian's merits his work as writer and orator, but the Hellenism he praised in him was the exclusively intellectual and cultural force, so vital to the Byzantines.

As a united principle Hellenism and *Romanitas* inspired Julian's administrative reform[124] just as much as it moulded his conception of how to exercise imperial power. By nature and upbringing Julian had a 'democratic' manner, which, from his position as emperor, he made a point of displaying in a rather obvious fashion; yet the feeling behind the pose was genuine. Diocletian, the son of a slave, had introduced to Rome the oriental practice of προσκύνησις, and Constantine, the grandson of a peasant, had approved of it and reinforced the complicated ceremonial first adopted by his predecessor. Julian was quick to abolish these odious innovations and proclaim that he was subject to the laws of his country like any other citizen.[125] He continued long after he had entered Constantinople to address his subjects as 'fellow-citizens',[126] and to give an account of his actions to his soldiers.[127] In being the 'genuine guardian of power'[128] he showed that his own rule was *potestas* rather than *licentia,* lawful power rather than the despotic rule that Constantius had exercised.[129]

---

[124] It is noteworthy that Julian, the Easterner, relied heavily on the Roman aristocracy, cf. Amm. XXIII. 1. 4.

[125] Amm. XV. 5. 18; see Lib. XIII. 38; XVIII. 183, 190–2.

[126] *ep.* 60. 380d; cf. Him. XLI. 15.

[127] Amm. XXIII. 5. 16 ff., esp. 22.

[128] Lib. XVIII. 181.

[129] Amm. XIX. 12. 18 referring to Constantius' *licentia.* See also Amm. XXII. 5. 2.

He chose to exemplify this attitude by behaving in all circumstances in what was, by fourth-century standards, an 'unkingly' manner.[130] He made a point of dressing simply[131] and of treating his collaborators publicly as equals, but the consequences of this behaviour were very grave for him. The subtle distinction that Julian made between a theocratic conception of kingship and the democratic manner he assumed in daily life was lost on the great majority of his subjects, who were disappointed by a ruler whose public persona did not correspond at all to the image of imperial dignity they had in their minds.

Had Julian kept to the beaten track of Greek and Roman political philosophy he would, as well as behaving democratically, have championed a democratic theory of kingship, such as modern scholarship considers him to have held.[132] Yet Julian was no Libanius. A typical product of his century and of the House of Constantine, he saw the last remnants of the old democratic political theories swept away without feeling the least regret, and tried to find a plausible means of linking the new political theology propounded by his own family to the ideals of Hellenism and *Romanitas*.

The central figure around which monotheistic paganism had crystallized for over a century now was Sol, the same 'Deus Invictus' whom in 275 Aurelian had proclaimed to be the 'Dominus Imperii Romani', and the Second Flavian dynasty had adopted as its special protecting divinity. The more involved Julian became with the world of Roman politics the more deeply he felt that he belonged to a house over which Helios was keeping watch—a belief that harmonized with the pronouncedly heliolatric character of both his Neoplatonic and Mithraic creeds. Yet the connection was not obvious to everybody, and Julian undertook to stress the links that united his metaphysical with his political thought-world, an attempt that resulted in the formulation of a mystical theory of kingship in tune with the spirit of his age.[133] From this theory none of the

[130] Cf. Mamert. 28; 30; Amm. XXII. 7. 3; Lib. I. 129.

[131] Mamert. 29. 5.

[132] See, *inter alia*, F. Dvornik, 'The emperor Julian's "reactionary" ideas on kingship', *Late Classical and Mediaeval Studies in Honor of A. M. Friend, Jr.*, Princeton 1955, 71–81; G. Dagron in *T&MByz* iii; G. W. Bowersock, 'Greek intellectuals and the imperial cult in the second century A.D.', *Entretiens Hardt* xix, 1973, 186.

[133] See below, pp. 174 ff.

elements that were vital to Julian's thought and reform is absent; and while Hellenism is blended with Mithraism on a metaphysical level, Mithraism itself, a popular cult with the army and one which asserted the practical values of *Romanitas*, was given official status by Julian through its identification with the cult of Sol Invictus (XI. 155b).

Indeed the army was a class in which Julian was particularly interested for political reasons,[134] and it is conceivable that, as other emperors had done before him,[135] he tried to encourage its members to perform their duty conscientiously by professing openly the religion that a substantial majority of soldiers and officers had embraced and whose values were so much in tune with the requirements of their profession.

Somewhat unexpectedly Julian was to proclaim that, while 'military service was of primary importance to the State', the protection of letters constituted but '*the second* adornment of peace'.[136] In view of his ardent desire to add to his surnames that of 'Parthicus',[137] Julian needed the support of the army more than that of any other class, and for that reason he was prepared to flatter the soldiers and even make concessions to them: he raised their pay, and showered on them gifts in kind,[138] while he chose to emphasize the importance of the military class by appointing to the consulship for 362 Nevitta, a man who proved 'uncultivated, boorish and . . . cruel in his high office'.[139] Acting in the same spirit, Julian nominated four *magistri militum* as against only two civilians to sit on the extraordinary tribunal that judged the political crimes committed in Constantius' reign.[140] All the defendants were civilians, for it would have been an offence to the eastern army, whose support Julian needed so badly, if any of their leaders had been arraigned. Foremost among the judges, on the other hand, sat Arbetio, Constantius' trustworthy collaborator, and a man whom Julian

---

[134] See *C.Th*. VI. 26. 1.

[135] Cf. the important inscription (AD 307) in Vermaseren, *CIMRM* 1698. As has already been mentioned, p. 88, Julian had a Mithraeum built in his palace and visited it daily (Lib. XVIII. 127).

[136] *C.Th*. VI. 26. 1.

[137] Amm. XXII. 12. 2.

[138] Amm. XXII. 12. 6; 9. 2.

[139] Amm. XXI. 10. 8.

[140] Amm. XXII. 3. 1–2.

still feared.[141] Arbetio soon imposed his will on the tribunal, but the emperor dared not interfere with its decisions—he did not even react in any way to the execution of Ursulus, the State treasurer, a crime for which, as Ammianus put it, Justice herself wept.[142] That was a typical case of military vengeance, for Ursulus' only offence was that before the ruins of Amida he had lamented the incompetence of the Roman army[143]—a sentiment with which Julian was in complete agreement, if we judge from the reform of the army that he undertook immediately after the trial.

'A general hardened by experience and study of the art of war',[144] Julian knew how to put an end to indiscipline: he reintroduced regular training[145] and entrusted the leadership of the army to experienced generals. He repaired the fortifications on the Thracian border and took personal care that the troops along the banks of the Danube lacked nothing in arms, clothing, pay or supplies.[146] Finally he excluded all convinced Christians from the army by requiring that all soldiers should offer sacrifices to the traditional gods.[147]

Through his reorganization of the army Julian aspired to bring back the old days of military discipline, which Ammianus so nostalgically evokes just before narrating and praising his reforms in this field.[148] In those reforms Julian was inspired by the old-fashioned Roman values which are advertised in the only surviving manual of Roman military institutions:[149] courage, diligence, modesty, loyalty, honesty, justice and constant training in order to attain both physical and moral excellence. Particular stress is laid on discipline, which in turn depends on the leader's *severitas*, a military and administrative ·

---

[141] Amm. XXII. 3. 9.

[142] Amm. XXII. 3. 7.

[143] Amm. XX. 11. 5; cf. Lib. XVIII. 152: ὀργῇ μὲν τῆς στρατιᾶς ἀνηρπάσθη.

[144] Amm. XXIV. 1. 2; cf. XVI. 5. 10.

[145] On the state of the army, Amm. XXII. 4. 6; Zos. II. 34. In this connection see R. Macmullen, *Soldier and Civilian in the Later Roman Empire*, Cambridge, Mass. 1963, who makes the interesting point that under S. Severus the Roman army began to lose its professional edge, a process which lasted for about two centuries and resulted in the dissolution of military discipline through loss of specialization.

[146] Amm. XXII. 7. 7.

[147] Socr. III. 22. 2; cf. *ELF*, No. 50.

[148] Amm. XXII. 4. 7–8.

[149] In his *Epitoma Rei Militaris*, Flavius Vegetius Renatus—a late-fourth- or, possibly, early-fifth-century bureaucrat—collected material from all periods.

virtue which should not, however, be pushed to extremes, thus provoking mutiny, but be tempered by such allowances as gifts in money and kind, as Julian understood.[150] It is coincidental, but significant, that these are also the virtues and principles on which rested the ideal Mithraic life, which Julian continued to practise as a private individual.

While Julian laid the foundations for the creation of a class of guardians that would protect his state against external dangers, he also took measures against inner dissolution: he undertook to reorganize the system of public justice and, more generally, to eradicate corruption from the administration. This was a problem of which Julian had become acutely aware during his years in Gaul. Though his power was limited and the reaction he encountered great, he had even then attempted to check abuses.[151] Now he could at last engage in open war against corruption. First he exposed one aspect of patronage— that of *suffragium*.[152] In a brief, nervous, military style—which is characteristic of all his laws—Julian denounces a situation which he knew to be 'too deeply rooted a feature of Roman life to be prohibited or abolished'.[153] The only weapon that he had in his hands was to stop encouraging as emperor so shameful a practice. With a pragmatism that verges on cynicism he makes clear his position: the man who gives money or property to a *suffragator* in order to obtain a benefit should be unable to reclaim what he gave away in 'an impudent and dishonest spirit' if his request failed.[154] Here is a characteristic specimen of Julian's cruel sense of humour at the expense of those he believed to be in the wrong: just as he had let loose heretics against orthodox, believing that that was the best way to exterminate Christianity, he was now abolishing every partial rule of fairness in a game which was essentially dishonest.

Another class whose corruption Julian sought to curb were

---

[150] See above, p. 114 n. 138; also Amm. XXV. 4. 12. Cf. Julian's lenient attitude when, on the eve of the Persian campaign, a mutiny broke out among his troops: Lib. XII. 84 ff.; XVI. 19. On Julian's *severitas*, see Amm. XXIV. 3. 2; 5. 10; XXV. 1. 7–9.

[151] See above, p. 59.

[152] *Suffragium* was the practice of paying money to influential people in order to obtain appointment: see Jones, *LRE*, 391–6.

[153] T. D. Barnes, 'A law of Julian', *CPh* lxix (1974), 290.

[154] *C. Th.* II. 29. 1.

the *numerarii*, the accountants working for municipalities. Following Constantius, he debased them to an ignoble status, so that they might be tortured if found guilty of corruption; yet as a Mithraist, he also took care to institute a reward for those who throughout their career performed their duty conscientiously.[155]

Having passed so many beneficial laws on behalf of the taxpayer,[156] Julian legislated severely against those who still attempted to swindle the State,[157] while he hit in exemplary fashion those who usurped the property of proscribed persons.[158] Greed was the one human weakness Julian found very hard to take. Here was a man who through constant effort had conquered for himself the four cardinal virtues,[159] a Platonist and a Mithraist who burned with ambition to build a state on the principle of τὸ δίκαιον.[160] Julian was accustomed to point out that the poet Aratus had painted Justice flying up to heaven because of her impatience with men's sins, and he would add that under his own rule the goddess had returned to earth.[161] Yet the emperor's copious and extremely detailed legislation on public justice amply confirms Aratus' pessimism: with rare exceptions, late Roman magistrates were dishonest men, and Julian does not hesitate to advert to this situation in an official document, in which he attempts to put an external brake on the doings of the 'prava conscientia' of imperial governors.[162]

Coupled with this passion for equity, a spirit of immobile traditionalism is apparent in many of Julian's laws concerning the administration of justice. As he clearly states in one of them, there was nothing he desired less than a break with the past.[163] In harsh and contemptuous words, Julian abolishes Con-

---

[155] *C.Th.* VIII. 1. 6–7.
[156] See above, pp. 103 ff.
[157] *C.Th.* XI. 3. 3–4; I. 16. 5.
[158] *C.Th.* IX. 42. 5.
[159] I. 10c; III. 79b; Amm. XXV. 4. 1. In his article 'Les quatre vertus païennes et chrétiennes: Apothéose et ascension', *Hommages à Marcel Renard* i, Brussels 1969, *Latomus* ci, 652, J. Préaux makes the interesting point that the doctrine of the four Platonic virtues is closely linked with the theme of Julian's apotheosis.
[160] The vision of the Platonic Republic was always lurking at the back of Julian's mind (cf. III. 98b).
[161] Amm. XXV. 4. 19.
[162] *C.Th.* XI. 30. 31.
[163] *C.Th.* V. 20. 1.

stantinian decrees in favour of the Hellenistic or even Roman-republican constitutions that they had replaced. 'Secutus consultum Claudianum firmum esse censemus, omnibus constitutionibus quae contra id latae sunt penitus infirmatis':[164] thus he thundered against innovations, while expressing with enviable clarity and attention to detail what he wished either to be done or to be left undone.[165]

The other major characteristic of Julian's laws on public justice is hatred of procrastination: with his personal experience as a judge, he understood how delays in doing justice may well result in some dishonest compromise being reached.[166] Thus, in tune with his more general policy, Julian made a serious attempt to decentralize justice.[167] 'A multitude of lawsuits were brought under Julian, while men drank in his justice open-mouthed, for no deferments were allowed, which under a pretence of lawfulness encourage the unjust, and favour those who know which string to pull.'[168] This was an emperor who 'guided the whole world by justice and the other virtues',[169] a true philosopher[170] who, in his role as a king, saw himself above all as a fair and mild judge[171] and a lenient legislator.

For the reader of the Theodosian Code—that unique monument of human brutality—Julian's laws stick out as islands of humanity in a sea of cruelty.[172] His philosophical disposition and religious convictions are nowhere more evident than in his abundant legislative work, in the whole corpus of which capital punishment is mentioned but once.[173]

Yet in his attempt to reorganize the empire Julian did not rely entirely on his own judgement and capacities. One of his major preoccupations was to find the right collaborators, men who

---

[164] See *C.Th.* II. 5. 2; IV. 12. 5, cf. III. 1. 3.
[165] Amm. XXV. 4. 20.
[166] *C.Th.* I. 16. 8; II. 5. 2; XI. 30. 29–31 and *Cod. Just.* VIII. 35. 12.
[167] *C.Th.* I. 16. 8.
[168] Suda I. 437; cf. Amm. XXII. 10. 4 ff.
[169] *OGIS* 520.
[170] *ILS* 751.
[171] *Cod. Just.* VIII. 35. 12; Amm. XXV. 4. 8–9 and 15.
[172] Amm. XXV. 4. 20; Lib. XVIII. 151.
[173] For the principles Julian followed in his legislation, see II. 128d, III. 89cd; 'For it is by reason that we ought to persuade and instruct men, not by blows and insults and bodily violence' (*ep.* 114. 438b). Like Plato (*Gorgias* 470e), Julian felt that the truly unhappy man was the unjust.

would be able to advise and even correct him.[174] The time had
come at last for him to put into practice his boldest dreams and
theories:

And though the good ruler will in person oversee and direct and
govern the whole, he will also see to it that those of his officials who
are in charge of the most important works and management, and
who share his counsels for the general good, are virtuous men and as
far as possible like himself. And he will choose them not carelessly
or at random, nor will he consent to be a less rigorous judge than a
lapidary or one who tests gold plate or purple dye. For such men are
not satisfied with one method of testing, but since they know, I
suppose, that the wickedness and devices of those who are trying to
cheat them are various and manifold, they try to counter as far as
possible, and they oppose to them the tests supplied by their art. So
too our ruler apprehends that evil changes its face and is apt to
deceive, and that the cruellest thing it does is that it often takes men
in by putting on the garb of virtue, and hoodwinks those who are
not keen-sighted enough, or who in course of time grow weary of the
length of the investigation; and so he will rightly be on his guard
against any such deception. But when once he has chosen them, and
has about him the worthiest men, he will entrust them with the
choice of the minor officials. (III. 91b–d)

Julian's criterion of selection was excellence combined with
diligence. Like a competent jeweller, he could tell a real pearl
from a fake, and, as a good diplomat, he knew how to avoid
tactfully the silly intellectuals who knocked on his door expecting to obtain a position of power simply on the strength of their
religious convictions and veneer of classical education;[175] yet at
the same time he encouraged men of no fortune to arm themselves with the four Platonic virtues and go straight to him if
they desired, and were prepared for, positions of responsibility.[176] With belligerent enthusiasm Julian purged the administration of all the illiterate and inefficient: by 1 January 362
Mamertinus could already congratulate him on his nomina-
tions,[177] adding: 'you choose as provincial governors not your
most intimate friends, but the men of the greatest integrity.'[178]

[174] Amm. XXII. 10. 3; XXV. 4. 16.
[175] See *ep.* 40; cf. *ep.* 8 (for Gaul) and the *Letter to Themistius*; Greg. Naz. *or.*
V. 20.
[176] Mamert. 21. 4; cf. 17.
[177] Ibid. 25. 3.
[178] Ibid. 25. 5; cf. Lib. XVIII. 104, 158.

E

To a contemporary panegyrist Julian's collaborators were the divine crew of the ship of state, and he felt that it would not be blasphemous to liken it to the crew that Athene herself had chosen for her own ship, the *Argo*.[179] Soon the ship of state would have to sail through less calm waters under new steersmen, yet the crew was to remain for a time substantially unchanged.[180]

As well as appointing able administrators Julian summoned to his court those whom he regarded as his own spiritual guides or as the priests of Hellenic *paideia*,[181] though he did not intend to invest them with any public office. He even addressed reassuring messages to some outstanding Christians,[182] wishing to show thereby that he was inaugurating a reign in which gifted men of whatever creed would be honoured and respected.

The extraordinary good sense and general tolerance that Julian showed until the autumn of 362, based as it was on genuine goodwill and on self-confidence, is the most reassuring trait of his behaviour and the one element thanks to which Julian's policies could have been crowned with success.[183]

Those who share the task of administration with me are, I am convinced, honest and reasonable men, intelligent and entirely capable of all they have to do. So they give me leisure and the opportunity of resting without neglecting anything. For our intercourse with one another is free from that hypocrisy of courts ... which leads men to praise one another even while they hate with a hatred more deadly than they feel for their worst enemies in war. But we, though we refute and criticize one another with appropriate frankness, whenever it is necessary, love one another as much as the most devoted friends. Hence it is that I am able—if I may say so without odium—to work and yet enjoy relaxation, and when at work to be free from strain, and sleep securely. For when I have kept vigil it was less on my own behalf than on behalf of all my subjects. (*ep.* 32)

---

[179] Him. XLI. 13; cf. Lib. XVIII. 158; *ep.* 1224.

[180] Petit, *Libanius*, 203; add the evidence of Eunap. *V. Phil.* VII. 4. 10: ὁ Ἰοβιανὸς ἐβασίλευσε καὶ τιμῶν τοὺς ἄνδρας διετέλεσεν. For Julianic administrative appointments surviving into Valens' and Valentinian's reign, see J. F. Matthews, *Western Aristocracies and Imperial Court A.D. 364–425*, Oxford 1975, 37–8.

[181] Lib. XVIII. 288.   [182] *epp.* 31; 46. See below, p. 127.

[183] A. H. M. Jones's bold hypothesis that 'if after a victory over Persia, he [Julian] had enjoyed a prosperous reign of thirty years, it seems possible that he could have reached his objective' (*The Decline of the Ancient World*, London 1966, 62), makes good sense in the context of that first period of Julian's reign. In this connection see Greg. Naz. *or.* V. 19, 26.

IV. PAIDEIA

Λόγῳ δὲ πείθεσθαι χρὴ καὶ διδάσκεσθαι τοὺς ἀνθρώπους, οὐ
πληγαῖς οὐδὲ ὕβρεσιν οὐδὲ αἰκισμῷ τοῦ σώματος. *ep.* 114. 438b

In his attempt to restore order to the Roman *oikoumene*, Julian
started from the assumption that it was possible to re-establish
the perfect balance that had been maintained between Hellenism and *Romanitas* during the Antonine period. Realizing that
this balance had been irrevocably shifted by the mid-fourth
century through the emergence of new attitudes, and thus of a
new political reality, he tried to bridge the gulf that had now
opened up between imperial and local ideologies, by exploiting
Hellenism as a cohesive force. Yet his attempt to impose from
above a religion which he faced *a priori* as a uniting principle,
meant that he necessarily advocated an imperial rather than a
local policy. His democratic ideology found expression only in
his personal relations with other individuals, and failed to affect
substantially either his legislation or his treatment of individual
cities, in which Julian proved that his idea of the empire was
Byzantine rather than Antonine, with Hellenism instead of
Christianity fulfilling the role of the State cult.

This 'Hellenism' was a much more complex and all-
embracing force than the paganism the empire had hitherto
known as its official religion. It was made up of many hetero-
geneous elements, whose theoretical inconsistencies Julian
undertook to explain to his subjects. As a good Platonist, he
conceived of *paideia* as a long process by which individual men,
and indeed the empire in general, might attain to a goal of
perfection which Julian identified with ἐπιστήμη. In the spiritual sphere ἐπιστήμη meant to him the salvation of the soul; in
cultural terms it coincided with the acquisition of exact knowledge; while in the socio-political field it denoted the happiness
of the State. Yet these three goals, which the commentator of
Julian's thought must separate for the sake of clarity, are for
him one; ἐπιστήμη, the supreme end of human existence, is a
unity and *paideia* forms the only possible path to it. And as
ἐπιστήμη displays many natures in one essence, so too *paideia*

has its intellectual, moral and political as well as its religious aspects.

For the Platonic thinker that Julian was, everybody is able to attain to ἐπιστήμη, because of the essential kinship of Man's nature with truth,[1] manifested in his innate inclination towards learning, research and study (IX. 206b), from which even those whose souls are deeply buried in materiality are not hopelessly estranged (IX. 189c). Yet this merciful vocation of human nature is no guarantee that Man will ultimately reach his objective, for in his pursuit of knowledge he may easily be led astray. This is the reason why Julian lays such emphasis on the definition of *paideia*. For him true *paideia* means an understanding of the Graeco-Roman cultural tradition in all its aspects and implications; only through this knowledge can man hope to begin to know himself, and thus ultimately be led to union with the divine.[2]

Like all truly great human achievements, Graeco-Roman culture is for Julian the product of divine revelation, and in its historical progress it is constantly watched over by God.[3] Thanks to the revelation of Apollo–Helios the Greeks developed an admirable religious, philosophical and artistic tradition which their kinsmen, the Romans, were to perfect by enriching it with the best political constitution the world had known.[4]

In this way, the Graeco-Roman civilization—Hellenism and *Romanitas* inextricably fused into one cultural and political principle, that of the Julianic *paideia*—finds its historical justification in theological terms, while Julian's own sense of worldly mission and of his spiritual salvation appear as interrelated ideas, as indeed he himself perceived them to be (VIII. 180ac).

Only a few decades before Julian, the Christian Eusebius had described the Roman *imperium* and the Christian gospel as the combined forces which, having grown together 'by one divine

---

[1] IX. 197a: ἔχουσι γὰρ ἄνθρωποι φύσει πρὸς ἀλήθειαν οἰκείως. Cf. IX. 194d; 196d, 197b. A Platonic axiom espoused also by Iambl. *Myst.* I. 3.

[2] VII. 225d. This conception of *paideia* as a general process leading from the concrete to the abstract is already to be found in Minucius Felix, *Octavius* XII. 7: 'quibus non est datum intellegere civilia, multo magis denegatum est disserere divina.'

[3] For the idea of Apollo–Helios as the Ἑλλάδος κοινὸς ἡγεμὼν καὶ νομοθέτης καὶ βασιλεύς, see IX. 188a.

[4] XI. 152d–153a, quoted above, pp. 84–5.

command', were God's gift to mankind.[5] In other words, Eusebius rejected the theological and cultic content of the Hellenic
tradition and replaced it by the teachings and practices of
Christianity. Like Eusebius, Julian attempted to establish an
indissoluble link between a particular political system and a
particular religion, except that the emperor's ideal of *paideia*
can be said to be more complete and homogeneous than the
bishop's, since it embraced and sanctioned the whole historical
achievement of the Graeco-Roman world. Far from dividing
paideia into sacred and profane or even into theoretical and
practical, Julian emphasized its organic unity and encouraged
the constant study of the whole for the sake of a higher end.

From studying our scriptures every man would become better than
before, even if he were utterly inept. But when a man is naturally
well endowed, and moreover receives the education of our literature,
he becomes actually a gift of the gods to mankind, either by kindling
the light of knowledge, or by founding some kind of political constitution, or by routing great numbers of his country's foes, or even
by travelling far over the earth and sea, and thus proving himself a
man of heroic mould. (*C.G.* 229de)

Julian never distinguishes between sacred and profane letters.
The literary culture of the Hellene is one and united; it is the
same store of learning that enables each individual to realize
his particular vocation, as scientist or philosopher, statesman or
general, explorer or priest. When, on moral grounds, Julian
forbids pagan priests to read Epicurean and Pyrrhonian literature, he hastens to add that most of it has perished anyway by
the work of divine providence:[6] priests as well as laymen should
avoid the reading of literature which encourages materialism
or scepticism.

Seen in this light all the literature produced by the Greeks
—poetry and prose alike—is sacred: 'What! was it not the gods,
who revealed all their learning to Homer, Hesiod, Demosthenes,
Herodotus, Thucydides, Isocrates and Lysias? Did not these
men think that they were consecrated, some to Hermes, others
to the Muses?'[7] This was the great asset of Hellenism. Religion
was one and coextensive with culture, whose various aspects

[5] *Tric.* XVI. 4.
[6] *ep.* 89b. 301bc.
[7] *ep.* 61. 423a; cf. VII. 236b.

sprang out of the need for a fuller expression of religious feeling. Epic, lyric and dramatic poetry, philosophy, rhetoric and history were closely connected with the Olympians—would in fact have been impossible without them.

In a still more obvious sense, all Greek art is sacred and ideologically consistent. Never in a Greek temple could one come across the blatant self-contradiction with which we meet in so many Christian churches: Greek philosophers, portrayed in their traditional garb and accompanied by their attributes, side by side with Christian saints. This persistent phenomenon in Christian iconography shows that men felt that culture was not merely an intellectual, but also a spiritual force, that it was true culture only in so far as it was endowed with religious overtones. Thus Homer, Plato and Aristotle, the main influences on the intellectual life of the eastern empire, soon ceased to be regarded as the enemy in religious matters, and were tacitly accorded citizenship in the kingdom of Christ.[8] This was a development anticipated by Julian's edict on education. Homer and Plato could not possibly be fully appreciated unless they were thought of as saints.

For Julian the sanctity of Greek culture was ensured by the fact that Apollo–Helios, the patron of culture and god of truth, acted as the παιδαγωγός of humanity and, in special cases, could also bestow his divine grace through instant illumination.[9] In his role as educator Apollo had been responsible for sending mankind its great philosophers (IX. 188b); and now at the crisis-point in the history of Hellenism, caused by the accession to the throne of the first Christian emperors, he had intervened once more. As Helios–Mithra, he addressed himself personally to the child Julian, and, raising him to the rank of emperor and *pontifex maximus*, ordered him to show to his subjects the road of true *paideia*.

This road was none other than the path opened up by Plato's metaphysical intuition and broadened by the contribution of

---

[8] A list of frescoes representing Greek philosophers in Christian churches is provided by K. Spetsieris, Εἰκόνες Ἑλλήνων φιλοσόφων εἰς ἐκκλησίας *EEAth* xiv (1963–4), 386–458. Cf. Ivan Dujčev, *Heidnische Philosophen und Schriftsteller in der alten bulgarischen Wandmalerei*, Rheinisch-Westfälische Akademie der Wissenschaften Vorträge G 214 (1976). See also John Mauropous, *epigr.* 43 (Lagarde), asking God to exempt Plato and Plutarch from his wrath.

[9] IX. 206bc; cf. VII. 231c.

his spiritual heirs. For in his general belief that wickedness is ignorance, and that training and goodwill are the prerequisites for the acquisition of knowledge, Julian was a Platonist:[10] he had read in the *Republic* that *paideia* was the only process by which the eye of the soul could be turned towards the contemplation of the Good (518b ff.), cause and source of all knowledge (509b); and he knew better than anybody else that this theme had remained an essential part of Platonic teaching ever since. Plotinus had emphasized the spiritual element in *paideia*,[11] while Porphyry had stressed its moral and cathartic aspects, as opposed to the mere accumulation of knowledge.[12] Yet it was only with Iamblichus that the concept of *paideia* began to acquire both the complexity and importance it has in the writings of Julian.

In his *Vita Pythagorica*, Iamblichus presents the paradigmatic pagan saint as a man who spends endless years in cultivating his mind by seeking to master those disciplines which are apprehended by man's discursive intelligence.[13] *Paideia* in the sense of intellectual achievement is described as Man's only sure acquisition in this life, as also the possession thanks to which ἀθάνατος δόξα may be attached to his memory long after he has passed away (42). In this sense *paideia* embraces also the theory and practice of politics, a domain in which the Iamblichan sage may actively involve himself. For Pythagoras was 'the originator of the whole of political *paideia* as well' (130); in historical terms he became the liberator and legislator of Magna Graecia (33), and trained his pupils in the social virtues of justice and affability (168). Yet the moral and intellectual aspects of the Iamblichan notion of *paideia* do not alone make the true sage: they must be matched by a profoundly spiritual disposition, for it was on account of his extensive knowledge of the cults and mysteries of the ancient world (151), and his constant involvement with them, that Pythagoras was considered

---

[10] V. 271d–272a. For the idea that *paideia* is the path to salvation in Plato, see *Leg.* 897b. The most famous exponent of the opposite theory that knowledge and virtue are not teachable was Pindar, see *Ol.* II. 86.

[11] *Enn.* VI. 9. 11.

[12] *Marc.* 9; 15; 24; 30; 34.

[13] *V. Pyth.* 17–19; cf. 28: Pythagoras leaves Samos according to one tradition τὴν περὶ παιδείαν ὀλιγωρίαν τῶν τότε τὴν Σάμον οἰκούντων παραιτούμενος; also 70: the human *dianoia* can be purified only by submitting to *paideia*.

to be a god by his contemporaries and by posterity. Iamblichus often implies that the perfect knowledge to which the path of *paideia* leads is the characteristic quality of divinity, a hint which Julian will not leave unexploited: for it is 'in so far as ἐπιστήμη is concerned that the gods differ from us' (IX. 184c).

With varying nuances of emphasis, *paideia* is the central theme of all of Iamblichus' writings.[14] As either philosophical training or theurgical proficiency, it illuminates the sage in his search after the divine. Julian took over Iamblichus' conception of *paideia*, but, while in its specific form of theurgical proficiency he meant it to be the exclusive privilege of one caste of people within the empire, the priesthood, in its broad sense he wanted it to be the privilege of all mankind. While Iamblichus had set out to instruct a limited number of people who were led towards the study of philosophy of their own accord, Julian felt that it was his duty to set all his subjects on the road of *paideia*, whether they wanted it or not. Only those stubborn few, the Christians, who denounced in his ideal of *paideia* a system of cultural totalitarianism, were to be condemned to the condition of the intellectual pariah.

It is in a passage in which Julian expresses his gratitude towards the masters of his youth, Mardonius and Maximus, for the education that they gave him,[15] that the emperor best defines the 'right education': it is the mastering of the Greek language and of the different genres of literature, the acquisition of virtue, and the entry into the realm of philosophy. In a later text Julian complemented his account of *paideia* by prescribing the rites and ascetic practices that the pious man should perform as part of his training towards the attainment of illumination.[16]

Yet, despite his predilection for definitions, Julian's general conception of the way of *paideia* seems to have been far from narrow, for he fully approved of those pagan conservatives who, unlike himself, respected the religious tradition of Hellenism only in its unadulterated form. Such a man was Salutius who, presumably at Julian's prompting, composed and circulated a pagan catechism which advocates a very different kind of

---

Hellenism from the emperor's.[17] Next to such men, with their decent religious preoccupations, Julian seems to have approved of all those who, without necessarily being able to appreciate its spiritual core, professed genuine respect and admiration for the cultural heritage of Greece and did not seek in any way to undermine its foundations by using the methods and spirit of Hellenism to further alien causes.[18] An outstanding representative of this category is Libanius, a man who spent a lifetime promoting the cause of Greek letters and shed genuine tears over the cultural wreckage of Hellenism.[19] Less obvious instances are two Christian intellectuals, Aetius and Prohaeresius, both of whom enjoyed Julian's favour as emperor.[20] Unfortunately we have no explicit comment by a pagan writer on Aetius' personality, other than Julian's letter, but on Prohaeresius we have the biography that Eunapius incongruously included in his collection of *Lives* of pagan saints, in which the Armenian rhetor, because of his respect for Hellenic *paideia*, appears as the Christian counterpart of Libanius. Both were men of a classical education, the degree and quality of whose respect for Hellenism Julian had had the opportunity to appreciate during long hours spent in their company. Julian's criterion for judging Greekness was indeed unerring; during the years of his studies he had also met two other Christians steeped in classical letters—Basil of Caesarea and Gregory of Nazianzos—both of whom he pointedly ignored, realizing that theirs was an irreverent attitude towards his thought-world, one of exploitation of Hellenism in order to serve Christianity.[21]

Yet, though he approved of all those who loved Greek culture (VII. 236bc), Julian knew who were those worthy of the title of the true Hellene—men like Iamblichus, Maximus, Chrysanthius, Priscus, who saw tradition as a living force in

[17] See below, pp. 154 ff.

[18] This may seem at variance with Julian's professed belief that the religious and cultural aspects of Hellenism are intermingled. Yet one could hardly expect Julian to be fully consistent in all his ideas and actions. Here again is an instance of that *levitas* that Ammianus remarked in him.

[19] A phrase like the following sums up Libanius' attitude towards contemporary literature: Ἦν ὅτε ἐγίνοντο λόγοι χρυσοῖ. τὰ νῦν δὲ σιδηροῖ πάντες καὶ ἢ μικρὸν ἢ οὐδὲν ἕτερος ἑτέρου διαφέρων (*ep.* 1340).

[20] *epp.* 31, 46. The addressee of *ep.* 32, a certain Basil, who was a close collaborator of Constantius (cf. *ep.* 32. 381b), may have been Christian too.

[21] See *ep.* 90 on Diodorus of Tarsus.

continuous and fruitful contact with reality. Like them, Julian
was a syncretist; yet he embraced in his sphere of interest not
just religion, but equally the fields of political theory and social
institutions. In the imperial throne Julian saw the chair from
which he was to preach as the apologist and apostolic father of
Hellenism. In a series of writings which he began to issue as
early as March 362, he at once defended the principles of his
syncretistic *paideia*, and presented it as the best road to worldly
happiness and spiritual salvation. He considered his message to
be of the utmost importance for 'all things that breathe and
move upon the earth',[22] but in his task of educating mankind
he proceeded by stages. The most obvious enemies of his
ideology—the Christians, whom Julian was soon to deprive of
the right of participation in his *paideia*—were to be left for a
time in blissful ignorance. Less evident and more insidious
underminers of his thought-world were to be dealt with first.
For within the camp of Hellenism itself there were heretics
whom the *pontifex maximus* had urgently to convert to more
orthodox views. Next to isolated cases, such as Themistius,[23]
there existed a whole class of people, the Cynics, whom Julian
disliked intensely and attacked several times with the fundamental accusation that they had lost their roots.

As a confirmed syncretist, Julian naturally believed that the
various currents in classical Greek philosophy (with the exception of the Epicureans and Sceptics) were in essential accordance with each other, not only as regards their metaphysical
principles, but also in their ethics and methodology. It may be
that Julian's accusation, in apparent violation of his syncretistic

[22] XI. 130b, cf. Hom. *Il.* P 447 and *Od.* σ 131; also the prayer that Julian
addresses to his patron god: 'may great Helios grant that I too attain to perfect
knowledge of Himself and that I may instruct all men in general, but especially
those who are worthy to learn' (XI. 157d).

[23] Themistius was regarded as a traitor by his contemporary Hellenes on account
of his having used his Greek *paideia* to promote a new conception of the vocation
of the empire. See Palladas' characteristic epigram, *Anth. Gr.* XI. 292:

Ἄντυγος οὐρανίης ὑπερήμενος, ἐς πόθον ἦλθες
Ἄντυγος ἀργυρέης· αἶσχος ἀπειρέσιον·
Ἦσθά ποτε κρείσσων, αὖθις δ᾽ ἐγένου πολὺ χείρων.
Δεῦρ᾽ ἀνάβηθι κάτω, νῦν γὰρ ἄνω κατέβης.

See also G. Dagron, *T&MByz* iii. 60–73. In 355 Constantius announced Themistius' entry into the Senate of Constantinople in the following words: μεταλαβὼν
παρ᾽ ἡμῶν ἀξιώματος ῥωμαϊκοῦ ἀντισφέρει σοφίαν ἑλληνικήν (*Dem. Const.*
21a).

principles, that the Cynics were rootless, was justified by the behaviour of some contemporary representatives of the sect; but the emperor's real concern is with the realm of abstract ideas, and here we see that he treads faithfully in the paths already marked out by the polemic of the classical Schools. Julian attacks the Cynics of his own day in tones strongly reminiscent of the attacks made by Socrates, Plato and Aristotle on Antisthenes;[24] and, if the founder of the sect is in Julian's eyes such an admirable representative of Cynicism, that too, along with much else that the emperor says about contemporary Cynics, has its precedent in writers of the second century AD.

In his *Fourth Discourse on Kingship*, Dio Chrysostom had drawn a picture of Diogenes as the ideal sage,[25] which is almost identical with that drawn by Julian: αὐτάρκεια, ἐλευθερία and παρρησία were the principles of Diogenes' life of constant training with a view to the attainment of that ideal state in which the human being, liberated from all passions and sorrows, conquers truth. His scorn for social conventions was not an end in itself, but the expression of the moral battle in which he engaged on an individual level in order to fulfil what he regarded as the end of human existence. Both Dio and Julian emphasize that Diogenes' nonconformism was not meant to shock his fellow-humans—for whose opinion he cared little anyway—but was just his personal way of expressing his innermost beliefs and tendencies, the genuine ascetic tastes of a strong nature striving to obtain salvation.[26] Strangely enough, this view was shared by Lucian,[27] who, while expressing his respect for the moral principles of Cynicism, attacks mercilessly whoever appears to him to have deviated from the norm best represented by Diogenes and occasionally revived since—as for instance, by his own contemporary Demonax.

In the later Cynics the values of αὐτάρκεια, ἐλευθερία and

---

[24] For Socrates on Antisthenes' κενοδοξία see Diog. Laert. *Vit. Phil.* II. 36. For the hostility between Plato and Antisthenes, ibid. III. 35; see also Plato, *Soph.* 251b, where Antisthenes is alluded to as γέρων ὀψιμαθής. Aristotle attacked Antisthenes on account of his εὐήθεια, see *Met.* 1024b, 32 ff.; cf. ibid. 1043b, 24: οἱ Ἀντισθένειοι καὶ οἱ οὕτως ἀπαίδευτοι. For Julian's own attack on Cynicism as a philosophy and way of life, see VII. 210c–211a.

[25] Esp. 16 ff.

[26] VII. 238 ff.; IX. 202c ff.

[27] *Dial. Mort.* I. 1. 2. See also R. Höistad, *Cynic Hero and Cynic King* (diss.), Uppsala 1948, 64 ff.

παρρησία were felt to have degenerated into misanthropy[28] and impudence.[29] Ἀπαιδευσία was their hallmark,[30] leading them into a fatal contempt and even hatred for the tradition into which intellectual laziness had prevented them from being integrated.[31] Thus, through their failure to understand them, they despised all the social, cultural, national and religious values on which the empire stood, and even made a positive attempt to discredit them: wandering from town to town they preached the denial of these values.[32] Yet, at the same time, despite their profession of indifference towards all worldly honours and material goods, they knew how to flatter the powerful in order to obtain favours[33] and satisfy their enormous appetites.[34] The Cynics' moral baseness[35] was thus the complement of that unkempt appearance they considered to be the hallmark of the true philosophy.[36]

Interestingly enough, both Lucian and Aelius Aristides had linked Christianity with this degenerate Cynicism, the first implicitly, by showing Peregrinus moving from the one thought-world to the other, the latter explicitly by remarking on the similarities between the habits of the two sects.[37] This point could hardly have been missed by Julian who, seeking a parallel for the Cynics, found it in the ἀποτακτῖται, the followers of the most misanthropic Christian heresy of the fourth century, who

[28] Aelius Aristides XLVI. 308 (Dindorf ii. 399–400); Lucian, *Demon.* 21; cf VII. 209a–c.

[29] Ael. Ar. op. cit. 309, p. 402; Luc. *Bis. Acc.* 33 ff.; cf. VII. 224c ff.

[30] Ael. Ar. op. cit. 307, p. 398: πλείω μὲν σολοικίζουσιν ἢ φθέγγονται. Cf. VII. 225a, 235a; IX. 201a.

[31] On Cynic laziness: Ael. Ar. op. cit. 307, p. 398: Ἡσιόδου κηφῆνες. Cf. VII. 223c.

[32] Luc. *Per.* 3; cf. VII. 210bc, 224a. Origen, *C.C.* III. 50, draws an analogy between Christian and Cynic preachers. On the history of the diatribe as an instrument of philosophical propaganda and its relationship with Christian teaching see P. Wendland, *Die hellenistisch-römische Kultur in ihren Beziehungen zum Judentum und Christentum*, Tübingen 1972⁴, 75 ff.

[33] Ael. Ar. op. cit. 309, p. 402; Luc. *Symp.* 12 ff.; cf. VII. 225a; IX. 198bc.

[34] Cf. Porph. *Abst.* I. 42, where some contemporary Cynics are described as being παντορέκται.

[35] On the Cynic ταπεινότης, Ael. Ar. op. cit. 309, p. 402; cf. VII. 208a, 224cd.

[36] Luc. *Per.* 15, 24; cf. VII. 225bc; IX. 198a; Epictetus, III. 22. 50 and the same description in John Chrysostom, Εἰς τὴν ἀποστολικὴν ῥῆσιν, *PG* 51. 274.

[37] See in particular *Per.* 13, 16; Ael. Ar. op. cit. 309: τοῖς ἐν Παλαιστίνῃ δυσσεβέσι παραπλήσιοι τοὺς τρόπους. See J. Bernays, *Lucian und die Kyniker*, Berlin 1879, 36–9.

condemned every aspect of secular life.[38] A particularly
ἀπαίδευτος Cynic seems to have associated even with nuns,
'admiring the dead existence of those wretched women'
(IX. 203c). Julian castigates him publicly for his lack of taste.[39]
Yet if we compare Julian's systematic invectives against the
Cynics with the attacks that Lucian and Aristides had launched
against them, we discover that, though the points they make
are the same, there is a great difference in the manner in which
they construct their argument: for the two second-century
writers, everything that they criticize in the Cynics is of equal
importance, with a slight emphasis perhaps on misanthropy,
whereas for Julian all the errors these men commit and preach
have but one source: ἀπαιδευσία.[40] This is why he undertook to
demonstrate their error, in the hope that they might draw some
profit from his teaching.

The emergence of Julian's syncretistic religion

The opportunity to launch a general attack on the Cynics was
provided by the talk given by an itinerant philosopher of the
sect, Heracleius, before a large audience in Constantinople in
March 362.[41] Heracleius had invited Julian and the intellectuals
of his entourage to listen to his lecture, which consisted of an
allegory in which, it seems, the gods were treated irreverently.[42]
What especially shocked Julian, and made him regret his having
ever accepted the invitation, was that the Cynic used the opportunity to teach the emperor a lesson in the art of governing,
Heracleius himself disguised as Zeus offering advice, with Julian
listening in the role of goat-like Pan (VII. 234cd). With wicked
cunning Heracleius seems to have accepted the tenets of Julian's
imperial theology in order the better to attack him: in his

[38] VII. 224ab. On ἀποτακτῖται, see Basil of Caesarea, *ep.* 199. 47. For their
condemnation as heretics together with the Manichaeans, see *C. Th.* XVI. 5. 7
(AD 381) and 11 (AD 383); and for attitudes common to Christians and Cynics,
see Greg. Naz. *or. Εἰς Ἡρῶνα τὸν φιλόσοφον.*
[39] The late Neoplatonist David mentions another Cynic who was worsted by
Julian in an exchange of epigrams, *Proleg. Phil.* 11, *Comm. Arist. Gr.* xviii(2), pp.
32. 30–33. 5.
[40] On ἀπαιδευσία as a great sin, see *ep.* 82. 444c, and cf. Plato, *Leg.* 863c. For
παιδεία and ἄσκησις as the most important themes in Cynic teaching, and on
their Socratic origin, see R. Höistad, op. cit., *passim.*
[41] Lib. XVIII. 157.
[42] VII. 204bc, 223b, 226d.

allegory the inexperienced son of King Helios had tried to drive his father's chariot, but displayed the same aptitude for his task as the legendary Phaethon (VII. 208ab). Doubly insulted, the pious and conscientious emperor seized this opportunity to launch a manifesto concerning the unity of theology, philosophy and politics within the empire, and at the same time to denounce the Cynics as enemies and underminers of this unity.[43] The declaration of a political manifesto and the defence of sacred mythology are the two main themes of the *Contra Heracleium*. And, while Julian's political views are clothed in an abstruse theological allegory, he uses a language of surprising immediacy to emphasize the traditional role of theurgy in the context of the classical Greek religion.

According to Julian, the τελεστικοὶ μῦθοι, since they are connected with initiation into the mysteries, carry the same supernatural power and have the same effect as the magic acts and words that the theurgist utters when invoking divinity to appear.[44] The emperor illustrates the function of a τελεστικὸς μῦθος in connection with the mysteries by providing two examples of his personal choice—one associated with the life and deeds of Heracles, and the other referring to the birth of Dionysus. Not only are the particular myths on whose symbolism Julian expands drawn from the classical tradition, but their heroes—mortal men who earned divinity by the slow process of unremitting labour in the complementary fields of ethics and metaphysics[45]—are singularly apt to suggest to the attentive reader analogies with the author himself.

Heracles, of course, was the special hero of Cynicism,[46] as

---

[43] VII. 210bc, 224c; cf. Lib. XVIII. 157.

[44] VII. 216c and 227ab; cf. Macrob. *Comm. in Somn. Sc.* I. 2. 6–21; Procl. *In Remp.* I. 78. 25–79. 4. For the various kinds of allegory, once it becomes a literary genre, see J. Pépin, *Mythe et allégorie: les origines grecques et les contestations judéo-chrétiennes*, Paris 1958, 95–104 and 176–214. The book is useful for the evidence that it contains and for the classification of sources.

[45] VII. 219ab; cf. VIII. 167a.

[46] For Heracles as worshipped by the Pythagoreans, see Iambl. *V. Pyth.* 155, where Heracles is said to symbolize τὴν δύναμιν τῆς φύσεως. See also J. Bayet, *Les origines de l'Hercule romain*, Paris 1926, *passim.*; also J. Carcopino, *Aspects mystiques de la Rome païenne*, Paris 1942, 173–206, who follows Bayet in tracing the origins of the Roman Hercules back to the Pythagoreans of southern Italy. For Heracles as a religious phenomenon in Roman life and literature, see G. K. Galinsky, *The Herakles Theme*, Oxford 1972, 126–52. For Heracles as a theurgist in the Neoplatonist tradition see Procl. *In Remp.* I. 120. 12 ff.: ὁ μὲν Ἡρακλῆς

also the Roman hero *par excellence*.[47] Introduced to Rome in the
third century BC from southern Italy by some Pythagorean sect,
he had established himself as the god of victory. The particular
myth on which Julian chose to comment deals with a secondary
deed of Heracles already known to the ancients but not much
exploited by them. In his interpretation of the myth, Julian's
primary intention seems to be to draw a parallel between the
Greek demi-god and Mithra, for what he does not mention in
his brief development, but is to be found in his sources, is that
Heracles challenged Helios to a fight; the fight did not take
place, but the Sun, marvelling at the hero's courage, offered
him as a present a golden cup on which Heracles crossed the
ocean.[48] Again, through his description of Heracles as the
saviour of the world, thanks to the constant guidance of Athene-
Pronoia (VII. 220a), Julian aims at establishing a double link:
in his role of mediator and saviour Heracles is associated with
Mithra, but also, at another level, with Julian himself, who
emerges as a second Heracles-Mithra, destined to restore order
to the Roman world with the constant aid of his special deity
Athene-Pronoia. This order had been disrupted mainly by the
Christians, and Julian takes this opportunity to denounce their
unoriginality. His disdainful reference to the Gospels, and the
implication that they borrowed important incidents in the life
of Christ from the Hellenes can hardly be lost on any reader;
and with the story of Christ walking on the waters in mind,
Julian remarks bluntly: 'my belief is that Heracles did not cross
the sea on a cup but walked on it as if it were dry land'.[49]

This line of thought is pursued even more systematically
through the analysis of the myth of Dionysus. Born human,

διὰ τελεστικῆς καθηράμενος καὶ τῶν ἀχράντων καρπῶν μετασχὼν τελέας
ἔτυχεν τῆς εἰς θεοὺς ἀποκαταστάσεως.

[47] See Livy, I. 7.

[48] We know from Pausanias (VIII. 31. 7, where he describes an image of Helios
Soter Heracles at Megalopolis in Arcadia), that the identification of Heracles with
Helios Soter had already been made, but what is important is that Julian here
attempts to emphasize the connection between the Roman Hercules and Mithra
by referring to a well-known episode from the *vita* of the Iranian god; cf. *MMM*
i. 172–3, 304.

[49] VII. 219d; cf. *C.G.* 213b and Matthew 14:25; Mark 6:48; cf. Philostrat.
V. Apoll. I. 38. For similarities between the Pauline language of Phil. 2:6 ff. and
the Heracles language, see W. L. Knox, 'The "divine hero" Christology in the
New Testament', *HThR* xli (1948), 229–49.

killed by the Titans, and buried only to be resurrected, the god appears as the perfect counterpart of Christ. With this thought at the back of his mind, Julian describes his manifestation on earth not only in dogmatic terms borrowed from contemporary Neoplatonic vocabulary—as a 'demonic revelation' ($\delta\alpha\iota\mu o\nu\acute{\iota}\alpha$ $\check{\epsilon}\kappa\phi\alpha\nu\sigma\iota\varsigma$, VII. 220b) or an epiphany (VII. 221ab)— but also in a language deeply familiar to the ears of large numbers of fourth-century men: the god's 'future manifestation' (VII. 221b) had been announced to mankind by prophetic lips long before his actual 'ungenerated birth in the cosmos' ($\acute{\alpha}\gamma\acute{\epsilon}\nu\nu\eta\tau o\varsigma$ $\tau\acute{o}\kappa o\varsigma$ $\acute{\epsilon}\nu$ $\tau\hat{\wp}$ $\kappa\acute{o}\sigma\mu\wp$) took place (VII. 221c). Predictably enough, a lacuna of several words follows after this phrase: the sentence which, we cannot help feeling, must have ended with an explicit parallel between the birth of Dionysus and that of Christ, doubtless appeared too irreverent to the Christian copyist of the oration.

Julian's public, as he admitted himself, consisted of 'minds disposed to anything rather than the study of philosophy' (VII. 221d). His was the combined task of a preacher, a vulgarizer and a polemicist, and, like earlier coreligionists who had attacked the Christians, he attempted in formulating the dogmas of Hellenism to prove, as if by the way, that all the essentials of the Gospels had been borrowed from the mythology and theology of paganism—his irreverent allusions to Christianity were hardly obscure and must have sounded infuriating to the ears of contemporary Christians. Yet this was only a secondary objective. The emperor's primary aim was to establish in the popular mind a link between the traditional Graeco-Roman religion and the semi-official mystery cults, of many of which he himself was an adept; he also wanted to make his public gradually aware of the roles that the Olympians had now assumed within the framework of a theology as new to mankind as Christianity itself. Thus the Mother of the gods Cybele is closely associated with both Dionysus and Athene, two other crucial deities in the late Greek pantheon. It is Cybele (whose essential kinship with Athene Julian emphasizes elsewhere[50]) who arrives and heals the new-born Dionysus of the madness with which Hera in her jealousy had stricken the illegitimate offspring of Zeus (VII. 220c), just as she also cures

[50] VIII. 179ab.

Attis of a similar affliction (IX. 175a). It is likewise Cybele who raises the child of Semele to the rank of a god (VII. 220c). 'And I discern also the divided creative function of Dionysos, which great Dionysos received from the single and abiding life of mighty Zeus. For from Zeus he proceeded and he bestows that life on all things visible, controlling and governing the creation of the whole divisible world' (VIII. 179b).

As a part of his tendency towards a broad syncretism, Julian sought to associate or even identify the 'intelligent' (νοερός) god Mithra with all those Greek deities who in some sense were emanations of the First Principle and held an intermediary rank between the transcendental and sensible worlds. At the same time Julian's particular emphasis on Dionysus' Indian origin (VII. 221b)—in accordance with the immemorial Greek conviction that all wisdom, sacred and profane alike, had reached Greece from the East—serves a double purpose: it may be seen as an attempt to connect Roman Mithraism with its remote roots (for Mithra had been the genius of light in both Indian and Iranian cosmology[51]), but it is also an implicit assertion of the link that united late antique with classical Hellenism.

Dionysus' Aryan origins had in fact already been emphasized —in contradiction of the traditional version of the myth—by Euripides, whose *Bacchae* was undoubtedly at the back of Julian's mind as he expounded his own interpretation of the Dionysus myth.[52] Euripides had been the one man in the context of the classical Greek tradition whom the sophists of the fifth century had claimed as their own because of his religious scepticism; by quoting his poetry and by referring to him in connection with τελεστικοὶ μῦθοι, Julian makes a deliberate attempt to prove that the tragic poet was a man of piety and that the literature that he produced was sacred.[53] This attempted rehabilitation of Euripides is particularly interesting, because it is part of a more general process at work in Julian's oration. The philosophy of Heraclitus and Empedocles was considered by the ignorant to be irrelevant to mysticism.

[51] See Cumont, *MMM* i. 225.
[52] *Bacchae* 13–22; cf. the treatment of Pentheus in the two texts.
[53] VII. 214b and *Phoen.* 469; VII. 220b and *Bacch.* 288 ff. See esp. VII. 221b ff. and *Bacch.* 13 ff.

Julian showed that, if Heraclitus had explained with the utmost
clarity that theurgy was the only process by which the pious
man could attain to divine illumination,[54] Empedocles, for his
part, imbued with the same mystical knowledge as Julian, had
described the miserable condition of those whose minds are
closed to theological truths.[55] As for Orpheus, Julian repeatedly
associates him with Plato, Aristotle, Plotinus and Iamblichus,[56]
in this way stressing simultaneously the Orphic-Pythagorean
character of the mysteries and the essential unity of all Neoplatonic teaching. He even makes a point of defending theurgy
by using Plotinian language,[57] while he chooses to have recourse
to Pythagorean formulas when he feels that, carried away by
divine frenzy, he has revealed to the uninitiated more than he
ought to.[58]

Albeit in a fragmentary and allusive way, the emperor conveyed in his invective against Heracleius the idea that theurgic
Neoplatonism was firmly based on the age-old tradition of
Greek theology. In doing so he was only following in the footsteps of the great syncretist and exegete, Iamblichus, who was
responsible for two major developments within the School. By
adopting the theurgical principles and hidden practices of the
Chaldean Oracles, Iamblichus had succeeded in transforming
Neoplatonism from a philosophy with mystical connotations
into a mystery religion with δρώμενα, while at the same time he
had managed to present his own system as the only possible
development of classical Greek philosophical thought, a claim
at least partially justified by the subsequent development of
Neoplatonism. If the master of Apamea was the pagan Father
par excellence, Julian saw himself primarily in the role of the
apostle of his teachings.[59] In the religious sphere he was anxious
to bring to the notice of all men that the best of classical Greek
philosophy—that great school of morals and theology—had
sound oriental roots (VII. 237a), and that Pythagoras and

---

[54] See VII. 216c, cf. Heracl. fr. 123; IX. 185a, cf. Heracl. fr. 101; IX. 187d,
cf. Heracl. fr. 40; VIII. 165d, cf. Heracl. fr. 36.

[55] VII. 226b, cf. Emp. fr. 121; see VII. 226c, cf. Heracl., fr. 96.

[56] VII. 215bc, 216d, 217bc.

[57] VII. 217d and *Enn.* V. 3. 12. 47–9.

[58] VII. 217d: οὐκ οἶδ᾽ ὅπως ἐπῆλθέ μοι βακχεύοντι μανῆναι, cf. Theognis,
815; Aeschylus, *Ag.* 36: etc. See also IX. 196c and *Aur. Carm.* 47.

[59] See Lib. XVIII. 125.

Plato and Aristotle did nothing more than sanction through Hellenic rationalism a process which the ensuing centuries of Greek thought continued and amplified (VII. 236d, 237cd).

But this was not an easy task. Julian's impressive public condemnation of the pseudo-Cynics did not succeed in exorcising them. The followers of Diogenes, not in the least shaken by the imperial attack, continued wandering throughout the empire in their coarse cloaks and long unkempt hair, preaching disrespect for any human or divine law. Before three months had elapsed after the composition of his invective against Heracleius, Julian was again presented with an opportunity of attacking the Cynics.[60] Another itinerant philosopher had in the course of a lecture ridiculed Diogenes by presenting him as vainglorious and second-rate (IX. 180d; 202d), and in his extravagance had not even hesitated to discredit his own School. Julian now felt that he had to teach the 'uneducated dogs' once and for all what were the principles of Cynicism and why its followers had to respect them. He wrote a much shorter, essentially theoretical and far more homogeneous oration in which, by integrating Cynicism into the Greek philosophical tradition, he demonstrated the deep unity of Hellenic thought.

Echoing Plato, Julian describes the Promethean fire as a particle of the sun sent by the gods to the world to become the λόγος and νοῦς, through which humanity shares in divinity.[61] The incorporeal reason that is in man[62] pushes him towards philosophy, 'the art of arts and science of sciences' (183a), which consists of nothing less than knowledge of oneself and assimilation to the divine.[63] Through knowledge of our own soul we eventually come to 'investigate whatever exists in us nobler and more divine than the soul itself, that something which we all believe in without being taught and regard as divine and all in common suppose to be in the heavens.'[64] This preliminary exposition, resting on the Plotinian scheme ψυχή–νοῦς–τὸ ἕν, leads Julian to treat of discursive philosophy as a path to salvation. It is through philosophical training and

---

[60] For the date of composition of Julian's second invective against the Cynics, see IX. 181a.

[61] IX. 182c and *Philebus* 16c ff.

[62] IX. 182d; cf. IX. 197b.

[63] IX. 184a, 192a; cf. VII. 225d, 234c.

[64] IX. 183bc.

speculation that one comes to perceive more and more about oneself, until one acquires the perfect knowledge that is proper to the gods (184a), for 'it is in knowledge only that the gods surpass ourselves' (184c), given that we all carry within us a spark of divinity.

This essential truth constitutes one of the major themes of this oration, in which Julian attempts to prove that philosophy —the one and indivisible discipline which leads through many paths to the same goal—forms *another* sure road to salvation. In his previous oration he had extensively discussed the theology of the mysteries, and through many complementary passages had shown that theurgy may lead a human being right to the end and justification of his existence. More orthodox by classical criteria, more rational and theoretical, this second oration complements the first by demonstrating the essential unity of all principles and all methods in the sphere of the spirit. The religious syncretism that Julian had preached in his invective against Heracleius represents the mystical aspect of the process that leads to the divine light; the philosophical syncretism preached in the attack on the uneducated Cynics is the rational aspect of the same process. As truth is one, so too is philosophy, which realizes its profound unity beyond the seeming multiplicity of form and its own systematic diversity (IX. 185a); for each of its apparent variations, classified under the name of some different system or School, regards assimilation with the Divine as its ultimate goal, and considers the knowledge of the self as its first principle.[65] Despite its coarse appearance, even Cynicism does not deviate from this rule: 'It is', Julian explains borrowing the beautiful image that Alcibiades had used about Socrates, 'exactly like those images of Silenus that sit in the shops of the statue-makers, which the craftsmen represent with pipes or flutes in their hands: when their two halves are pulled apart, they are found to contain statues of gods.'[66] How sad it would be, the emperor continues, if we were to stop at Cynicism's outward characteristics without ever realizing what Oenomaus of Gadara grasped, that, far from being 'Antisthenism or Diogenism' (IX. 187c), it is, like any other system, but

[65] IX. 184c, 185c, 186a, 188bc; cf. Them. 236ab; cf. also VII. 225d; IX. 185a,d.

[66] IX. 187ab, cf. Plato, *Symp.* 215ab; see also IX. 188a–c, 190a, 199b.

one of many expressions of the universal aim of philosophy. The founder of this School, as of all others, says Julian, is none other than 'He who is the cause of all the blessings the Greeks enjoy, the universal leader, law-giver and king of Hellas, the god of Delphi' (IX. 188a). Apollo is the prince of philosophy by the common confession of all,[67] Antisthenes and Diogenes and Crates being the leaders (κορυφαῖοι) in the divine chorus,[68] together with Plato, Pythagoras, Socrates, the Aristotelians and Zeno, who all dedicated their lives to encompassing truth with their whole understanding (IX. 188c).[69]

As a good Platonist, Julian draws a sharp distinction between the ἐπιστήμη possessed by these philosophers and the δόξα of the multitudes. In words borrowed from the *Laws*, he describes the knowledge that leads to truth as 'the beginning of all good things for gods and men alike' (*Leg.* 730bc), a saying which Julian finds characteristic of the Cynic philosophy as well. But the late Cynics are like the sophists of Socrates' day: their only preoccupation seems to be the pursuit of vain opinion and false praise,[70] when the quest of truth is a pursuit innate to mankind (IX. 197a). Wishing to prove, in accordance with his syncretistic principles, that Cynicism is essentially akin to Platonism by virtue of the identity of the ends that the two philosophies pursue, Julian juxtaposes evidence drawn from Diogenes' life and from Plato's writings which effectively illustrates the same principles (IX. 188c). Then, he asks: 'Are we now to ignore all this evidence, and without further question fence off

[67] Diogenes seems to have subscribed explicitly to this view (IX. 191b, cf. 192d).

[68] IX. 188b; cf. VII. 211b.

[69] The use of the term κορυφαῖοι to designate the great philosophers, and thus emphasize the unity of all philosophy, is extremely common in late Neoplatonic vocabulary: cf. IX. 197d–198a for the adepts of Pythagoras, Plato and Aristotle; Lib. LII. 21 referring to Iamblichus; Damascius, *V. Isid.* fr. 124, p. 107 (on Proclus); Procl. *Theol. Plat.* I. 1; *In Remp.* II. 96 on the myth of Er, whose hidden sense the κορυφαῖοι of the Platonists, namely Numenius, Albinus, Gaius the Nicaean, Maximus, Harpocratio, Euclid and, above all, Porphyry, had, according to Proclus, succeeded in detecting. The origin of both this image and of Julian's assertion that Apollo is the philosopher *par excellence* is to be found in Plato who, seeing the philosophers as a tragic chorus, assigns to them Apollo, the Muses and Dionysus as συγχορευτάς τε καὶ χορηγούς (*Leg.* 665a).

[70] IX. 188b, 193d, 197b. In his previous invective Julian had already made a point of drawing a parallel between fifth- and fourth-century sophists and late Cynics; cf. VII. 206bc, 216a, 224b and Plato, *Protag.* 314e ff.

from one another and force apart men whom passion for truth, scorn of opinion, and unanimity in zeal for virtue have joined together?' (IX. 189a); for what Plato taught by words Diogenes illustrated in his actions, facing every moment of his life on earth as a preparation for death, according to the famous Socratic definition of philosophy.[71]

Diogenes' entire life was an incessant battle for the acquisition of ἀπάθεια and the conquest of that true εὐδαιμονία which consists in living according to nature and not the opinions of the multitude.[72] The quintessential freedom achieved by the true philosopher is nothing else than the Cynic αὐτάρκεια, complete liberation from the tyranny of the body: this state, once obtained, is the equivalent of the bliss experienced by the gods (IX. 196c). Significantly enough, Julian asserts the truth of this statement by a Pythagorean oath,[73] and then proceeds to expound for the sake of the false Cynics the values preached by Diogenes.[74] Most of the key-words of Hellenic philosophy appear in this passage which draws even-handedly on the teachings of all the major classical schools: ἐλευθερία, αὐτάρκεια, δικαιοσύνη, σωφροσύνη, εὐλάβεια, χάρις (IX. 202a) are the qualities which have to be cultivated if a man would achieve happiness either for himself or for his fellow-humans. Such is the meaning of the apparently enigmatic sentence in which Julian states that 'if Socrates and many others devoted themselves to theory, this was only in view of practical ends' (IX. 190a); for through the acquisition of self-knowledge they learned precisely what should be assigned to the soul and what to the body.[75]

In his previous invective the emperor gave full rein to indignation and used a sharp language which did not seem to bear fruit. Lucid, determined and obstinate as he was, Julian realized his mistake, but refused to abandon the battle after the first signs of failure; experience advocated a change of policy and now Julian set out to expound his views in a calmer tone. This effortless change of attitude suggests that until June 362 at least Julian was an adaptable and versatile person: once he had

[71] IX. 190c; Plato, *Phaedo* 81a.
[72] IX. 193d; another biting remark along the same lines as those referred to above, p. 139 n. 70.
[73] Cf. *Carmen Aureum* 47–8.
[74] IX. 200 ff., cf. VII. 238 ff.
[75] IX. 190ab, cf. IX. 183d–184a.

perceived that the method followed in pursuit of a certain aim was not the right one, he did not hesitate to acknowledge his error and humbly reconsider what was the best means to achieve his objective.

By convoking the Council of Nicaea in 325, Constantine had sought to obtain agreement on the formal essentials of Christian belief, while as ἐπίσκοπος τῶν ἐκτός—bishop of those outside the Church—he saw that all laymen were duly instructed in those dogmas.[76] Henceforth the unity of the empire was to be considered by its rulers to rest on the unity of its religion. Julian grasped the importance of this point, and in turn attempted to formulate the dogmas of paganism. Accordingly, at the same time as he issued his bitter invective against the Cynic Heracleius, Julian also composed his first dogmatic speech, a hymn addressed to the Mother of the gods, Cybele.[77] This coincidence in the date of the two works is paralleled in the community of their subject matter: theurgy as the path to salvation, and Roman patriotism as a duty at once worldly and spiritual. Both the *Contra Heracleium* and the dogmatic treatise were composed while Julian was still resident in the imperial city of Constantinople, and not unexpectedly they reflect better than any other of his writings his idea of the mission of a Roman emperor and of a *pontifex maximus*.

The two main themes of the *Hymn to the Mother of the gods* are the defence of Hellenism as a systematic theology which, having absorbed all the wisdom of the Orient, still bears the hallmarks of its Greek origin, and of *Romanitas* as a synthesis of ancient traditions handed down to the Roman people by the gods, and to be preserved at all costs. *The Hymn to the Mother of the gods* should be regarded as an encyclical addressed to the higher pagan clergy by their hierarch: οἱ ξυνιέντες ... κοινούμεθα τοῖς ἐπισταμένοις θεούς (VIII. 177cd), 'we who comprehend share our understanding with those who know the nature of the gods', declares Julian, who writes here as 'a philosopher

[76] See Constantine, *Ad Sanct. Coet.*, PL 8. 402–78. For the expression ἐπίσκοπος τῶν ἐκτός, see *V. Const.* IV. 24 (cf. ibid. II. 69, 72; III. 17); for a discussion of its meaning, see R. Farina, *L'impero e l'imperatore cristiano in Eusebio di Caesarea: la prima teologia politica del Cristianesimo*, Zurich 1966, 312–19.

[77] Lib. XVIII. 157; VIII. 178d; see also *Julien* II(1). 102.

and a theologian' (VIII. 161ab). His text is at once a φυσικὸς and a μυθικὸς ὕμνος.[78] It is a combined attempt to define the true nature (φύσις) of divinity and to provide an original allegorization of the myth of Attis and the Mother of the gods.[79] Such hymns, through the deliberately obscure elements that they are bound to contain and through the necessarily elevated and often enthusiastic tone of their composition, are by nature unsuitable to the masses.[80] They are exegetical works presupposing a sound knowledge on the reader's part of the divine mysteries with which they deal, and destined to serve as sacred books used largely by the priests of the cult, who in their turn were presumably intended to draw material from them for the instruction of their flock. This explains why Julian inaugurates his catechetical work by explaining the myth that was at the very core of the first oriental cult to reach Rome, that of the Phrygian Magna Mater Cybele and of her youthful lover Attis.[81]

Julian begins his oration by investigating the historical origins of the cult, stressing the fact that the Athenians had adopted it before the Romans (VIII. 159a). He relates in vivid language the miracle that occurred when the statue of Magna Mater was brought to Rome, dwelling particularly on the piety of the city's population, who went out in immense crowds to receive the goddess ἐν κόσμῳ τῷ πρέποντι κατὰ τὰ πάτρια (VIII. 159d)—in befitting decorum, according to the ancestral tradition. We are left in no doubt that Julian regards this miracle as a historical event: and in making this point he both calls attention to the importance of mythological tradition (VIII. 159c ff.), and establishes that Rome has enjoyed the protection of Cybele for six whole centuries. To this important theme he will return at the end of his oration, which closes with the addressing of a prayer to the patron of the City.

[78] Menander in *Rhet. Graec.* iii. 333–7.

[79] Julian's interpretation of the myth is faithfully reproduced by Salutius in his *De diis et mundo* IV.

[80] Menander, op. cit. iii. 337: ἐπιτηρεῖν δὲ χρὴ καὶ μὴ εἰς τὸν πολὺν ὄχλον καὶ δῆμον ἐκφέρειν τοὺς τοιούτους ὕμνους· ἀπιθανώτεροι γὰρ καὶ καταγελαστικώτεροι τοῖς πολλοῖς φαίνονται.

[81] This mystery religion, of an orgiastic character, was officially introduced into Rome in 204 BC at a critical moment in her history, and subsequently always had a strong following among the Roman aristocracy; cf. Origen, *Contra Celsum* (trans. H. Chadwick), p. 336 n. 3.

Such is the historical context in which Julian's dogmatic treatise is soundly integrated. Rome and her eternity are always at the background of all Julian's systematic theology, providing the only reason why the pagan religion should be crystallized into a dogma. The myth of Cybele and Attis being an apparently obscene story and, on moral grounds, one much condemned by the opponents of the traditional religion, the *pontifex maximus* of paganism undertakes to reveal the true symbolism lying behind the paradoxical and incongruous elements in the myth (VIII. 170a).

In this first dogmatic speech Julian carefully defines his theological affiliation by mentioning Plato and the *Chaldean Oracles* (VIII. 175bc). Both authorities are distilled through the channel of Iamblichan exegesis, and yet not fully so, for Julian is anxious on the one hand to stress the classical roots of contemporary religion by referring all Neoplatonic teachings to their primordial source, and on the other to give currency to the fundamental dogmas of the *Chaldean Oracles*, which should be regarded as voicing verbatim divine traditions.[82]

Adopting Iamblichus' tripartite division of the universe into the intelligible, the intellectual and the sensible spheres,[83] Julian places Cybele in the intelligible domain. Being the motherless maiden (VIII. 166b) and the *pronoia* of the intelligible region, she appears as the perfect counterpart of Athene (VIII. 179a), the encosmic (= intellectual) providence under whose special protection Julian places himself.[84] She is likewise the source of the intellectual and creative gods, the mother and spouse of mighty Zeus, who bears in herself the causes of all gods both hypercosmic and intellectual (VIII. 166ab, cf. 179d).

[82] See XI. 148ab, where Julian states explicitly that the word ὑπόθεσις should be applied to scientific knowledge, while the word δόγμα should be reserved for the beliefs of the Chaldeans; cf. VIII. 178d; *ep*. 89b. 299c, 302a. Borrowing Chaldean vocabulary, Julian describes the material world as σκύβαλον (VIII. 170d, 175b, 179c), and the Sun that rules over it as ἑπτάκτις (VIII. 172d); cf. Lewy, *Chaldaean Oracles*, 199–200 n. 97; Turcan, *Mithras Platonicus*, 118; F. Cumont, *Études syriennes*, Paris 1917, 106–7 n. 2.

[83] Iambl. *Protrepticus* XXI, p. 112, 4 ff.; cf. *Myst*. I. 19, where the νοεροὶ θεοί are called δεύτεροι θεοί. It was Iamblichus, and not Julian, who integrated this Chaldean dogma into the Platonic theology, despite Julian's remarks at XI. 148ab. For the Chaldean origin of this distinction, see Procl. *In Crat.*, p. 72, 10 ff. For its attribution to Plato by the Neoplatonists see Syrianus, *In Met.*, *Comm. Arist. Gr.* VI(1). 4. 5 ff. and 83. 26–7.

[84] See below, pp. 173, 176.

As such, the Mother of the gods is explicitly identified with Rhea, Demeter (VIII. 159b) and even Hecate, for Julian is anxious to remind his readers of his Chaldean affiliation.[85] This affiliation is brought home in even more striking fashion by his description of Helios as the ἀναγωγός of the soul during theurgic union;[86] but in propounding this crucial dogma of Chaldean theology, Julian takes his precautions, for he is fully aware of its innovatory character: 'if I were to touch on the arcane teachings of the Chaldean mystagogy . . . I would speak of things unknown—yea wholly unintelligible—to the common herd, but familiar to the blessed theurgists' (VIII. 172d), the privileged class to which the emperor himself belongs.

With the superior knowledge that he now possessed and the constant help of the Mother of the gods—the true holy virgin[87]—Julian hoped to be able to cleanse his people from 'the stain of atheism' (VIII. 180b), so that 'the most impious among men' (VIII. 174b) would stop hurling base slanders against all that is most holy. Yet the emperor's attack on Christianity is not always conducted in this enraged tone. The *Hymn to the Mother of the gods* also contains passages in which the dogma of incarnation is rejected on purely theological grounds. Whereas for Hellenism anthropomorphism is only a crude way of speaking about the divine to the uninitiated, Christianity promotes anthropomorphism from the level of myth to that of history by presenting its mediator-god as a human being, and the drama of his *vita* as a chain of actions, which actually happened at a particular place and time. To a Greek mind this was the great scandal of the Semitic religion and, accordingly, Julian undertook to denounce the folly of those who might conceive of any metaphysical myth in historical terms.[88]

Against this resolutely Hellenic background Attis emerges as

---

[85] Cf. *Chaldean Oracles* fr. 56:

'Ρείη τοι νοερῶν μακάρων πηγή τε ῥοή τε
πάντων γὰρ πρώτη δυνάμει κόλποισιν ἀφράστοις
δεξαμένη γενεὴν ἐπὶ πᾶν προχέει τροχάουσαν.

For the identification of Cybele and Hecate in the Chaldean–Neoplatonic theology, see Lewy, *Chaldaean Oracles*, 362–3.

[86] VIII. 172d; cf. 172a: ἀναγωγοὶ ἀκτῖνες. VIII. 173c: σωτὴρ καὶ ἀναγωγὸς θεός.

[87] VIII. 166ab; cf. VII. 230a.

[88] VIII. 169d–170a, 171cd.

the lowest being in the divine hierarchy. Thanks to the transformation wrought by his will-power, he is the leader of all the tribes of divine beings (VIII. 168a); while he is also the creator 'of all things down to the lowest plane of matter' (VIII. 161c), in the sense that he bears in himself the principles and the causes of all material forms. As the emanation of the third creator (VIII. 161d, 168a), Attis becomes one with the rays of the sun (VIII. 165c), while in his role of connecting link between all the forms embodied in matter in the sublunar region (VIII. 166d), he can be seen as the very symbol of human nature. Forgetful of his divinity, he traversed the zone of the Milky Way, beneath which there extends the world subject to change (VIII. 165c), and, descending to the lowest level of the material universe, he reached a cave—symbol of the dampness of matter—where he had intercourse with a nymph (VIII. 165cd). But this act of self-degradation on the part of the intellectual god (VIII. 167b) was discovered by the omniscient fiery principle, the lion,[89] cause of all motive force and symbol of the salvation of the soul (VIII. 168bc). In a fit of repentance and divine frenzy Attis mutilated himself, in this way putting an end to his degradation (VIII. 167c), and preparing himself for a gradual re-ascent towards the pure region of Ideas.

By his exegesis of the Attis myth, Julian allegorized the doctrine of the solar descent and ascent of the soul which was one of the fundamental dogmas of the *Chaldean Oracles*, and the mainspring of Iamblichan theurgy.[90] Attis, identified by Julian with the rays of the sun, could thus be seen as the personal principle operating during the descent and ascent of the soul; while his sudden transition from the world of movement and change and limitedness to a state of passionless fixity, symbolized in the mysteries by the halting of Helios over the vernal equinox (VIII. 168cd, 171c), could be seen by sinful humanity as an example and a guarantee of spiritual salvation (VIII. 169cd; cf. 175b) and of the certainty that those whose eyes are constantly turned 'towards the heavens, or rather beyond the heavens' (VIII. 175c), 'those who learn to mount

---

[89] The lion was the symbol of fire in the theology of the Mithraic Mysteries, *MMM* i. 101, Gordon, *Religion*, ii. 99; it was also the middle degree of initiation, corresponding to the planet Sun, *MMM* i. 315 ff.

[90] Iambl. *Myst.* III. 6; V. 26.

upwards' (VIII. 172c), can indeed 'attain the goal and summit
of all human questing' (VIII. 170bc), 'escape from limitedness
and generation and inward storm to be translated up to the
very gods' (VIII. 169d).

This theme of ἐπιστροφή (VIII. 168a ff.), of the ultimate
union of the purified soul with the divine, runs throughout the
Hymn to the Mother of the gods and culminates in a clear description of the state of bliss in which a human being may participate
through the constant exercise of will-power and the minute
observance of all the prescribed ritual acts and purifications.[91]

When the soul abandons herself wholly to the gods and entrusts her
own concerns absolutely to the higher powers, and then there follow
the holy ceremonies just after the performance of sacred rites, at that
point, I say, since there is nothing to hinder or prevent, for all things
reside in the gods, all things subsist in relation to them, all things
are filled with the gods, straight away the divine light illuminates
our souls. (VIII. 178b)

As one reads Julian's works in an attempt to trace the principle
by which he seeks to unite all ancient philosophy and religion,
one realizes more and more that it is on account of the common
end pursued by all ancient theology—identification with the
divine through individual effort—that he is able to produce
this impressive edifice of syncretism.

The Mysteries of the Magna Mater, of which Julian himself
was an initiate (VIII. 158d, 173a), formed one of the many
ways that led to the truth. The *pontifex maximus* of paganism,
'who had communicated with the divine through thousands of
ritual ceremonies',[92] and had been invested with the power to
perform miracles,[93] was anxious to prove the essential unity of
the pagan religion, and so associated the cult of Cybele with
the only mystery cult practised in classical Athens, the Eleusinian Mysteries (VIII. 173). Performed over the vernal and
autumnal equinoxes respectively, the two mysteries had many
of their cultic features in common, expressing the same occult

[91] VIII. 173d–177d.
[92] Lib. XXIV. 36; for an interesting parallel, see Eus. *Tric.* XVIII: Constantine
had had μυρίας θεοφανείας of Christ.
[93] By standing immobile under the rain for several hours, Julian succeeded in
putting an end to an earthquake, Lib. XVIII. 177; cf. Him. XLI. 8: Βασιλέα
λέγω τὸν ἔνθεον, οὗ μυρίαι μὲν καθ' ἑκάστην ἡμέραν αἱ χάριτες εἰς τὴν
γειναμένην.

truth (VIII. 173, 179a). In this light Julian undertakes to explain the symbolism of the ritual practised by the devotees of Cybele, while as a typical Neoplatonist he minutely prescribes the process of abstinence and asceticism by which the faithful will seek to purify his body before being admitted to the mysteries.[94]

The essential unity of all pagan religion is further illustrated by Julian's attempt to bring together all the main god-*logoi* of Hellenism. Thus Attis is associated with Heracles and Dionysos—the two intermediary figures *par excellence* in the classical Greek tradition, who both, like Attis, ascended from a state of semi-divinity and ultimately achieved union with the divine (VIII. 167a, 173c). Along the same lines, Julian undertakes to justify in theological terms the close interrelation already established between Attis and Helios.[95] Helios, 'the living, animate, reasoned and beneficent image of the intelligible Father' is the true Logos,[96] as also is Attis, who through the rejection of the world of the senses regained divinity:[97] 'Is not this Logos Attis, who not long ago was out of his senses, but now through his castration is called wise? Yes, he was out of his senses because he preferred matter and presides over generation, but he is wise because he adorned and transformed this refuse, our earth, with such beauty as no human art or cunning can imitate' (VIII. 179cd).[98]

Here, at the very end of the oration, the emperor introduces another important theme which is further expanded in his second dogmatic hymn addressed to King Helios: that of the unspeakable beauty of the world and of its incorruptibility. The thesis of the eternity of the world, which, more than any other, in the first centuries of our era separated the antique way of thinking

[94] VIII. 173d ff. For the importance of asceticism in the Neoplatonic tradition, see Porph. *Abst.* I. 36 and 45; *Marc.* 7 and 34–5; in the *Chaldean Oracles*, Lewy, *Chaldaean Oracles*, 276; cf. C. A. Lobeck, *Aglaophamus*, 40–1, 57, who associates the Neoplatonic and the Eleusinian rites and shows that in both cases καθαρμοί are a preparatory stage to ἐποπτεῖαι.

[95] Cf. Firmicus Maternus, *De errore* VIII. 3, and Cumont, *Mystères*[3], 189 ff.

[96] *ep.* 111. 434cd. For the phraseology see Procl. *In Remp.* II. 212. 22 ff.

[97] This should be connected with VII. 219d and 221c, and considered as a further attempt by Julian to prove that all the essentials of the Christian theology were borrowed from paganism.

[98] *Orac. Chald.* fr. 158. For a commentary on the oracle in connection with Julian's text, see Lewy, *Chaldaean Oracles*, 213 n. 144.

—and in particular Neoplatonism—from the Christian thought-world, has its firm roots in Plato.[99] Julian, following Plotinus,[100] ardently defends this dogma, which provides the corner-stone both of his theory of the ethnic gods,[101] and for the construction of his heliolatric theology. The few lines that precede the dogmatic discussion of the nature of Helios convey this Platonic truth with classical power and immediacy: 'This divine and wholly beautiful universe, from the highest vault of heaven to the lowest limit of the earth, is held together by the continuous providence of God, has existed ungenerated from all eternity and is imperishable for all time to come' (XI. 132c).[102]

The eternity and indestructibility of the universe is by no means the only Platonic dogma that Julian echoes in the hymn he composed at Antioch to celebrate the *Dies Natalis* of the Invincible Sun (XI. 131d). The influence of Plato is stronger here than in any other of his writings. Before setting out on the Persian campaign, the emperor would ideally have wished to leave behind a unified empire with a strong sense of spiritual tradition reflected in a coherent and systematic theology. The *Hymn to King Helios*, if compared with that to the Mother of the gods and considered from the stand-point of the Persian campaign, can be regarded as Julian's definitive attempt to crystallize the Roman religion. It is no mere coincidence if in this lengthy work the two sources on which Julian draws most abundantly, and to which ultimately he refers every single major statement, are Plato and 'the Wisdom of the East'. These are the two pillars of his thought, the two poles determining his theology more conclusively even than Iamblichus himself, though he too receives his due share of homage.[103]

First of all Julian puts a Platonic seal on his Hymn by addressing it to 'King' Helios. The royal nature of the planet sun, the ruler of the sensible universe, had already been asserted by

[99] *Timaeus* 41ab.
[100] *Enn.* II. 1, II. 9. 7; cf. above p. 136. On pre-existence, see XI. 139b.
[101] See below, pp. 163 ff.
[102] Cf. 139b, 145d; VIII. 164d, 170c; and III. 80d.
[103] The *Hymn to King Helios* anticipates in many ways the work of Proclus who is reported to have said that, if he had the power, he would conceal all philosophical works with the exception of two: the *Timaeus* and the *Chaldean Oracles* (Marinus, *V. Procli* 38).

Plato in a famous passage where he developed the analogy that exists between the worlds of the senses and of the spirit: the luminous principle reigning over the physical universe, the un-generated source of all life,[104] is but the direct emanation of the idea of τὸ ἀγαθόν, the supreme principle of the metaphysical world and the origin of truth and all science.[105] The clear, strong and direct physical light with which Plato's eyes were familiar appeared to him as the only symbol fit to convey the ineffable beauty of transcendental truth shining over the regions beyond (*Rep.* 508bc), while the healthy eyes, able to sustain the vision of light, served to denote the soul illuminated by truth.[106]

Julian had instinctively grasped the terms of this Platonic proposition when, in early youth, he had recognized in the celestial light at once an indication and a proof of the divinity of both the cosmos and his own soul. Now, in his mature years, rich with the knowledge gained through so much reading and so many initiations, the emperor recalled the experience of his adolescence (XI. 130cd), but in the hymn that he composed in honour of King Helios he expressed himself in traditional philo-sophical vocabulary rather than in the language of his private intuitions. Accordingly he reproduced *in extenso* the passage from the *Republic* in which an analogy is established between the two distinct universes to which every human being belongs actually and potentially,[107] while in order to convey effectively the way in which the soul can reach the transcendental sphere, where everything is ineffable, he introduced the intelligent world of Iamblichus and the *Chaldean Oracles* (XI. 148a) as an explicit link between the two Platonic regions (XI. 133c).

The basic Platonic dichotomy is always at the back of Julian's mind, but, belonging as he did to a period when Hellenism had become but the commentator of its own spirit,[108] Julian was bound to conceive and present in an exegetical manner what he knew in his heart to be but a simple and straightforward truth.

[104] See 142a and cf. Plato, *Rep.* 509b.
[105] Plato, *Rep.* 508bc: τοῦ ἀγαθοῦ ἔκγονος, ὃν τἀγαθὸν ἐγέννησεν ἀνάλογον ἑαυτῷ. Cf. Plato, *ep.* II, 312e; Plot. V. 1. 8.
[106] Plato, *Rep.* 508cd; cf. J. VIII. 172d.
[107] XI. 133a and *Rep.* 508bc.
[108] See Seneca, *ep.* 108. 23: 'quae philosophia fuit facta philologia est'; cf. Porph. *V. Plot.* 14, where Plotinus is reported as saying: φιλόλογος μὲν . . . ὁ Λογγῖνος, φιλόσοφος δὲ οὐδαμῶς.

It is the period when the notion of salvation becomes inextricably linked in men's consciousness with that of a mediating Logos—Christ or Mithra, Attis or Asclepios—and Julian is a genuine child of this period. He may address his prayer to Zeus, seen as the conventional symbol of the First Principle, but he knows that the First Principle itself, being beyond both essence and intellection, can only be reached through a mediator. Thus it is Helios, in his specific hypostasis as Mithra, who acts as a *saviour* for Julian (VII. 231ac).

If, in his autobiographical myth, the emperor expressed this idea in purely anthropomorphic terms, as befits a myth, in his *Hymn to King Helios* he has recourse to philosophical analysis. Thus, in describing the substance, powers and energies, both visible and invisible, and the blessings that the Sun in his three hypostases bestows throughout the Intelligible, Intellectual and Sensible worlds (XI. 132b), Julian concentrated largely on the second hypostasis of Helios, the one manifested in Mithra the Mediator (μεσίτης) (XI. 138c ff.). By doing so, he laid particular emphasis on the moral struggle that each devotee should be prepared to engage in if he wishes to comprehend and enjoy fully all the marvellous things of which the beauty of our sensible world is but a faint hint.[109] This is the sphere where continuous revolution symbolizes the incessant struggle of the human soul to attain to moral excellence. When the soul, which ascends the grades of the planetary ladder, leaving aside on the way all passions and desires, at last enters into the intelligible zone of the fixed stars, then the truth of which Plato speaks may be grasped for all eternity.[110]

In his *Hymn to the Mother of the gods* the *pontifex maximus* had prescribed the acts of lustration and abstinence to be followed by the adepts of the cult. In this second work, which could well be described as a 'Hymn of the All',[111] Julian completed his task of moral instruction on a subtler level. Nothing is explicit, no precise orders are given as to how the devotee should purify his

---

[109] Cf. *Timaeus* 37c and J. XI. 145a: 'all that is only at times beautiful here is always beautiful in the intelligible world'; see also XI. 144d ff.; IX. 185b: ὃ γὰρ ἡμεῖς ποτέ, τοῦτο ὁ θεὸς ἀεί.

[110] XI. 146cd; cf. XI. 132cd and above, p. 39.

[111] Ὕμνος τοῦ παντός. The expression, referring to the *Timaeus*, was to be found in the lost part of the *Critias* (cf. Menander op. cit. iii. 337).

soul, yet what is continuously suggested to the reader's mind by the constant comparison of the values of the sensible and intelligent worlds and by the emphasis laid on their unity, is the necessity for the elevation of the soul and its progression along a path which runs straight and uninterrupted until it reaches the highest vault of heaven.[112] The fundamental Chaldean dogma of the elevation of the soul[113] by the help of the rays of the sun, which, guided by angels, draw it upwards, is the only path of salvation Julian can recommend to his flock.[114] And the sun, 'bringing to union the last with the first things' (XI. 142a), confirms the unity of the universe.

The mysterious unity of the cosmos, which transcends not only time but the rest of the Aristotelian categories too (XI. 143b, 145d ff.), is expressed through the ubiquity of the Platonic Ideas, but it is to Helios alone—cause of the sharing out of the Forms and of the ordering of matter (XI. 141a)— that the human being owes his ability to intuit the intelligible Ideas and to perceive their visible manifestation on earth (ibid.). This Platonic teaching allows Julian to proceed one step further and associate Helios with the most contradictory pair of deities in the Greek pantheon, Apollo and Dionysos, symbols of the incessant conflict between the divine and earthly elements in Man. For Julian, 'Apollo coexists and communicates with Helios through the singleness of his thoughts and the stability of his substance and the consistency of his activity';[115] but at the same time the king of the intelligent universe 'shares

[111] XI. 139bc. Good generalization of this way of thinking by J. Trouillard, 'Raison et mystique chez Plotin', *REAug* xx (1974), 9–10: 'Tandis-que la pensée judéo-chrétienne s'efforçait de penser la création en sublimant et en purifiant le modèle artisanal, la tradition pythagoricienne et platonicienne développait de son côté une théorie de la procession illustrée par un modèle mathématique . . . Ils ont préféré le schème mathématique à l'image artisanale sans doute parce que ce schème suggérait une intériorité plus stricte entre les dérivés et le principe, comme entre le nombre et l'unité . . . Le schème mathématique a donc une valeur polémique et corrective contre l'anthropomorphisme technique'; cf. A. H. Armstrong, 'Man in the Cosmos: a study of some differences between pagan Neoplatonism and Christianity', in W. den Boer *et al.* (edd.), *Romanitas et Christianitas: Studia Iano Henrico Waszink . . . oblata*, Amsterdam 1973, 5–14.

[113] J. indicates that this is a dogma when he says: ἀφ' ἡμῶν πιστευέσθω μᾶλλον ἢ δεικνύσθω (XI. 152b).

[114] XI. 134ab; 141a; 142a; 154d; cf. V. 275b; VII. 229d; VIII. 172.

[115] XI. 144a (I would suggest κατά for καί, so that the passage reads: ἐπικοινωνεῖ κατὰ τὴν ἁπλότητα τῶν νοήσεων).

F

his creative function with Dionysos, the god who controls divided substance'.[116] Here Julian does nothing more than follow the teaching of the god of Delphi, whose oracle he had already cited when he first announced the theme of the unity of all divine principles (XI. 136a). The association of Apollo—the negator of plurality, according to the Pythagorean tradition[117]—and Dionysos—the god torn asunder by the Titans[118]—is an idea which, significantly enough, was first expressed by an outstanding representative of Middle Platonism, and high priest of the god of Delphi, Plutarch.[119] It is at once an echo and an illustration of the famous prelude in the *Timaeus*, where Plato contrasts the notions of Being and Becoming, unity and plurality, as they are displayed respectively in the divine and the human spheres.[120]

In this oration, which not inappropriately contains a truly beautiful hymn to light as a physical and spiritual blessing (XI. 133d–134b; cf. VIII. 172), all ideas are connected together with exemplary clarity,[121] while its every page is inspired by a tone of serenity and otherworldliness. Coherent ideas, unmarred by polemical aggressiveness, are here conveyed in a Greek which effortlessly runs back to Plato's day. Form and content match perfectly, expressing the unity and eternity that Julian attributes to the cosmos. The spirit is Platonic through and through: and, while Greek philosophy and poetry acquire validity through Plato alone,[122] the wisdom of the Orient,

---

[116] XI. 144c, cf. VIII. 179b.

[117] Theme adopted by the Platonists, Plut. *Mor.* 381 f, 388 f; for the etymology ($\dot{a}$ + πολλοί) see ibid. 393c.

[118] On the possible associations between the myth of Dionysos–Zagreus as expounded by the Neoplatonists and that of Mithra Tauroctonus, see Bidez–Cumont, *Mages hellénisés* i. 97.

[119] Cf. *Mor.* 388e–389b and 393 ff.

[120] *Tim.* 27d–28a. See Procl. *In Tim.* 200c ff., who says explicitly what in Julian is only implicit.

[121] *Pace, inter alia,* Bidez, *Vie,* 253 and Lacombrade, *Julien* II(2), 79, who, thanks to their failure to perceive that Julian's development unfolds on two levels, confuse what is important with relatively immaterial details, and consequently accuse the emperor of obscurity and irrationality. For a more understanding approach see G. Mau, *Die Religionphilosophie Kaiser Julians,* Leipzig 1907, and J.-C. Foussard, 'Julien philosophe', *L'Empereur Julien: de l'histoire à la légende (331–1715),* (edd. R. Braun-J. Richer), Paris 1978, 189–212.

[122] XI. 132d, 133a, 136a, 146a, 152b; cf. VIII. 172d.

together with the teaching of the Mithraic Mysteries, becomes
meaningful only through its integration in the Platonic
cosmos.[123] It is certain that most of what Julian has to say
about Chaldean theology comes from Iamblichus' lost commentary on the *Oracles*.[124] It is also well known that the Neoplatonists were dedicated to the worship of the Sun, that
Porphyry had already composed a treatise on the subject,[125]
and that Iamblichus regularly celebrated the feast of the god.[126]
Yet, neither had gone so far as to admit Mithraism into the
sphere of Platonic theology.[127] Possibly with this in mind, the
pontifex maximus declares that up to his day Mithraism had
remained a *religio externa*, and warns his flock that, at the cost
of appearing an innovator,[128] he is attempting through his
speech to provide the Roman world with a consistent and
viable religious system, made up of all the current traditions
and practices of solar worship: ἐξ ἑνὸς μὲν προῆλθε τοῦ θεοῦ εἷς ἀφ᾽
ἑνὸς τοῦ νοητοῦ κόσμου βασιλεὺς Ἥλιος, τῶν νοερῶν θεῶν μέσος ἐν
μέσοις τεταγμένος κατὰ παντοίαν μεσότητα . . . εἰς ἕνωσιν ἄγων τὰ
τελευταῖα τοῖς πρώτοις (XI. 141d–142a). This language, which
is strangely reminiscent of the terms in which the Logos-
Christ is proclaimed in the Nicene creed, must have sounded
familiar to fourth-century ears, while the theology of a creation
held together by the salvific action of transfigured light had by
that time taken deep root in men's consciousness.

What his uncle had done with Christianity, Julian dreamed
of repeating with Mithraism: they both turned to a young and
popular religion and lent it their full support, not merely on
the crude financial level, but also on the subtler plane of
dogmatic articulation.

[123] XI. 134a, 148a, 150b–d, 155b, 156b.

[124] See *ep.* 12; also the acknowledgement of Julian's debt to Iamblichus in his
Hymn to King Helios, XI. 146a, 150cd, 157d.

[125] See G. Heuten, 'Le "Soleil" de Porphyre', *Mélanges F. Cumont*, Brussels 1936,
253–9.

[126] Eunap. *V. Phil.* V. 1. 12–14. Proclus also made a point of προσκυνῆσαι
ἥλιον ἀνίσχοντα, μεσουρανοῦντά τε καὶ ἐπὶ δύσιν ἰόντα, Marinus, *V. Procli* 22.

[127] See my article, *JThS* xxviii (1977), 360–71. This point is completely neglected
by R. E. Witt, 'Iamblichus as a forerunner of Julian', *Entretiens Hardt* xxi (1975),
35–63, who depends for his understanding of 'le Roi Soleil of fourth century
paganism's pantheon' (35) on the introduction to W. C. Wright's edition of
Julian's works, and on Gore Vidal's novel.

[128] XI. 155b: ἐρῶ νεώτερα, cf. Him. XLI. 8: τελετὰς δὲ θείας καθιδρύων τῇ
πόλει ξένας, an allusion to Julian's Mithraeum in Constantinople.

While Julian was engaged in defending the unity of Greek philosophy and of all theology, carefully linking the sacred mythology of Mithraism with Hellenic piety, the established Roman religion, and the so-called 'oriental wisdom', the new prefect of the East, Salutius, issued a brief catechism in which he treated *Of the gods and the cosmos*.[129] Julian's close friend and collaborator, who had spent so many nights in Gaul discussing with him not only affairs of state, but also the great problems of human destiny (IV. 241cd), cannot have circulated his treatise without the approbation of the *pontifex maximus*. Yet this initial assumption ought not to influence our understanding of the treatise.

In tune with the spirit of an age which had not yet lost sight of the fact that παιδεία and παιδαγωγία are 'the most beautiful and most perfect possessions in this life', and inspired by the selfless love that once filled the classical man when he thought of his most beloved,[130] Salutius makes of *paideia* the leading theme of his treatise.[131] His Platonic affiliation makes him accept as axiomatic that wickedness is due only to ignorance (XII. 4) and that human nature is, even in the worst men, at least potentially good (X). He enumerates the varieties of education that may, in his opinion, lead a man to master ἀρετή (XII. 6), and all the punishments to which the human soul will be subjected if it fails to achieve this objective (XVIII. 3; XX).

The public that the praetorian prefect addresses is a cultured one consisting of men who, through the acquisition of the right *paideia*, have developed the innate good qualities of the soul—in other words, the four cardinal virtues as defined by Plato.[132] These are the men who are able to understand Salutius' λόγοι—

[129] For the identification of the author of the *De Diis et Mundo*, see p. 68 n. 74.
[130] Clem. *Ped*. I. V. 16. 1.
[131] See Salutius, I, X, XII. 4, etc. In the following pages in the text Roman numbers refer to chapters in Salutius' treatise; Arabic numbers denote sections within chapters.
[132] At X Salutius adopts the Platonic division of the soul, assigning to each of its three parts the cardinal Socratic virtues, and seeing justice as the fourth one which belongs to the indivisible soul. Following Plato's discussion in the fourth and eighth Books of the *Republic*, he associates the three kinds of government and their respective degenerate form with the three parts of the soul (XI). In this context, following Plato again, Salutius stresses the importance of *paideia*.

the rational, straightforward way in which he treats of the fundamental mysteries of being.[133] Here lies the first significant difference between the methods followed by Salutius and by Julian. The emperor teaches his public primarily by using μῦθοι, and providing a personal exegesis of them, whereas his prefect speaks in λόγοι. He too concedes that μῦθοι are the highest means of theological teaching, used by the gods themselves, by the divinely inspired prophets and by the best philosophers (III. 1), but as for himself he has recourse to λόγοι. And when he wishes to give an example of a theological myth, Salutius faithfully reproduces Julian's interpretation of the myth of Attis (IV).

His conception of *paideia*, on the other hand, agrees with Julian's. For Salutius does not only expand the notion of *paideia* in the Platonic sense, but also defends theurgy. With Iamblichus, he stresses the importance of prayer,[134] and of religious practices.[135] He speaks of worship (λατρεία) performed by means of all manner of symbols such as prayers and sacrifices, statues of gods and temples, amulets and sacred signs, all of them objects that 'imitate' either what we wish to be rid of or the condition to which we aspire. These symbols, if used aright, make of us the ὑποδοχή that will allow the human soul to be united with the divine;[136] this notion of συναφή, of ἐπιστροφή (XIV. 2. 3), of mystic union, which is achieved after one has performed the right ritual acts (τὰ δρώμενα) and thus been enabled to travel through all the spheres that are interposed between the First Principle and Man in his fallen state, is crucial to Salutius.[137]

Cosmic sympathy and the notion of a divine hierarchy—two other important Iamblichan teachings directly concerned with

[133] Λόγοι as opposed to Μῦθοι, for which Salutius proposes a classification of his own (IV), and to oracles (III. 1).

[134] Salut. XVI; cf. Iambl. *Myst.* V. 26. In later Neoplatonism the importance of prayer, as a theurgical process and partial cause of *unio mystica*, is even more accentuated; cf. Procl. *In Tim.* 65a: πρὸς δὲ τὴν ἐπιστροφὴν ταύτην ἡ εὐχὴ μεγίστην παρέχεται συντέλειαν.

[135] Salut. XV; cf. Iambl. *Myst.* I. 11, II. 11, V. 23, etc.

[136] Contrast with this passage Porphyry's conception of the mystical union achieved through constant training of the soul, through ἄσκησις and contemplation, until the νοῦς becomes εἰς καταδοχὴν τοῦ Θεοῦ ἐπιτήδειος (*Ad Marc.* 19). Cf. the identity of terms with Salut. XV and Iambl. *Myst.* V. 23.

[137] For a systematization of the relevant passages and Salutius' sources, see Nock, *Sallustius*, pp. xcviii–ci.

ἐπιστροφή and δρώμενα and further propagated by Julian—likewise hold a prominent position in this manual of the pagan
religion. Indeed, as befits a work of this genre, they are more
thoroughly analysed here than anywhere in Julian's work.
Through his reconciliation into a coherent system of the most
abstract notions of the Platonic and Chaldean theology, the
gods of the traditional religion, the demons of popular belief
and the divinities of the oriental cults, Iamblichus was responsible for the introduction into Neoplatonism of the idea of a
pyramid of divinities, with the One at its apex.[138] Yet the
Iamblichan gods had been distinguished as 'pericosmic' and
'hypercosmic',[139] without any further elaboration; and it was
left to Salutius to classify into triads the endless chain of intermediary gods and lesser divinities between the First Cause and
Man (XIII. 5), dividing the 'encosmic' (= pericosmic) gods
into four categories, and to assign each of the four elements of
nature to its respective divine category (VI). That in Neoplatonism we witness a transposition of the Stoic principles
from a physical plane onto a metaphysical[140] is a point well
illustrated by this classification, which should be seen as an
attempt to refute the Christian accusation that the pagans
divinized the elements of nature.

In this rigorously hierarchical system, where all the gods
possessed different but complementary functions, the theoretical
basis for the close interrelationships that obtained between gods
and demons was provided by the doctrine of cosmic sympathy;
and the natural corollary of this doctrine was the acceptance
of theurgy as the science best able to lead Man towards union
with the First Cause.[141] The First Cause, which the human
spirit can grasp through its essential kinship with it,[142] is defined
by Salutius, according to contemporary theological belief, as
being beyond essence (V), ineffable (V), indivisible (II), totally
good (XII), omnipotent (XII), immutable and impassible
(XIV).[143] This passionlessness of the divine, which places it
beyond the need of prayers and sacrifices (which man needs to

[138] See *Myst.* Book II and VIII. 2.
[139] *Myst.* VIII. 8; for different appellations see VIII. 3 ἐπουράνιοι θεοί,
VIII. 7 ὑπερουράνιοι, VIII. 8 ἐμφανεῖς.
[140] See P. Hadot, *Histoire des religions*, ii. 90.   [141] See above pp. 6–7 n. 18.
[142] Cf. VII. 206b, 217d, etc.   [143] Cf. Porph. *Marc.* 17.

perform only for his own sake, XIV, XV) is a Greek concept
through and through, to be found for the first time perhaps in
Plato,[144] and further expounded by the Neoplatonists. Yet
Salutius' thought does not run parallel with Julian's in all
respects. Iamblichus had adopted the Hermetic doctrine of the
coexistence in man of an irrational soul subject to fate, and a
rational soul participating in the power of the creator.[145]
Salutius, who, like any other Neoplatonist, accepts the fundamental Plotinian scheme τὸ ἕν–νοῦς–ψυχή (V), is unique among
the members of his School in taking over the Iamblichan
theory about the two souls in man (VIII).[146] Equally Salutius
borrows from Iamblichus his conception of Εἱμαρμένη as the
force ruling the planetary universe to which man's irrational
soul is subject (IX). This view, that the power of fate is confined to the planetary universe (IX. 4) and that the sphere of
fixed stars can be reached by man through his divine soul, is a
major theme of Neoplatonism.[147] Here lies the great difference
between the Stoic and Neoplatonic thought-worlds. Stoicism
ultimately sanctioned the fatalistic determinism of the East,
while Neoplatonism, despite all the oriental influences it under-
went, despite all minor compromises, remained Greek in
essence, and never gave up the concept of Man's free-will.

If Salutius conceives of Εἱμαρμένη as Iamblichus does, and of
Providence in the manner of Plotinus, as the totally good principle responsible for cosmic order,[148] his concept of Tyche is his
own. The subtle dialectician distinguishes between two forms of
Tyche, the one, in accordance with traditional Greek belief,
identical with the individual's personal demon, and the other
with a city's collective genius (as distinct from her patron god)

---

[144] Cf. Plato, *Rep.* 364b–e; *Leg.* 905e ff. For a collection of passages illustrating
the classical Greek belief that God is not ἐνδεής, see E. R. Dodds, *Proclus, The
Elements of Theology*, Oxford 1963², 197. This point need hardly be made, yet see
A. D. Nock, op. cit., p. lxxxv: "it need hardly be said that this view that the gods
need nothing from a man is foreign to early Greek thought, as is also the passionless state ascribed to them". On the latter, see *Tim.* 29e; *Phaedr.* 247a.
[145] Iambl. *Myst.* VIII. 6–7.
[146] G. Rochefort, *De diis et mundo*, 37 n. 4, seeing in J. XI 142d a confirmation of
this view, bases his remark on a careless reading of a passage where Julian simply
refers to the antagonism between soul and body.
[147] See useful references in Nock, op. cit., p. lxxii nn. 149–53.
[148] Salut. IX; cf. Plot. *Enn.* III. 2. 3.

(IX. 7).[149] Anxious to introduce his public to the Neoplatonic theology of the Syrian School, in which Selene as a cosmic force holds a crucial position, the prefect of the East presents the Tyche that rules the destinies of the empire as drawing her power from the Moon (IX. 7). Yet exactly because Salutius' demonology does not admit that any evil powers may have authority in the universe (XII. 3), the cosmic character of the Genius Publicus appears as the guarantee of the felicity of the empire. This optimistic theory was not shared by Julian, for whom (as for Porphyry and Iamblichus) the world was subject to wicked as well as beneficent powers.[150] Evil demons haunt it, and it is the task of the individual to escape their influence both by cultivating his innate good qualities and by performing the correct rituals. Indeed both Platonic and Chaldean belief make of our planet the refuse of the cosmos, the theatre of evil (VIII. 175bc). Exiled in it, the wise ruler will concentrate all his efforts on 'purging almost the whole earth and sea of the evil spread all over their surface' (VI. 254a). This Mithraic conception of the exercise of power was also deeply Neoplatonic, for Julian declared explicitly that their Tyche was likely to help cities and nations only if they lived according to the traditions and particular laws received from their ethnic tutelary gods when they first came into existence.

Unlike Julian, who was conscious of the essentially tragic character of history and faced cultures as fragile things,[151] Salutius had an optimistic view of both the world and history. To him the entire cosmos, and the human world in particular, were perfect and eternal like their creative principle (VII); they were constantly guarded by divine Providence (IX) and

[149] This latter hypostasis of Tyche may represent an attempt towards a redefinition of the concept of the Genius Publicus: G. Rochefort, 'Le Περὶ θεῶν καὶ κόσμου de Saloustios et l'influence de l'empereur Julien', *REG* lxix (1956), 63. See also the introduction to his edition of Salutius, p. xvi.

[150] On the ambivalence of cosmic powers in Porphyry, see *Abst.* II. 36: δαίμοσι δὲ ἄλλοις ἤτοι ἀγαθοῖς ἢ καὶ φαύλοις. Cf. ibid. 38, 40, 42. On evil demons see *Marc.* 11, 16, 21. In Iambl. *Myst.* III. 31; IV. 13: τὸ τῶν πονηρῶν δαιμόνων φῦλον; IV. 7: τὰ ἄδικα καὶ αἰσχρὰ ἀπεργάζονται οἱ φύσει πονηροὶ δαίμονες; cf. IX. 7. In Julian, III. 90ab; VIII. 175b; etc. It is interesting to note that Julian wrote a treatise Περὶ τοῦ πόθεν τὰ κακά, cf. Suda I. 437. As Lewy saw, *Chaldaean Oracles*, 381, 'the demonological explanation of the evil of the world possessed for the Platonists the advantage that it permitted the maintenance of a philosophical monism.'

[151] *C.G.* 143c. See also below, pp. 162–3.

were necessarily exempt from evil (XII). For Salutius utterly rejected Mazdean dualism,[152] just as he condemned Egyptian theology (IV. 3). A. D. Nock may well find 'this rejection of Egyptian ideas . . . somewhat surprising in view of the fact that Julian was a warm adherent of the cult of their gods',[153] but in fact Salutius' spurning of Egyptian theology is wholly predictable in a man who ignores all foreign cults, and condemns *a silentio* whatever is not Greek either by origin or by plausible adoption. It is true that in a period of extravagant intellectual promiscuity, when Hellenism was vigorously assimilating extraneous influences, a pagan catechism which deliberately ignores these trends appears an oddity. Yet Salutius' book was not an isolated phenomenon. In Porphyry's *Letter to Marcella*, which was designed for similar purposes, we find the same absence of any notion that is not Greek by orthodox standards. Yet in other works Porphyry's thought shows many oriental influences. The same is true of Iamblichus' *Protrepticus*, where the bulk of the material is drawn from Plato, Aristotle and the Orphic–Pythagorean tradition. Perhaps it is legitimate to speak of a convention of the genre, though no other brief catechism of the pagan religion survives from late antiquity, and we cannot know what the generally accepted rules for this genre were—if indeed it was a genre at all.

In view of the wide diffusion for which it was designed, a catechism obviously had to be clear and simple, eschewing subtle nuances which might be misunderstood and even breed controversy.[154] Yet this still leaves unanswered the problem posed by Salutius' bold rejection of Egyptian theology, which appears all the more puzzling if we recall that Julian must have approved the treatise before it was circulated, and, more importantly, that he later dedicated to his prefect the *Hymn to King Helios*. Certainly, Salutius was of a conspicuously independent cast of mind, as we can see from the way in which he uses Iamblichus, on whom he draws abundantly. It is notable that Salutius often borrows from Iamblichus views not to be found

---

[152] G. Rochefort, 'La démonologie de Saloustios et ses rapports avec celle de l'empereur Julien', *REG* lxx (1957), p. xiv; see also the same author's, 'Le Περὶ θεῶν . . .', *REG* lxix (1956), 65.

[153] A. D. Nock, op. cit., p. xlix.

[154] F. Cumont, 'Salluste le philosophe', *RPh* xvi (1892), 49–56, and G. Rochefort in both his articles.

in any earlier Platonic philosopher, such as the principle of the two souls in man, or that of the importance of prayer. In both these cases one is bound to admit that Iamblichus' innovation consists of nothing more than a mere expansion or interpretation of concepts already fully in accord with the Greek tradition. On the other hand, Salutius justifies theurgy in a fragmentary manner which Iamblichus would scarcely have found satisfactory. As for the great theme of divine epiphanies —that key-notion of Syrian and Pergamene Neoplatonism— not a hint of it is to be found in the *De diis et mundo*. In short, Salutius' exploitation of Iamblichus is markedly one-sided; his prime object is to defend Hellenism as he, rather than Iamblichus, saw it. Salutius' most recent editor has observed: 'il appuie son exposé sur les bases encore solides des antiques croyances pour ramener l'empire à la Religion des Ancêtres.'[155] In his approach to Iamblichan Neoplatonism, Salutius proved that he had his own distinctive criterion of Hellenism. Yet he knew that he was a bureaucrat typical of his age, and, being conscious of his own limitations and of the magnitude of the cause he was defending, he saw it as a matter of honesty not to dabble in anything beyond his understanding. Julian realized this, but even so, he gave Salutius his full approbation. As for himself, he went one step further: though beginning from the same presuppositions as his prefect, he aimed at a complete Hellenization of oriental wisdom, so far as that was possible. And if Julian wrote a treatise—*Against the ἀπαίδευτοι Cynics*—in which he dealt exclusively with Greek philosophy, demonstrating its essential unity and presenting it as a road to salvation, this simply serves to remind us that his religious policy unfolded itself on two distinct levels: first Julian defended the unity and autonomy of Greek religion (and Salutius' contribution at this stage was of inestimable value), and attempted to identify the oriental deities and cults of the Hellenistic and Roman world with the classical gods and their mysteries. Then, when he judged that this process of dogmatic syncretism was complete, the emperor wrote the *Hymn to King Helios* in which he explicitly connected Mithraism with Plato, and raised Helios-Mithra, the god who was the tutelary divinity of his own dynasty, to be the supreme deity of the Roman empire.

[155] Rochefort, *REG* lxx (1957), p. xv.

V. THE PRIEST KING AND THE
PHILOSOPHER PRIEST

Before the Edict on Education was published, Julian had already proclaimed the indissoluble unity of Hellenic culture and religion in three major didactic works, *Against the Cynic Heracleius, The Hymn to the Mother of the gods* and *Against the uneducated Cynics*. Yet his message to his people would not have been complete, had he not at the same time stressed the sociopolitical aspect of his educative ideal, both on the practical and the theoretical level. For Julian now faced himself as at once πολιτικός and πολυπράγμων,[1] just as much a philosopher as a man of action, and this balanced conception of himself and of life in general found its clearest reflection in the manner in which he attempted to impart his ideal of *paideia* to his flock.

Nowhere else is this ideal as clearly delineated as in his polemical work *Against the Galileans*.[2] Composed in unfriendly Antioch during the long winter nights of 362–3, this treatise, which sadly survives only in fragments, illuminates better than any other Julianic text the emperor's conception of Hellenism. Here Hellenism is defined apophatically, by contrast with foreign ways of thought and life, both traditional and revolutionary. Unlike his two famous predecessors in the field of anti-Christian polemic, Julian is preoccupied in his work much more with politics and social issues than with doctrinal points, so that from the pages of his attack on Christianity there emerges a philosophy of history rather than a theory of metaphysics. Behind the evolution of this philosophy of history are recognizable all the social, intellectual and spiritual trends that worked on Julian's mind—often against his own will—at various stages during his lifetime. Born in a universal state at a moment when a highly centralized political system was finding its practical adaptation in a form of government based on the

---

[1] IX. 203b; cf. VII. 211b.

[2] Julian always calls the Christians Galileans, in order to deny to their creed any claim to universality. For the date of the *Contra Galilaeos*, see C. I. Neumann, *Iul. Imp. Libr. C. Christ. quae supersunt*, Leipzig 1880, 6–8. In his refutation of the C.G., Cyril of Alexandria admits that it was a dangerous piece of propaganda and that it caused many Christians to apostatize, *Contra Iulianum, PG* 76. 508c.

principle of minute hierarchization and its theoretical justification in the development of an ideology that transformed the
princeps into the awesome and almost transcendent figure of a
dominus, Julian also happened to belong to the family that ruled
the *oikoumene*. If this coincidence of birth proved the source of
personal suffering for the young prince, it also impressed on him
a sense of the uniqueness of his destiny. And the circumstances
of his physical existence, which he pretended to ignore by taking
refuge in the timeless Platonic universe, ultimately conditioned
his understanding of Plato's teaching at least as drastically as
the innate force that nurtured in him the spark of Platonism.

It was typical of a man with a Platonic mould of mind, whom
experience had acquainted with the *modus vivendi* of many
peoples,[3] that he should have viewed each individual culture as
the terrestrial expression of a heavenly archetype. Julian placed
every nation under the special protection of a national or ethnic
god,[4] whom he saw at once as an emanation of the First Cause[5]
and as the first principle in a hierarchy of national powers, consisting of an angel, a demon, a hero and a 'peculiar order of
souls' which obey and serve the higher power.[6] Each nation's
characteristics are the visible manifestation of the character of
its ethnic god (*C.G.* 115de), so that, for example, the nations
under the special protection of Ares are predominantly war-
like, while those under Hermes are more shrewd than adven-
turous. Once the character of a nation has found its expression
in time—in other words, once a culture has been created—
there naturally emerges the concept of national tradition, which
ideally should be as perennial as the divine prototype whose
concrete representation it is. Consequently each nation has a
divinely allotted duty to maintain its specific character at all
costs.[7] At this point Julian's sense of tragedy comes into play:
Adrasteia is ever vigilant (*ep.* 84). Cultures are fragile things
(*C.G.* 143c) facing constant challenges from without; if they
fail to respond to these challenges, while at the same time
remaining true to their own character, they begin to show the
first symptoms of disease. The existence of an eternal prototype

[3] Cf. I. 13a, 13d–14a.
[4] *ep.* 89b. 292cd.
[5] *C.G.* 115de.
[6] *C.G.* 143ab; XI. 145c.
[7] *ep.* 89a. 453b.

for each individual culture, and the nation's implied responsibility to be faithful to that prototype, rules out for Julian the
notion of inevitable decadence. Yet self-deception is endemic
to humanity, and there are instances in history when entire
races have lost sight of their tradition. Those individuals who
attack the traditions of their nations become the tragic heroes
who, by consciously ignoring divine law, draw the wrath of
heaven not only upon themselves but also upon their progeny
and their whole race, thus bringing divine nemesis to its inevitable fulfilment.[8] Mercifully enough though, the drama of
human history always carries within itself the possibility of
catharsis, through those men who at critical moments appear
and save a culture from doom by setting it anew on its old
foundations.[9]

This is Julian's message to Hellenism as expressed in his
pastoral letters, as it is also his message to Judaism in his
polemical work against Christianity.[10] Yet while the emperor
recognizes that Jehovah is one of the many tutelary gods
emanating from the First Principle (*C.G.* 100c), and that he is
responsible for the destiny of the Jews, he rejects the idea that
the children of Israel are an elect people (*C.G.* 99e–106d), and
denounces Paul's inconsistency in this matter (*C.G.* 100ab ff.).
Julian criticizes too the god of the Old Testament, and especially his jealousy (*C.G.* 106de), which he takes pleasure in contrasting with the impassibility of the Greek deities.[11]

As is natural, the race over which a jealous god rules is one
subject to a 'harsh and stern, savage and barbarous law' (*C.G.*
202a), a race condemned to perpetual servitude (*C.G.* 209d–
213a; 218b), which, on account of its mediocre qualities, never

---

[8] *ep.* 89a. 453cd.

[9] See *ep.* 89a. 453c, where Julian uses the proverbial expression ἀφ' ἑστίας
ἐπιμεληθῆναι to refer to his restoration of Hellenism. The best illustration of this
theory is provided by Julian's autobiographical myth (VII. 227c–234c): Constantine had brought down the wrath of heaven upon himself and his progeny by
betraying his country and its tutelary gods. Then his sons acted as the agents of
divine νέμεσις; finally Julian appeared to save his culture from extinction.

[10] *A la rigueur*, Julian might be described as a 'Zionist' (for a selection of evidence
illustrating this, see *ELF*, No. 134), yet he was by no means a 'philo-Semite' (*pace*
M. Avi Yonah, *The Jews of Palestine*, Oxford 1976, 185–207, esp. 190.)

[11] *C.G.* 171de; cf. Plato, *Phaedr.* 247a: Φθόνος ἔξω θείου χοροῦ ἵσταται.
Tim. 29e: ἀγαθὸς ἦν [sc. ὁ δημιουργός], ἀγαθῷ δὲ οὐδεὶς περὶ οὐδενὸς
οὐδέποτε ἐγγίγνεται φθόνος.

achieved anything great in the military domain or in that of public administration and institutions or in the higher spheres of medicine and intellectual and artistic life (*C.G.* 218b–224d). In all these fields, the Greeks are immensely superior to the Jews (ibid.). A quick comparison between the cosmogonies of the two races, as related in the *Timaeus* and in Genesis, suffices to illustrate the perfection of the Greek god and of the Greek idea of the universe as opposed to the naïve and incomplete vision of the Jews.[12] Towards the Israelite Julian feels the double contempt of a Greek intellectual and a Roman states-man. Yet, he hastens to add with the superiority of one who is fully aware of the privileges Destiny has squandered upon him, even to the Jews the divine economy has allotted their due place on the earth. Albeit inferior to the Greeks, who, on the evidence of history, have a much better claim to be God's chosen race,[13] the Jews ought, none the less, to remain faithful to the commandments of their god, if they wish to be pre-served as a cultural and religious entity. In his magnanimity the emperor will help them to fulfil this duty by lending them his full support. In practical terms Julian assisted the Jews by undertaking to rebuild the temple of Jerusalem[14]—a generous gesture, which was certainly not motivated exclusively by philo-sophical considerations. Political speculation must have played an important role in Julian's decision, for he could not have forgotten the unsuccessful Jewish revolt against his brother in 351 or have been unaware of the favour that the rival Sassanid empire displayed towards the Jews. This material and moral succour that the emperor afforded to a particular ethnic minority had its correlative in the spiritual sphere too, for Julian devoted considerable attention to the exegesis of Hebrew religious traditions, which for didactic purposes he paralleled with Greek customs and beliefs, pointing out that both races regarded divination and sacrifices as methods of communicating with the divine (*C.G.* 358d), and, at a deeper level, shared a sacred mythology whose function was initiative ($\tau\epsilon\lambda\epsilon\sigma\tau\iota\kappa\acute{\eta}$).[15]

---

[12] This was probably a common theme. Galen, *De usu partium* XI. 14 (G. Helmreich), Leipzig 1909, 158 ff. had already compared the cosmogonies of Moses, Epicurus and Plato to the advantage of the last.

[13] *C.G.* 184b–190c; *C.G.* 218b–224d, 235b ff.

[14] Amm. XXIII. 1. 2.

[15] *C.G.* 44b–75a; cf. VII. 216c–217b.

Indeed the only way in which the Jews could aspire to appre-
hend the true nature of divinity was through the study and
allegorization of the fundamental myths contained in their
sacred books, for a hidden meaning can be detected behind the
incongruous elements in Genesis (*C.G.* 44a–94a).

It is along these lines that Julian interprets the myth of the
tower of Babel (*C.G.* 134d–138a), in which he sees a clear
reference to his theory of the national gods, 'which neither
Moses nor anyone else took care to elucidate' (*C.G.* 138a).
According to Julian's own exegesis of the myth, the divergence
between the customs and the political constitutions of individual
nations serves as proof, even more than the different languages
by means of which the gods divided mankind, of the existence
of a variety of national types (ibid.). It was the ethnic gods
themselves, assisted by the whole hierarchy of their subordi-
nates (*C.G.* 146b, 148c), who bestowed upon the races under
their protection customs and laws to fit their peculiar character,[16] while the climate of each region supplemented the
influence of the gods in further determining the idiosyncrasies
of the race inhabiting it (*C.G.* 143e). Seen in this perspective,
the law-givers of each country were merely the interpreters of
what was communicated to them through divine inspiration,[17]
so that the so-called $\theta\epsilon\tau\grave{o}\varsigma$ $\nu\acute{o}\mu o\varsigma$ is a god-sent gift to humanity,
and should be preserved at all costs.[18]

Once the principle of the invariability of national types has
been proclaimed, and the Jews have been praised for the
tenacity with which they cling to their national traditions,[19] the
emperor feels that he has laid the foundations on which his
argument against Christianity may rest. Indeed, Julian makes
a point of exploiting all the standard weapons of Jewish anti-
Christian polemic before he mobilizes his private indignation
and the disgust natural to a Neoplatonist thinker and a Roman
patriot.

Julian presents Christianity as 'a human fabrication, wrought

[16] *C.G.* 143d; cf. *ep.* 89a. 453b.

[17] *C.G.* 131c, 193d–194b. See below, pp. 175–6.

[18] For a different, and more pessimistic, view of the $\theta\epsilon\tau\grave{o}\varsigma$ $\nu\acute{o}\mu o\varsigma$, see Porph.
Marc. 25 ff.

[19] This point is not original. Celsus also praises the Jews for their respect for
tradition, cf. Orig. *C.C.* V. 25: 'their worship may be peculiar, but is at least
traditional' (trans. H. Chadwick).

by wickedness and devoid of any divine element' (*C.G.* 39ab).
It is a monstrosity contrived by men 'to appeal to the childish
and foolish part of the soul' (*C.G.* 39b), an enormous deceit
which can only be classified as a heresy of Judaism.[20] Those
embracing it are rootless individuals who have deserted the god
of Moses and denied the traditions of Hellenism (*C.G.* 238a–d).
They have merely adopted the worst characteristics of each
race, 'the rashness of the Jews, the indolence, indifference and
vulgarity of the Gentiles' (*C.G.* 238b, 43b), and this extraordinary mixture has produced the Galilean 'atheism', a way
of living and thinking for which there are no divine patterns.[21]
A band of outlaws on earth, the Galileans have no place anywhere in the cosmic order.

This last point, which, next to the usual clichés of anti-
Christian polemic, provides the bulk of his argument against
Christianity, reveals how little 'reactionary' Julian's idea of
the Roman empire was. The last representative of the Second
Flavian dynasty faced the empire as an epitome of the divine
cosmos, built and functioning according to as strict and complicated a hierarchy as those of the last Neoplatonist philosophers. His ethnic gods, subordinate to their δεσπότης, are but
the governors of provinces who, subject to their βασιλεύς,
administer each his own region, and restore it when it falls on
hard times (*C.G.* 148b; *ep.* 89a. 453c).[22] 'Of course we do not
make the supreme being the sectional rival of the gods whose
station is subordinate to him' (*C.G.* 148c),[23] explains Julian, lest
the suspicion should enter the mind of his subjects that any
emperor might fail to display the moral superiority appropriate
to his status. But the most quintessentially Byzantine of Julian's
teachings is still to come: if particular nations within the
empire, if even individual cities are allowed to cultivate their

---

[20] *C.G.* 43a.

[21] With reference to their historical tradition, Celsus wrote about the Christians:
'I will ask them where they have come from, or who is the author of their traditional laws. Nobody, they will say', Orig. *C.C.* V. 33.

[22] The analogy between God and the great King of Persia on the one hand, and
demons and satraps on the other, had been developed at length by the author of
the *De Mundo*. Aelius Aristides further elaborated this point (XLIII. 18, Keil
ii. 343) and Celsus (Orig. *C.C.* VIII. 35) vaguely alluded to it. It is Julian, however, who is responsible for the formulation of a cogent theory of ethnic gods and
their connection with the governors of the Roman empire.

[23] Like God, whose terrestrial image he is, the emperor is exempt from all envy.

local customs and traditions under the vigilant eye of their
governor, it is only because at a higher level both people and
governors are subject to a universal law represented by the
supreme authority of the emperor.[24] The principle of the invariability of particular cultures is thus co-ordinated with that
of the universality of the empire and of its mission. But into
this forceful vision the Christians do not integrate. They are
rootless individuals, living according to no accepted norms
(*C.G.* 305e);[25] and, having no sense of continuity or discipline,
they feel not merely strangers in this world, but even hostile
to it.

Yet Julian could not disregard Christianity's greatest asset:
the fascination exerted over the human spirit by its personal
god—one who, like so many late antique deities, was an emanation of the First Principle and who, through his life on earth,
had accomplished a series of brilliant deeds which had been
engraved in the memory of men. To this hero the pagan
emperor clearly had to oppose some analogous figure in the
Hellenic tradition. Julian chose Asclepios, the healer of
humanity's body and soul,[26] the saviour *par excellence*, a deity
whose popularity had steadily increased ever since the fifth
century BC. Julian was well aware of the fact that the φιλάν-
θρωπος θεός was regarded by the Christians themselves as a
dangerous competitor, a kind of Anti-Christ whose ancestry
and *vita* alike were strangely similar to those of their own god.[27]
As the son of Apollo, identified in later centuries with Helios-
Mithra, Asclepios came to be regarded as the direct emanation
of the Sun,[28] and the very guardian of the Immortals.[29] He was
also the patron of divination,[30] 'the most perfect mystagogue',[31]
who not only looked after men in this life but also assured
salvation to their soul in the next—a role in which he was

---

[24] See above, pp. 109–10.
[25] Cf. Cyril, *Contra Iulianum*, PG 76. 957bc.
[26] *C.G.* 235c; Ael. Ar. XXXVIII, XXXIX, XLII *passim*. For Asclepios' special place in Neoplatonism see Proclus, *In Remp.* I. 69. 6 ff.
[27] Cf. Tertullian, *Ad Nat.* II. 14. 42 (Oehler), who calls Asclepios 'tam peri-culosam mundo bestiam', and Clem. *Strom.* V. 1. 13, who regards Asclepios as a forerunner of Christ.
[28] XI. 144b; *C.G.* 200ab; Eus. *Praep. Ev.* III. 13. 15–16; Macrob. *Sat.* I. 20. 1.
[29] Ael. Ar. XLII. 4.
[30] *C.G.* 235cd; Macrob. *Sat.* I. 20. 4.
[31] Ael. Ar. XXIII. 16: ὁ τελεώτατος μυσταγωγός.

associated with Demeter. Through his initiation in the Eleusinian Mysteries (the most prestigious ancient Greek cult of a
pronouncedly other-worldly nature and characterized by ritual
acts[32]), Asclepios had also become the god who opened to man
the path into the Beyond.[33] It was in this spirit that he was
invoked by Socrates, whose very last words, 'Crito, we owe a
cock to Asclepios',[34] were with the passing of centuries to be
charged with a profoundly symbolic significance.

In Julian's choice of Asclepios as the rival of Christ political
considerations must have weighed at least as heavily as the
purely theological advantages of the Hellenic god-*logos*. When
he composed his anti-Christian polemic, Julian's popularity was
at its lowest ebb. Yet his panegyrists had not ceased to proclaim
in him Asclepios incarnate, greeting him as the superhuman
healer who had come to resurrect not just one man, but the
whole *oikoumene*.[35] The association of his own sacred person with
Asclepios would be wasted on his subjects, though, if they were
not aware of the specific qualities of the god, and if the story of
his life remained for the great majority buried in the mists of
an improbable, half-forgotten legend. Julian undertook to
acquaint them with the achievement of one who, born a mortal,
had gained divinity thanks to his *paideia* and the philanthropic
way in which he exploited it. His father, Apollo, had early in his
life entrusted Asclepios to the care of the 'deep-counselling'
Centaur Cheiron, 'who taught him the gentle-handed lore of
cures',[36] and Asclepios used the wisdom that he acquired, not
only to heal bodies, but also 'to raise up sinful souls' (*C.G.* 200b).
Yet, if his primary vocation is the spiritual salvation of
humanity, the god of medicine regards it also as his duty to try
to impart intellectual *paideia* to the souls of 'the descendants of
Cheiron' (*C.G.* 176ab). In this eminently Greek task, he is
assisted by the Muses, by Apollo and Hermes, whose combined
efforts have made of the nation under their protection the
educators of the *oikoumene*—just as it is on account of their lack

---

[32] For Asclepios' initiation at Eleusis, see Philostr. *V. Apoll.* IV. 18.
[33] For a full account of the Asclepios cult see E. and L. Edelstein, *Asclepius. A
Collection and Interpretation of the Testimonies* i–ii, Baltimore 1945.
[34] Plato, *Phaedo* 118a.
[35] See Lib. XIII. 42, from his address to Julian shortly after the latter's arriva
at Antioch; cf. Him. XLI. 8.
[36] Pindar, *Nem.* III. 53–5; see also *Pyth.* III. 45–6.

of *paideia* that the Jews have to be classified as a second-rate race:[37]

In my opinion there is no reason why their god should not be a mighty god, even though he does not happen to have wise prophets and interpreters. But the real reason why they are not wise is that they have not submitted their souls to be cleansed by the regular course of study (ἐγκυκλίοις μαθήμασι), nor have they allowed those studies to open their tightly closed eyes, and to clear away the mist that hangs over them. (*ep.* 89b. 295d)

The theme of *paideia* recurs in all its complexity throughout what pathetic fragments remain of the *Contra Galilaeos*—a work which was aimed more explicitly than any other of Julian's writings at the awakening of the national and political consciousness of its readers. In it a well-articulated theory of the universality of Roman rule found its metaphysical justification in Neoplatonic terms. Julian had come a long way since the days of his youth when he proclaimed unreservedly the supremacy of the contemplative over the practical life; and the intricacy of his mature reaction to this major problem was to make of him an innovator within the Neoplatonic tradition.

In the fourth century BC Plato had diverted the stream of philosophical speculation by transposing the First Principle from a physical onto a metaphysical level, when he proclaimed it to be 'beyond essence'—ἐπέκεινα τῆς οὐσίας. Yet Plato did more than simply state a transcendental truth; he linked his message with the spirit of the culture to which he belonged, both finding a place in his metaphysical scheme for the traditional Homeric gods and sanctioning through it the prevailing Greek political system—the *polis*. At the same time Plato, the καλὸς κἀγαθός Athenian citizen, did not find it incompatible with his theological views to compose the most lasting hymns to patriotism to be found in the classical Greek tradition.[38]

Six centuries later, Plotinus, the émigré from Egypt, whom Augustine called 'Plato redivivus', drew on Plato to formulate his transcendental theology, but also used his exegesis of the

---

[37] *epp.* 89a. 454a; 89b. 295d–296b; *C.G.* 202a. For *paideia* in a more modern sense, see Cyr. *Contra Iulianum, PG* 76. 857: ἐνισταμένῳ δὲ μετὰ τοῦτο, καὶ τὴν ἁγίαν τε καὶ θεόπνευστον κατασκώπτοντι Γραφήν, ἐπεί τοι τῇ Ἑβραίων συντέθειται γλώττῃ.

[38] Cf. *Crito* and *Menexenus*.

master to express his fundamental sense of alienation from the world; he commented exclusively on the metaphysical dialogues, ignoring those works in which Plato had expounded his civic philosophy, and in this he was followed by all other Neoplatonists, who became less and less inclined to admit any real links with society. The one notable exception in the history of the School is Julian, who imbibed the spirit of Plato's political works and translated it into terms of fourth-century AD reality. His originality consists in having substituted the empire for the *polis*, the oriental cults for the Olympians and *Romanitas* for Greek civic patriotism.

In the *Republic* we find the reconciliation of the two contending vocations in man: the tendency towards the Absolute which pushes him to reject his worldly existence in favour of the contemplative mode of life, and the urge to justify himself as a social and sociable being by adhering to the practical life and leading an active and even combative existence in society. The perfect philosopher is for Plato the *philanthropos* statesman and not the misanthropic hermit.[39] Likewise, the well-governed state is the best school in which to train men to achieve spiritual maturity. In his turn the individual must pay his tribute of gratitude to the *polis* by occupying himself with the κοινά.[40] It is only from a state assaulted by incurable evils and ruled by injustice that the righteous individual may flee, but not until it is clear that his own limited potentialities cannot be of any further use in the situation.[41]

This Platonic conception of the philosopher's obligations towards the terrestrial city, going hand in hand with the belief that collective and individual welfare are complementary notions, is clearly exemplified in Julian's life. Raised in the belief that the actual world in which he was living was less real than Homer's world,[42] and subsequently, through his adherence to Neoplatonism and his initiation in the Eleusinian Mysteries, brought into contact with a universe where Beauty and Truth shone in perpetuity, Julian naturally felt increasingly alienated from his immediate environment. He, if anybody, was in a position to know on how low, vicious and criminal a basis the edifice of the State stood (VII. 232bc).

---

[39] *Rep.* 540b.
[41] *Rep.* 496c–e.
[40] *Rep.* 497a.
[42] See pp. 15ff.

Yet personal resentment and even fear and disgust were soon superseded by an attitude of philosophical detachment, shaded by a certain sarcastic contempt for all the glory and grandeur of the Roman empire.[43] This attitude too eventually gave way to a much maturer one. Albeit with some sense of resignation, Julian first accepted the duty that Constantius imposed on him, and then sought to find some noble aim in the duty performed; because of his sense of commitment and sacrifice, he was enabled to perceive that the position of Caesar, for all its tribulations, was a mission divinely allotted to him and to be accomplished with dedication and enthusiasm.[44] Ultimately, when the Genius Publicus appeared to Julian on the night of his proclamation as Augustus, we witness a radical change in attitude which could justly be described as Julian's conversion to a theocratic idea of kingship.

Once converted, Julian attempted to articulate his new credo in the language of the tradition with which he was familiar. No other text conveys as effectively Julian's state of mind at that moment as the autobiographical myth in the *Contra Heracleium* (227c–234c). This myth is constructed in such a manner as to suggest close similarities with the spirit and the patterns of classical tragedy, an unconscious technique which Julian was to use again later in his *Contra Galilaeos*.[45] Of course in neither case does he state explicitly that he has recourse to the patterns of the tragic genre in order to legitimize a personal theory by linking it with the classical tradition, for he speaks as a man who does not even conceive of any other way of speaking.

When in the ninth century, the patriarch Photius wished to console his brother Tarasius for the loss of a daughter, he addressed a long epistle to him; their family, he wrote, was the tragic stage on which there played a band of evils led by Erinys, while Clotho supplied them with their material drawn from the lives of Photius' family.[46] In this Photius was typically Byzantine; he felt obliged to have recourse to the Hellenic tradition in order to strengthen his argument, and yet, as a

---

[43] V. 277a; Amm. XV. 8. 17.

[44] Amm. XVI. 1. 1.

[45] See above, pp. 162–3.

[46] Photius, Ταρασίῳ πατρικίῳ ἀδελφῷ παραμυθητικὴ ἐπὶ θυγατρὶ τεθνηκυίᾳ in N. V. Tomadakis, Βυζαντινὴ Ἐπιστολογραφία, Athens 1965, 82.

partial outsider to this tradition, he also felt that if he did not state his point clearly, it would be missed. Julian could afford to be subtle. Wishing to expound a theory of imperial authority of his own, he spontaneously had recourse to the thought-patterns of the tradition in which he had been brought up.

In his autobiographical myth, before introducing himself onto the stage, Julian outlines the history of the dynasty to which he belonged, as the rules of Attic tragedy required. He first presents Constantine as a man who, being ignorant of the art of governing (VII. 227d), failed utterly to administer the large patrimony he had received from his ancestors. His ignorance engendered unjustified pride and greed, and he found himself guilty of the most serious crime that a man may commit in society, that of injustice—ἀδικία (VII. 227c): in order to enrich himself he disregarded the principle of justice—τὸ δίκαιον —which in a well-organized society rules human relations (ibid.). Yet iniquitous behaviour towards one's fellow-humans is only the first step towards the tragic climax of *hybris*, the second being the violation of τὸ ὅσιον—divine law. Through his lack of education, Constantine was found guilty of *hybris* in the full sense of the term—he became both unjust and ungodly— thus raising the wrath of the gods against his House. His sons could only aggravate the situation: they had received a bad education (VII. 228a), and were fated victims by virtue of the tragic malediction (ἡ τραγικὴ κατάρα, VII. 228b) upon their father and his House, all of which was to share in the god-sent ἄτη (ibid.). The story of the Constantinian House is modelled on the core of the Theban cycle, the story of Eteocles and Poly-neikes, who, bringing to fulfilment their father's curse, had 'to divide their patrimony by the sharpened edge of the sword'.[47] Some members of the doomed family perished during a night of slaughter, but Constantine's sons survived to act as the agents of divine wrath.

The sons demolished the ancestral temples which their father before them had despised and had stripped of the votive offerings, which had been dedicated by many worshippers, and not least by his own ancestors. And besides demolishing the temples, they erected sepulchres both on new sites and on the old sites of the temples, as

---

[47] VII. 228b; cf. Eur. *Phoen.* 68; Aesch. *Sept. c. Th.* 816–17, 940 ff.

though impelled by fate or by an unconscious presentiment that they would ere long need many such sepulchres, seeing that they so neglected the gods. (VII. 228bc)[48]

When divine and human laws alike were profaned, and all was in a state of confusion (ibid.), Zeus himself, beholding the tragedy, was moved with compassion (τὸν Δία ἔλεος ὑπῆλθε, VII. 228d). Wishing to put an end to the misfortunes of the royal House, he sent upon the stage, according to the tragic conventions, a *deus ex machina* who was to resolve the drama by causing the last offspring of the Second Flavian dynasty to act in such a way as to bring catharsis.[49]

Julian now begins the story of his own life, emphasizing those moments that he himself regards as the landmarks in his development. Before Helios intervened personally to snatch the child Julian 'from the blood and turmoil of war and the slaughter of men',[50] Zeus had asked the Fates to implement this same plan, but the three sisters had replied to their father that they were prevented from doing so by 'Οσιότης and Δίκη, the two goddesses superior to them in the heavenly hierarchy, whom Constantine and his sons had insulted (VII. 229ab). Zeus had then interfered to ask the two most venerable goddesses, his daughters, to stop opposing his wish, himself guaranteeing that neither would in future be neglected among humans (VII. 229b). It was only then that the Fates were allowed to weave their loom according to the will of their father, and that Julian was trusted to Athene-Pronoia, the motherless maiden who shared with Helios the task of bringing him up (VII. 230a).

The restoration of the Roman empire is thus presented as the effect of predestination, the work of the fates complying with the will of the father of the gods. Helios—the tutelary deity of the Second Flavian dynasty—is presented as Julian's ancestor (VII. 229c–d) and spiritual father (VII. 229c, 231d), while Athene-Pronoia is the providence who had been specially allotted to him (VII. 230b) so as to enable him, through her

---

[48] Cf. Lib. XXX. 6 (on Constantine's attitude towards the ἱερά) and LXII. 11; XVIII. 158 (on Constantius).

[49] This passage could conceivably be seen as a parallel to *Tricennalia* VII, where Eusebius presents Constantine as the man who put an end to ἀσέβεια and to the crimes that were committed in the name of the ψευδώνυμος θεολογία of the pagans.

[50] VII. 229d and Hom. *Il. Λ* 164.

constant guidance and protection, to achieve the great re-
formatory task whose accomplishment Zeus had guaranteed to
'Οσιότης and Δίκη. Finally Hermes, in his double role of god
of eloquence and Psychopompus, appeared at the moment
when Julian was about to reach maturity (VII. 230a), to lead
him through the different grades of initiation[51] until the final
stage, when the devotee was granted a direct encounter with
God (VII. 230c–231b).

The spiritual journey towards illumination was not a short
one: it was like ascending a great and lofty mountain (VII.
230d), and the conferment of divine grace at the moment of
setting out was not enough to guarantee the completion of such
an enormous task (VII. 230b). An expert guide was needed to
point out at each stage what path had to be taken and why, till
the supreme moment of divine ecstasy dawned. Julian was
gratified with this transcendental vision (VII. 231b) and, when
he fell back into the state of ordinary humanity, he had been
enriched with divine knowledge. At the sight of all the vicious-
ness that reigned over the earth (VII. 232a ff.) he experienced
mixed feelings of pity and disgust; and the remembrance of
the supernatural glory that he had just contemplated made
him reluctant to exchange a state of spiritual bliss for one of
brilliant servitude in the service of humanity (VII. 232c).[52]
Only after much hesitation and resistance did he consent at last
to utter the words: 'Oh most mighty Helios, and thou, Athene
—and thee too, Father Zeus do I call to witness—dispose of
me as ye will' (VII. 232c).

Being appointed to rule by the will of heaven—*Dei gratia*—
Julian received from his tutelary gods the knowledge that would
allow him to govern righteously, together with the attributes of
kingship—the symbolic torch of eternal light from Helios, the
aegis and helmet from Athene, and the golden wand from
Hermes (VII. 234ab). Subsequently, Helios-Mithra gave his
commandments to his elect (VII. 234b).[53] Henceforth Julian

---

[51] Hermes Psychopompus leads the purified soul of the devotee through the
seven degrees of initiation in the Mithraic Mysteries. For his identification with
Helios in similar contexts, see Bidez–Cumont, *Mages hellénisés* ii. 284–5; cf. P. P.
Bober, 'The Mithraic symbolism of Mercury carrying the infant Bacchus', *HThR*
xxxix (1946), 84.

[52] See above, pp. 17, 53–4.

[53] See above, p. 39.

was to regard his personal salvation as being dependent on the successful performance of his duty as emperor—a duty which to his mind consisted in acting as the guardian of the laws and traditions that the race under his supervision had evolved in order to express its specific characteristics, and in being the interpreter of those traditions in the light of the changing mood of the age.[54]

Here lies the great difference between Julian's conception of the relationship between law and monarch and the Neopythagorean, Themistian and Christian mystique of kingship which conceives of the emperor as the ἔμψυχος νόμος placed beyond and above human law, which by its very nature is biased and imperfect.[55] Using Neoplatonic language, Julian explicitly states in one of his pastoral letters that the law is of divine origin (*ep*. 89a. 453b). The king, being in his earthly body half dust half deity, must, ignoring his mortal nature, strive to grasp the essence of the law by means of the element in himself that is akin to the gods. In support of his theory Julian cites *in extenso* and comments on the only passage from Plato where such a doctrine is implied, albeit veiled behind an ingenious allegory.[56] Far from being the law incarnate, the king is, for Julian, its ephemeral exegete, appointed to this office by the gods.[57] If he fails to rise to the circumstances, if

---

[54] Cf. III. 88d: φύλαξ δὲ ὢν ἀγαθὸς τῶν νόμων, ἀμείνων ἔσται δημιουργός, εἴ ποτε καιρὸς καὶ τύχη καλοίη. XII. 356d; *ep*. 89a. 453bc.

[55] See above, pp. 61–2. For the phrase νόμος ἔμψυχος in late Hellenistic and Roman times, see Oswyn Murray, '*Περὶ Βασιλείας*. Studies in the justification of monarchic power in the Hellenistic world', unp. diss., Oxford 1970, 251, 273–80. Following A. Steinwenter, 'Νόμος ἔμψυχος: zur Geschichte einer politischen Theorie', *Anz. der Akad. der Wiss. Wien, Philos.-hist. Kl*. xix (1946), 250–68, Murray holds that the doctrine of ἔμψυχος νόμος, as yet unformulated in Byzantium, first acquired wide currency in the thirteenth century. Also, together with L. Delatte and Steinwenter, he points out that the meaning of the phrase varies from one author to another.

[56] See above, pp. 92–3. VI. 258a–259a and Plato, *Leg*. 713c. Cf. J. VII. 209c on divine law being engraved on the human soul. For the Judaeo–Christian origin of this idea, see J. Daniélou, *Les Anges et leur mission d'après les Pères de l'Église*, Paris 1952, 14–15 and references.

[57] VI. 259a ff. It is not until the twelfth century that we find Julian's understanding of the law plainly stated in an imperial document, whose apologetic tone is reminiscent of the closing page of the *Letter to Themistius*; see J. and P. Zepos, *Ius Graecoromanum*, Athens 1931, i. 385 ff., and esp. the chrysobul of Manuel I Comnenos (AD 1159): Διορίζεται γὰρ διὰ τῆς παρούσης χρυσοβούλλου γραφῆς, ἵνα εἴ τι δι᾽ ὅλου τοῦ καιροῦ τῆς αὐτοκρατορίας ἡμῶν ἀγράφως

he does not seize upon the καιρός[58] so that the inert letter of tradition finds its right expression in time, then he betrays both the mission allotted to him and the spirit of his race.

The vocation of a Roman emperor in particular is for ever determined by the specific characteristics of the City's ethnic god, Quirinus, whose legend Julian relates in these words:

The founder of our City was sent down to earth not by Ares alone (though it is not unlikely that a demon with the characteristics of Ares has contributed to the physical formation of his body), visiting Silvia, as the legend has it, while she was carrying water for the bath of the goddess; yet the whole truth is that the soul of the god Quirinus descended from Helios; for we must trust the sacred tradition. And the minute conjunction of Helios and Selene—the powers who rule the sensible world—was responsible as much for his descent to earth as for his ascent, once the mortal element of his body was destroyed by the fire of a thunderbolt. Thus patently did she who creates earthly matter, she who is placed immediately under Helios, receive Quirinus onto this earth when he was sent down by Athene-Pronoia, and lead him back again to Helios, the King of the All, when he took his flight upwards. (XI. 154cd)

This is an autobiographical passage. Using the language of tradition Julian proclaims his own very modern theocratic conception of kingship. Romulus becomes a double of the emperor, placed under the special protection of Athene-Pronoia and watched over by Selene and Helios, to whom his fiery soul is bound to return at the end of his predestined journey on earth. There is a doublet of this passage in Julian's works: 'That the goddess [Athene-Pronoia] did not betray her suppliant or abandon him she proved by the event. For everywhere she was my guide, and on all sides she set a watch near me, *bringing guardian angels from Helios and Selene*' (V. 275b).

ἢ ἐγγράφως ὁρισθῇ παρὰ τῆς βασιλείας μου ἐναντίον τῷ δικαίῳ καὶ τῇ τῶν νόμων εὐθύτητι, ἄκυρον τοῦτο διαμείνῃ καὶ τὸ ἄπρακτον ἔξῃ παντάπασιν.

[58] Julian is categorical on this point. Again and again he expresses his deep conviction that man can and should indeed be taught by history (II. 124c), but that in the study of history the guiding thread should be provided by the actual circumstances of contemporary events. If the function of history is essentially didactic (*ep.* 89b. 301b), this is so only for those who are able to meditate on the past from the standpoint of the present: μέτρον δέ ἐστι τοῦ πλήθους τῶν φερομένων ὁ καιρός (II. 124d).

These angels, who are placed directly under the ethnic god himself (*C.G.* 143ab), naturally have a specifically 'national' character. Just before his arrival in Milan Julian had been entrusted to them. His mission on earth was determined by the divine will, as he stated in the autobiographical myth, once he had fully acknowledged his vocation. When in Gaul Julian put all his energies at the service of a cause, which he regarded as a divinely allotted mission, he had not yet articulated his imperial theology, nor had he seen himself as the last link in the divine chain that connected earth to heaven.[59] This was a realization that struck him only at the moment when the Genius Publicus of the Roman empire appeared to him.[60] From the moment when the ethnic δαίμων of Rome carried to Julian the mandate for his election, the prince knew that he belonged to the divine hierarchy of powers protecting Rome and that he was God's vice-gerent on earth. This conviction remained with him until the night in Mesopotamia, on the very eve of his death, when the *Genius* of the empire appeared again 'now with veil over both head and horn of Abundance, sorrowfully passing out through the curtains of his tent'.[61] Then Julian knew at once what fate awaited him.[62] Yet, confident in the principles of Neoplatonic and Mithraic theology, he passed away in the quiet belief that, just like Romulus, 'the heaven and the stars were calling him to union'.[63]

But the Romans are not Quirinus' sons alone—they are just as much the descendants of the pious Aeneas (XI. 154a), who, for Julian, is intimately and significantly related to the Sun, patron of Rome (XI. 153d): 'According to the legend, Aeneas is the son of Aphrodite, who is subordinate to Helios and is his kinswoman' (XI. 154a). Yet several generations had to pass by

[59] See Plut. *Romulus* 28. 10. Julian was particularly keen on Plutarch, as may be deduced from the large number of references to him in all Julian's works, especially the *Caesars*.

[60] Amm. XX. 5. 10. In the Neoplatonic hierarchy the *Genius* or Δαίμων corresponds to the power placed immediately under the angels and above the heroes (*C.G.* 143ab etc.). The heroes inhabiting the region just below the moon are the disembodied souls of the emperors (X. 307c, 312c). In the *Caesars*, Commodus' 'humid soul' pulls him down to the earth (X. 312c). See F. Cumont, *Lux Perpetua*, Paris 1949, 364 ff.

[61] Amm. XXV. 2. 3.

[62] Ibid. 4.

[63] Amm. XXV. 3. 22.

before Rome was founded and a philosopher king appeared who fully realized his vocation by instituting the worship of the Sun:

When after her foundation many wars encompassed Rome, she won and prevailed in them all; and since she ever increased in size in proportion to her very dangers and needed greater security, then Zeus set over her the great philosopher Numa who dwelt in deserted groves and ever communed with the gods in the pure thoughts of his own heart. It was he who established most of the laws concerning temple worship. (*C.G.* 193cd)[64]

In the *Hymn to King Helios*, written at the same time as this passage, Julian further specifies in what the legislation of the 'most divine king Numa' (XI. 155a) consisted. The legendary king of Rome founded the cult of Helios by appointing the Vestals 'to guard the undying flame of the sun at different hours in turn' (ibid.). In this, as in his reform of the calendar, Numa subtly anticipated Aurelian, who instituted the cult of *Sol Invictus Exsuperantissimus* (XI. 155b). Thus, Julian claims, the divine project was fulfilled over a period of exactly one millennium.

Nor was it only the worship of Helios that proved the continuity of Roman history and the perpetual vigilance that Providence exercised over it (*C.G.* 194c). The emperors themselves formed a royal chain which, even though often interrupted by impiety, had not yet been, nor indeed ever could be, irrevocably broken; for Julian believed that, whenever the innovating policies of some irreverent emperor clashed with the vocation of the empire and endangered its future, the gods in their magnanimity were bound to bring to an end the dynastic line and terminate the misfortunes of the State by bestowing power on some other family.

The death of Constantius removed the last obstacle that could prevent Julian from indulging in a feeling of family pride. Now that all real dangers were past, and the men responsible for his private misfortunes were either dead or powerless, Julian could formulate a dynastic theory which both drew inspiration from his Roman patriotism and was in accordance with his doctrine of national destinies. Julian felt

[64] Julian's source for the description of Numa's character and life-style is Plut. *Numa* 3. 6–8; 4. 1–2; 8; 10; 15. 11.

that, if his actions were determined to some extent by the fact that he was born a Roman, and more specifically by his royal origin,[65] what bound him most of all was his belonging to the Second Flavian dynasty, whose founder had set its particular tone. For over three generations this dynasty had been devoted to the cult of Helios, and it is exactly because of his identity as a Flavian that Julian feels entitled to address a hymn to the god (XI. 131c). Only once he has established this important connection can he assert his position in the long chain of emperors stretching back to Numa, with its incontestable solar affinities.

For Julian the dynasty is a mysterious force in the divine hierarchy of national powers: it subsumes in itself the will of its individual members, so that, consciously or unconsciously, they become bearers of the dynastic spirit. The example of Constantine and Constantius, who, without realizing it, behaved in many ways as Flavians owing allegiance to the Sun, is sufficient proof of his argument for Julian. His conversion to Christianity did not prevent Constantine, for example, from encouraging the diffusion of the cult of *Sol Invictus*,[66] whose terrestrial image he was. This latent allegiance of Constantine was to find permanent expression in the pages of the last panegyric composed in his honour by the bishop Eusebius in which the emperor is identified with the sun.[67] Following on this well-established tradition, the pagan rhetor Himerius made a point of recalling the solar origins of the imperial House when addressing Constantius II: 'Oh brightest eye of your race, you who play the same role towards it, as your ancestor Helios often did towards you' (fr. 1, p. 249). Julian himself reproduced the spirit of these words in his *Hymn to King Helios* where he specifically referred to the homage that his predecessors paid to the Sun (XI. 131c).

Yet next to obliging its members to behave in a certain way, the dynasty, as a mysterious spiritual force, may also have a salutary effect on the individual who fails to acknowledge his debt to it and to his race. Thus Constantine and his sons, 'who

[65] XI. 131b; cf. Eunap. *Hist.*, fr. 24: ὅτι ὁ Ἰουλιανὸς ἐν ταῖς ἐπιστολαῖς ἴδιον πατέρα ἀνακαλεῖ τὸν Ἥλιον . . . καὶ αὐτὸς εἰς τὴν ἡλιακὴν βασιλείαν τινὰ καὶ χρυσῆν σειρὰν ἀναφέρων καὶ συναπτόμενος.

[66] For evidence, see G. H. Halsberghe, *The Cult of Sol Invictus*, Leiden 1972, 167-9.

[67] *Tric.* III. 4; cf. *V. Const.* I. 43.

were delivered to the avenging demons (παλαμναῖοι δαίμονες) to be punished for their impiety and for the shedding of the blood of their kindred, were granted a respite by Zeus *for the sake of Claudius and Constantius* [Chlorus]' (X. 335b). The gods themselves, to Julian's mind, thought in terms of dynasties and did not want to see one extinguished ignominiously. When they invested Julian himself with the royal power, they stated this wish very clearly: 'Know that a frame of flesh was given to thee so that thou mightest discharge these duties; for we desire out of respect for thy ancestors to cleanse the house of thy forefathers.'[68]

In his attempt to fulfil the duty thus entrusted to him, Julian seems to have taken an initiative which he saw as fully compatible with the divine will. As he left for the Persian campaign, the childless emperor designated as his successor his nearest relative, Procopius, whom at the same time he also invested with command over a substantial part of the invading forces.[69] But in the course of the expedition Procopius acted with such cautiousness as to anticipate the disastrous behaviour of Grouchy at Waterloo. Ignorant of the movements of his general and fearing the worst, on his death-bed Julian did not even mention him as his successor, but 'seeing no relative of his near-by, he left the decision to the army',[70] which he saw as the surest channel for the expression of the will of heaven.

Julian's views on dynastic legitimacy, as he expressed them through his writings and actions, took a long time to crystallize. But in their final form they appear as the clearest formulation of the Byzantine mystique of kingship. Julian already lived in a world in which a ruler's individual destiny was felt to be inextricably linked with the fate of the universal empire. In his prayer to the Mother of the gods the pious emperor asked for himself perfection in the art of theurgy and true knowledge of divine doctrine together with perfect virtue, that he might successfully undertake the affairs of the State and the army; at the same time he prayed for the holy empire to be granted a

---

[68] VII. 234c. Julian further elaborates the 'teologia dinastica' that Eusebius had expounded for the sake of Constantine in his Τριακονταετηρικός. Cf. Calderone, 'Teologia politica . . .', *Entretiens Hardt* xix (1972), 215–61, and esp. 253 ff.

[69] Amm. XXIII. 3. 2; XXVI. 6. 2.

[70] Lib. XVIII. 273.

blessed lot for many thousand years (VIII. 180b). He further
developed this theme when in the *Hymn to King Helios* he identified not only his personal mission on earth, but also his spiritual
salvation, with the prosperity of Rome (XI. 157b), until in
his *Caesars* and *Contra Galilaeos* he introduced a further idea,
that of the eternity of Rome which he made absolutely dependent on the solar piety of her subjects.[71] The Middle Ages
had dawned.

The concept of a universal *ecclesia* embracing all the faithful
had now emerged thanks to Julian's didactic efforts. But if
Hellenism, the monotheistic universal faith systematized by
the emperor, was to be established as the State cult, then a
strictly organized church in the physical sense of the word was
needed as well. If his attempt to encourage his subjects to
advance along the road of *paideia* was to succeed, Julian clearly
needed to pay some attention to the practical implementation
of his plans.

The shock troops of Julian's religious reform were to be the
priests. Taking over from Iamblichus the concept of the philosopher priest, of the inspired mediator between divinity and
humanity, and conferring authority upon him (as Constantine
had invested his Christian bishop with δύναμις[72]), Julian hoped
to lay the foundations of a powerful and universal pagan
Church. In thinking thus he was not really departing from the
tenets of the Neoplatonic tradition. Rather he was pushing
some of its latest theoretical innovations to their natural
practical conclusion.

Already Porphyry had equated the philosopher with the
priest,[73] and had provided an accurate and extensive description of his ideal ἱερεύς by reproducing the Stoic Chaeremon's
account of the Egyptian priesthood. The main characteristic
of this sacred caste was the possession of ἐπιστήμη acquired by
the constant study of intellectual disciplines and the practice

---

[71] Augustus' speech from the *Caesars* (X. 326b): τὴν Ῥώμην οὕτω διεθέμην
... ὥστε εἶναι εἰ μὴ δι᾽ ὑμᾶς, ὦ θεοί, τὸ λοιπὸν ἀδαμαντίνην. XI. 157b:
δοίη [sc. divinity] ... κοινῇ ... τῇ πόλει τὴν ἐνδεχομένην ἀιδιότητα. *C.G.*
194c: τῆς πόλεως ἡμῶν εἰς τὸ διηνεκὲς προασπίσει .... XI. 131d: ἡ
βασιλεύουσα πόλις, etc.

[72] For Libanius' awareness of this fact, see *ep.* 1543.

[73] *Abst.* II. 3, 49.

of asceticism and contemplation.[74] Till the end of his life
ἐπιστήμη, achieved in this manner, seemed to Porphyry the
only prerequisite of sanctity: 'For an ignorant man, even if he
offers prayers and sacrifices, defiles divinity. The priest alone
is wise, he alone is loved by God, he alone knows how to pray.
And the man who exercises wisdom exercises ἐπιστήμη as regards God, not by perennial litanies and sacrifices, but by the
exercise of divine piety through his actions' (*Marc.* 16–17).

This view was taken over and expanded by Iamblichus, who,
though as a good Platonist he asserted that the knowledge of
God is innate in mankind,[75] also added that only the study,
theoretical and practical, of theurgy by a man already endowed
by divine grace with the priestly vocation[76] could activate that
knowledge.[77] Such a man would then become part of the onto-
logical chain through his position as link between the natural
and the supernatural. By addressing to God the right prayer
and by performing the appropriate rites and sacrifices, the
ἐπιστήμων θεουργός can overturn the action of the powers of
evil which often affect man's soul as well as his body.[78] Thus, by
virtue of the godly ἐπιστήμη he possesses, the Iamblichan priest
appears as the manifestation of the divine among men,[79] the
only repository on earth of divine *gnosis*, as Julian hastened to
explain for the benefit of his flock:

It is befitting to honour the priests as ministers and servants of the
gods; and because they accomplish for us our duties towards the
gods and contribute powerfully towards securing god-sent gifts. For
they sacrifice and pray on behalf of all mankind. It is therefore right
that we should pay them all not less, if not indeed more, than the
honours that we pay to the magistrates of the State. And if anyone
thinks that we ought to assign equal honours to them and to the
magistrates of the State, since the latter also are in some sort dedicated to the service of the gods, as being guardians of the laws,
nevertheless we ought to give the priests a far greater share of our
εὔνοια. The Achaeans enjoined their king to reverence the priest,

[74] Porph. *Abst.* IV. 6–8.
[75] *Myst.* I. 3.
[76] Ibid. III. 20.
[77] See Procl. *In Tim.* 65bc, who reproduces Iamblichan views. For the Chaldean
origin of this conception, id. *In Parm.* (Cousin), p. 990, col. 2, 27 ff.
[78] Iambl. *Myst.* V. 6, 10, 21; VI. 6; VII. 4; VIII. 6; IX. 6.
[79] Ibid. III. 18: ὁ ἐπιστήμων θεουργός. V. 21; VII. 4; etc.

even though he was an enemy; so should we refuse to respect friends, who pay and sacrifice on our behalf? . . . So far as he sacrifices for us and makes offerings and stands face to face with the gods, we must regard the priest with respect and awe as the most valuable chattel of the gods. (*ep.* 89b. 296b–d, 297a)

By circulating this text and the rest of his pastoral letters as much as by his efforts to create a model clergy, Julian sought to change the attitude of his contemporaries towards the social function of the priesthood, which had sunk considerably in public esteem.[80] Indeed the rapid debasement of the social status of the priesthood in late antiquity was not unconnected with the degradation of the old religion.[81]

The introduction of oriental cults into Rome had resulted in the emergence of a new priestly class (drawn by late antiquity from all social strata[82]), whose odd habits and behaviour shocked the middle classes.[83] Again and again in contemporary texts we come across descriptions of itinerant beggar-priests, stripped of all sense of dignity and self-respect.[84] Little by little these mendicant priests became associated in the popular con-sciousness with the members of the public priesthood, and this connection was not wholly unjustifiable in a period in which religious syncretism allowed a Praetextatus to be simultaneously a priest of Vesta and of Sol, a *curialis Herculis* and an Eleusinian hierophant, an initiate of the cult of Magna Mater and a Mithraic *pater patrum*.[85]

Thus at the time when the Christian bishop was beginning to exert his authority over the population of the province,[86] his pagan counterpart was despised even by the adherents of his

[80] On the moral and social debasement of the pagan priesthood, see *epp.* 84 and 89b. 296d ff. Cf. Julian's assertion of the superiority of the clergy over the civil magistrates: *ep.* 84. 431c; *ep.* 88; *ep.* 89b. 289a, 296c.

[81] See E. R. Dodds, *Pagan and Christian in an Age of Anxiety*, Cambridge 1965, 109 n. 1.

[82] Halsberghe, *The Cult of Sol Invictus*, 40 n. 2, for evidence.

[83] See Carmen Codicis Parisini 8084, *Anth. Lat.* i, Leipzig 1894, lines 57–62; [Cyprian], Carmen IV, lines 30–3, *CSEL* III(3).

[84] Apuleius, *Met.* VIII. 24 ff.; cf. also John Chrys. *De S. Bab.* 41 (ed. M. Schatkin, diss., Fordham Univ., New York 1967 (Ann Arbor) = *PG* 50. 544). This point is confirmed by Iamblichus, who also presents Porphyry as sharing the view: *Myst.* X. 2.

[85] *CIL* vi(1), 1779.

[86] See Garth Fowden, 'Bishops and temples in the eastern Roman empire 320–435', *JThS* n.s. xxix (1978), 53–78.

G

own cult because of the utter material degradation to which he had been reduced,[87] yet at the same time he was also feared because of his supernatural authority, which he could express in the form of curses. Thus the very society that invested the priest with his δύναμις, shifted that δύναμις onto the demonic level by failing to recognize the priest as god's representative on earth. Indeed by facing the priest as nothing less than the embodiment of the powers of evil, the ἄθεος καὶ σκοτεινὴ δύναμις (VIII. 173b)—'the godless power of darkness' (VIII. 175bc) which rules over the world of matter—society became responsible for his demotion to the level of a mere purveyor of curses. Julian who, if anybody, was aware of this misplacement of power, goes out of his way in a letter, probably addressed to the governor of Caria,[88] to reject the belief in the maledictions of gods on the grounds of the absence of any historical evidence in support of it (*ep.* 88. 451cd); and, speaking in his capacity of *pontifex maximus*, he states plainly that 'we are ministers of prayers', not curses.[89]

As wise men and links between mortals and the gods, the priests naturally deserved to be the most powerful men in the empire, argued Julian.[90] It has been aptly remarked that in the Roman world power, which still in late republican times belonged exclusively to the upper strata of society, was gradually disseminated over a wider area until, by the era of the Antonines, it had become just power, without social definition: 'once a share had passed from the more generous or slackening grasp of Tacitus' like to a wider circle, it was destined to appear embodied in a thousand shapes, some harmonious with the historic aims and character of Rome, some otherwise.'[91] Aware of this process, Julian undertook to *define* power once more. By conferring it upon the priesthood he sought—just as

[87] Cf. Julian's attempt to restore dignity to the priestly caste, *ep.* 89b. 302d–304d.

[88] For the addressee of the letter, see *Julien* I(2), 101.

[89] *ep.* 88. 451cd. On the right exercise of the curse by the Christian holy man in late antiquity in his role as mediator and arbitrator between God and Man, see Brown, *JRS* lxi (1971), 87–9.

[90] See above, p. 183 n. 80; also Soz. V. 3. 2: μύσταις τε καὶ ἱερεῦσιν, ἱεροφάνταις τε καὶ τοῖς τῶν ξοάνων θεραπευταῖς τὰς παλαιὰς τιμὰς ἀπέδωκε . . . λειτουργιῶν τε καὶ τῶν ἄλλων ὧν πρὶν εἶχον τὴν ἀτέλειαν ἐπεψηφίσατο.

[91] R. MacMullen, *Enemies of the Roman Order*, Cambridge, Mass. 1966, 244.

Constantine had done before him—to confine power within one class and to use it as an instrument of social control.

Julian planned his philosophical clergy to be a hierarchical body with a strict inner organization. At its apex stood Julian himself in his capacity of μέγιστος ἀρχιερεύς and prophet of Apollo Didymaeus,[92] even though informally he submitted to the spiritual authority of his καθηγεμών, Maximus of Ephesus,[93] as by implication he confesses: 'For my part I envy the good fortune of any man to whom God has granted a body built of sacred and prophetic seed and thus singled him out to unlock the treasures of wisdom; yet I do not despise the lot with which God has endowed me, to have been born in the dynasty that rules and governs the world at present' (XI. 131b).[94] That man of prophetic calibre was Maximus, to whom a vague but exalted place had been allotted in the ecclesiastical hierarchy.

Under the *pontifex maximus* stood the regional high priests, most of whom, if not all, were Neoplatonists of the Iamblichan type. Thus Theodorus, a pupil of Maximus, became on his recommendation the high priest of Asia,[95] while Chrysanthius of Sardis and his wife Melite—both intimate friends of Maximus—were appointed by Julian high priests of Lydia, after their refusal to join the emperor at Court.[96] Arsaces was the high priest of Galatia,[97] and Seleucus, the philosopher friend of Julian, was yet another high priest, possibly of Cilicia.[98] The hierophant of Eleusis, who had initiated Julian into the

[92] *ep.* 89b. 298d; *ep.* 88. 451b; cf. *ep.* 89b. 302d, where Julian alludes to his office as president of the Collegium Pontificale in Rome; cf. Lib. XII. 80: χαίρει καλούμενος ἱερεὺς οὐχ ἧττον ἢ βασιλεύς.

[93] *ep.* 89a. 452a; *ep.* 89b. 298b. Cf. p. 34 n. 96.

[94] For the idea that the prophetic soul is the gift of God see Procl. *In Remp.* II. 118. 4 ff.

[95] 'Theodorus 8' in *PLRE*. Julian addressed to him *epp.* 30, 89a and 89b, and probably *ep.* 79. He was appointed ἄρχειν τῶν περὶ τὴν Ἀσίαν ἱερῶν ἁπάντων ἐπισκοπουμένῳ τοὺς καθ' ἑκάστην πόλιν ἱερέας καὶ ἀπονέμοντι τὸ πρέπον ἑκάστῳ (*ep.* 89a. 452d). For Maximus as the κοινὸς καθηγεμών of both Julian and Theodorus, see *epp.* 89a. 452a and 89b. 298b.

[96] See Eunap. *V. Phil.* VII. 4. 9.

[97] On Arsaces, see *PLRE*, 'Arsacius 3'. Julian addressed to him *ep.* 84.

[98] See *PLRE*, 'Seleucus 1'. In his *ep.* 770, written in 362, Libanius says of Seleucus that before that date he occupied himself with civil administration, τὰ δὲ νῦν βωμοὶ καὶ νεῷ καὶ τεμένη καὶ ἀγάλματα κοσμούμενα μὲν ὑπὸ σοῦ κοσμοῦντα δέ σε καὶ γένος ... Σὲ ... βοηθοῦντα τῶν ἱερῶν τοῖς κειμένοις. After 351, Seleucus spent some time with Julian in Bithynia (Lib. *ep.* 13), and was among the emperor's intimate friends during his stay at Antioch, cf. J. *ep.* 86.

mysteries and had played an important role in his election as
Augustus in Paris,[99] had been entrusted by the emperor with
the supervision of the temples in Greece.[100]

In their turn, these high officials of the pagan Church were
entitled to appoint local priests,[101] who remained under their
authority.[102] Ideally these priests conformed to the image of
the Iamblichan sage, and indeed Hierax,[103] Hesychius,[104] Theodora,[105] Callixena,[106], and the anonymous recipient of Julian's
ep. 87, all seem to have done so. Yet, despite Julian's good intentions and efforts, men of questionable moral integrity seem
to have entered the ranks of the clergy, quite apart from the by
no means insignificant number of dubious priests already in
office.[107] This situation was soon to cause Julian distress, which
he expressed in a series of letters addressed to high priests,
reiterating what he conceived to be the spiritual, moral and
social duties of the priesthood.[108] He had no interest in the
material possessions or social background of candidates for the
priesthood, but he was most insistent that τὸ φιλόθεον καὶ τὸ
φιλάνθρωπον were absolute prerequisites for those who would
enter the sacred body.[109] This radical measure was fully in
character with a man who had proclaimed and already proved
by his actions that in all spheres of public life appointments
were to be made exclusively on the basis of merit—a policy
which caused much dissatisfaction and criticism.[110]

[99] See above, pp. 51; 74 n. 112. M. P. Nilsson, *Geschichte der griechischen Religion* ii,
Munich 1974³, 351 n. 5, suggests that the Eleusinian hierophant in question is
the same as *PLRE* 'Nestorius 2', grandfather of Plutarch. Saffrey and Westerink,
however, doubt it (*Théol. plat.* i, p. xxix n. 5).

[100] Eunap. VII. 3. 9: τὸν ἱεροφάντην ἀπέπεμψεν ἐπὶ τὴν Ἑλλάδα ... πρὸς
τὴν ἐπιμέλειαν τῆς Ἑλλάδος ἱερῶν.

[101] Eunap. *V. Phil.* VII. 4. 9; cf. *ep.* 89a. 452d.

[102] *epp.* 84. 430a; 89a. 452d.

[103] Hierax was a priest at Alexandria in Troas; cf. Lib. *epp.* 796, 1352.

[104] See Lib. *ep.* 724.

[105] See *PLRE* 'Theodora 3'; Julian addressed to her *epp.* 85–6 and possibly
ep. 87 too.

[106] From *ep.* 81 we learn that Callixena was priestess of Demeter and of the
Mother of the gods at Pessinus, Phrygia.

[107] Such as Pegasius, cf. *ep.* 79: see also above, p. 28.

[108] See *epp.* 84 and 89, where Julian announces that he will soon circulate full
instructions concerning the matter. See also Greg. Naz. *or.* IV. 111, possibly reproducing the main lines of a lost 'pastoral letter'.

[109] *ep.* 89b. 305a ff.

[110] Cf. above, pp. 98 and 119–20.

As an adept of Iamblichan Neoplatonism, Julian devoted considerable attention to the ritual of Hellenism. He even seems to have made an attempt to evolve a pagan liturgy composed mainly of religious hymns, which he held to represent the word of the gods themselves,[111] while he required priests to address private prayers to God at least at dawn and dusk each day, so as to assure divine protection for the empire.[112] In asserting the importance of prayer, Julian was reproducing the teaching of Iamblichus, for whom prayer was a magical act whose performance ensured that the soul was purged of all impure and mortal elements.[113] Julian also insisted that prayer should ideally be offered in the temples where the omnipresence of the gods was richly suggested by means of human art.[114] The worshipper's communion with the divine was to be further heightened by the spectacle of the officiating priest, dressed for the occasion in magnificent robes—a point on which Julian lays particular emphasis.[115] Here also Julian follows the Pythagorean–Neoplatonic tradition which requires the priest, when standing face to face with his god, to be an awe-inspiring figure. The full explanation for this practice (which was not unknown to the Christians) is given by a late representative of the Iamblichan tradition, Proclus: 'Whoever has an intimate knowledge of divine lore knows that in sacred mythology priestly robes symbolize incorporeal life' (*In Remp.* II. 246, 10 ff.). On the same page Proclus alludes to a clergy, no longer in existence, that dressed and officiated according to the Iamblichan ideal: 'And those devoted to the gods, when invoking them or possessed by them, used to wear variegated garments and girdles in imitation of the divine life towards which all their efforts were directed' (*In Remp.* II. 246, 23 ff.).

As the public man *par excellence*, the Julianic priest was expected to possess not only ἐπιστήμη, but also perfect virtue. As Porphyry observed: 'If they think that they honour the gods,

---

[111] *ep.* 89b. 301d–302a: Soz. V. 16. 2. Pletho, who was inspired by Julian in his attempt to revive Hellenism, as the patriarch Gennadius notes, also evolved a pagan liturgy; see M. V. Anastos, 'Pletho's Calendar and Liturgy', *DOP* iv (1948), 183–305.

[112] *ep.* 89b. 302ab.

[113] *Myst.* V. 26.

[114] *ep.* 89b. 297a.

[115] Ibid. 303b.

and if they believe in the existence of the gods, yet neglect to
be virtuous and wise, they negate and dishonour the gods'
(*Marc.* 23). This could almost have been Julian's definition of
the priest. His social role, dependent on his wisdom and goodness, was at once didactic and philanthropic, for his mission
was to diffuse all over the empire the Julianic notion of *paideia*,
at least in its religious aspect.[116] But outside the temple the
awesome officiant and the authoritative preacher was to become
a modest and affable human being, full of solicitude for his
fellow-men; for 'the gods have not made us so astonishingly
rich, that we may bring reproach on them by disregarding the
poor who go about in our midst.'[117] The Homeric notion of
φιλοξενία, the classical virtue of μεγαλοψυχία and the broader
Hellenistic ideal of φιλανθρωπία may have been at the back of
Julian's mind as he urged his priests to perform charitable
works. Yet his moving passages on universal brotherhood are
uniquely animated by the spirit of the age in which he lived:
'Whether he likes it or not, every man is akin to every other
man' (*ep.* 89b. 291d). For this reason

> we ought to share our money with all men, but more generously with
> the good, and with the helpless and the poor so as to suffice for their
> need. And I would add something which might appear paradoxical,
> that it would be an act dear to the gods to share our clothes and food
> even with the wicked. For it is to the humanity in man that we give
> and not to his specific character. (*ep.* 89b. 290d–291a)

The saintly disposition behind these words may be found in
all ages, but the way of expression is distinctly post-classical.[118]

The channels through which organized charity was to be
conveyed to society at large were welfare institutions for which
the emperor had already reserved generous subsidies.[119] In each
city there were to be founded orphanages, hostels for travellers,
asylums for the poor and colleges of study for men and women
who wanted to follow their philosophic vocation.[120] The parallel
with the methods of Christianity is obvious enough. Yet what
should capture our attention is not the sterile speculation on

---

[116] Greg. Naz. *or.* IV. 111.

[117] *ep.* 89b. 289d–290a.

[118] For a similar sentiment attributed by Diogenes Laertius to Aristotle, see
V. Philos. V. 17.

[119] *ep.* 84. 430c.

[120] *epp.* 84 and 89b. 289a ff.; Greg. Naz. loc. cit.; Soz. III. 16. 2.

whether or not Julian exploited Christian models for the further-
ance of the pagan cause, but the realization that we are here
dealing with a man deeply rooted in his century, able to think,
feel and act according to the categories imposed upon him by
his own environment.

At the same time as Julian regulated the duties of his priesthood, he also issued a law on temples, which decreed that provincial governors were not to undertake any new projects until
they had completed those started by their predecessors, 'ex-
ceptis dumtaxat templorum aedificationibus'.[121] Like the edict
on education, this law too may have been accompanied by a
document in which the emperor explained in detail the reasons
why he commanded the reconstruction of temples and expounded his theories on the artistic value of religious symbols.
For Julian the aesthetic aspect of *paideia* was of paramount
importance—but not for merely aesthetic reasons. To his mind,
art and literature were complementary concepts, expressing
one and the same thing: Greek *paideia* or Greek religion. In the
Misopogon, through his description of the traditional feast that
he was expecting to attend at the temple of Apollo at Daphne,[122]
the emperor conveys his deep respect for an art dependent for
its life on religious enthusiasm, and kindled by the study of
philosophy and the preaching of the priest. Certainly Julian
had a very definite idea of the function of art in religion. Indeed,
this Byzantine Hellene was the first to define the nature and
function of the symbols of worship in exactly the terms which
are to be found in the Acts of the Seventh Oecumenical Council
restoring the icons: 'Our fathers established statues and altars,
and the maintenance of undying fire, and, generally speaking,
everything of the sort as symbols of the presence of the gods, not
that we may regard such things as gods, but that we may worship the gods through them' (*ep.* 89b. 293ab). This passage is
further complemented by a definition—utterly Byzantine in
spirit—of the religious icon as neither wood nor stone nor yet
the god himself.[123]

---

[121] *C.Th.* XV. 1. 3 (29 June 362); cf. above, p. 111.

[122] Quoted below, pp. 205–6.

[123] *ep.* 89b. 294bc; cf. J. D. Mansi, *Sacrorum conciliorum nova et amplissima collectio*
xiii, Florence 1767, 377e: καὶ ὁ προσκυνῶν τὴν εἰκόνα προσκυνεῖ ἐν αὐτῇ τοῦ
ἐγγραφομένου τὴν ὑπόστασιν.

The same proposition holds true of God's representative on earth: 'We do not say that the imperial images are a piece of wood or stone or copper, still less that they are the emperors themselves' (*ep.* 89b. 294bc). The parallel between divine and imperial worship is significant. Indeed Julian's systematic exploitation of iconography and of all the other means of imperial propaganda at his disposal was yet another way of proclaiming his ideal of the unity of the spiritual, cultural and political life within the empire: 'And on the public images he took care that next to him should appear Zeus, as if descending from heaven and presenting to him the imperial insignia, the crown and the purple; he would also show Ares and Hermes gazing at him as if to testify that he was skilled in the art of writing and warfare.'[124]

Julian did not simply substitute his own *imago* for the Constantinian *labarum*; he also made a conscious attempt to reassociate the cult of the emperor with that of the traditional gods. Styling himself as Apollo and his dead wife as Artemis, he set up two gold-plated statues in Nicomedia where he expected them to be worshipped; ὅθεν καὶ ἄπειρον πλῆθος κλαπὲν εἰς εἰδωλολατρίαν κατέπεσεν[125]—'as a result of which an infinite number relapsed to idolatry, without their even realizing it.' The more articulate of Julian's contemporaries realized only too well what was the objective of his policy. Gregory of Nazianzos for one, admittedly after his enemy's death, fulminated against the man who had conceived of 'linking for ever the traditional Roman laws with the worship of idols'.[126] Yet the type of imperial cult that Julian championed was in spirit and execution alike as far removed from the 'traditional Roman laws' as the form of religion that the emperor had expounded. Gregory saw correctly that for Julian these two things had now become inextricably linked together, though he failed, or refused, to perceive how drastically they had both

[124] Soz. V. 17. 3. Bowersock shows a complete misunderstanding of the situation when he says that 'the arch pagan Julian ... used the imperial cult for laughs with just as much unselfconsciousness as Seneca'; 'Greek intellectuals and the imperial cult in the second century A.D.', *Entretiens Hardt* xix (1973), 186.

[125] Παραστάσεις σύντομοι χρονικαὶ (Preger) 47; cf. Soz. V. 17. 5: ἐσπούδαζε κλέπτειν τῶν ὑπηκόων τὴν προαίρεσιν. For the theme cf. the Orghidian cameo (R. Calza, *Iconografia romana imperiale da Carausio a Giuliano (287–363)*, Rome 1972, No. 486), if the figures represented there are indeed those of Julian and Helena.   [126] Greg. Naz. *or.* IV. 81.

been redefined before becoming a unity. Indeed the two fundamental principles of Julian's reform were hieratism, as expressed in his innovations in the fields of religion and of political
theology, and hierarchy, as illustrated in his organization of
Church and State. These two notions, strongly characteristic
of both Mithraism and Neoplatonism, were as foreign to the
classical world as they were crucial to Byzantium. It is indeed
paradoxical that Julian, who was regarded by posterity as the
man who dreamed of resurrecting the ancient religion and of
returning to obsolete forms of government, should in fact have
broken so completely with the religious and political patterns
of the ancient world.

His obsession with unity, wholeness and order was entirely
Byzantine. Significantly enough, Julian did not even conceive
of the possibility of sharing his power with an associate, but
faced himself as God's sole vice-gerent on earth: Εἷς θεὸς εἷς
'Ιουλιανὸς ὁ Αὔγουστος—Εἷς θεὸς 'Ιουλιανὸς βασιλεύς—'God is
one and one is Julian the emperor', as his votive inscriptions
proclaimed. And, just as God is immortal, so too is his representative on earth. The Roman empire over which he rules is
in principle at least coextensive with the *oikoumene*, for those
inhabited territories that happen still to be outside its limits,
will soon be integrated in it thanks to the victorious efforts of
the pious *basileus*.[127]

A bronze *exagium* from Geneva conveys the same message
even more clearly than these inscriptions. From it there gazes
out at us the grave face of an emperor-monk. Dressed in the
austere *paludamentum* of a Roman soldier, and encircled in a
sumptuous crown, the 'cosmocrator' Julian receives the wreath
of victory from a winged Nike. His prominent eyes stare into
infinity, while with his raised hand he bestows his blessing on a
world that he holds in his palm.[128] Unlike Marcus Aurelius,
who strove not to become drunk with power, and regarded the
Roman emperors as simple mortals,[129] Julian ultimately
adhered to a hieratic conception of kingship—ἀπεκαισαρώθη.

[127] See *CIL* 14176; 14175¹; 14172; 14172²: Αὔγουστε 'Ιουλιανὲ νικᾶν
ἐγεννήθης; *BCH* (1900), p. 577: 'Ιουλιανὸς ἐνίκησεν εὐτυχῶς τῷ κόσμῳ
cf. E. Peterson, Εἷς Θεός: *Epigraphische, formgeschichtliche und religionsgeschichtliche
Untersuchungen*, Göttingen 1926, 271–2; also *CIL* 14149³⁸⁻⁴⁰: Νικᾶν ἐγεννήθης
βασιλεῦ ἀθάνατε—'you were born for victory immortal king!'
[128] Calza, No. 472.   [129] M. Aurelius, VI. 30.

VI. TOWARDS THE PERSIAN CAMPAIGN

In 356 Julian had bitterly criticized Alexander for his monstrous arrogance in claiming that he was not really Philip's, but Ammon's son.[1] Yet before six years of his condensed existence had passed by, the young emperor officially declared that he was himself the son of Helios. Though this parallel between the behaviour of the two men may be purely fortuitous, there were plenty of other signs that Julian had now begun consciously to imitate Alexander.

The decision to attack Persia seems originally to have been conceived as a solution to Julian's political problems. Just as in Gaul it was thanks to his activity that Roman territories had been won back and the frontier stabilized,[2] so the emperor now hoped to be able to free the populations along the eastern frontier from the permanent threat of Persian invasion.[3] But if such were the considerations that occupied Julian's mind during the days that followed his entry into Constantinople and inspired the moderate tones of the *Letter to Themistius*, by early 363 this modest mood had been left far behind. For in his race along the road of Byzantinism Julian had passed the milestone of theocracy, and now thought himself responsible towards his God for the spiritual salvation even of those outside the embryonic pagan Church, whether Christians within the empire or pagans without.[4]

All these radical thoughts were effortlessly articulated by

[1] I. 45d–46a.
[2] Amm. XXV. 4. 14.
[3] Amm. XXII. 7. 8.
[4] See the revealing passage Lib. XVIII. 282: 'we expected the whole empire of Persia to form part of that of Rome, to be subject to our laws, receive its governors from us and pay us tribute; they would, we thought, change their language and dress, and cut short their hair, and sophists would turn Persian children into orators in Susa; our temples here, adorned with Persian spoils, would tell future generations of the completeness of the victory, while he who had accomplished all this would set up prizes for those who celebrated his exploits in panegyric with admiration for some and without disdain for others, with pleasure and without annoyance at their efforts, and there would be more delight in oratory than ever before; dead men's tombs would give place to temples, and every man of his own free will would make his way to the altars.'

Julian in the language of a tradition which, because of its very diversity and wealth, could easily be made to embrace and express a whole new world. Thus any expansion eastwards in which political motives were mingled with civilizing pretensions was bound to be conceived in terms of the heroic exploits of Alexander the Great, whose life-story had already passed into the realm of folklore. Rather than despising him for his folly, at this stage Julian regarded him as a model and a hero, as his uncle had done before him.[5] He was even to go beyond Constantine and see himself as a reincarnation of Alexander.[6]

In the gradual development of all these tendencies, and in the systematic articulation of his theories, Julian seems to have evolved in a straightforward and even predictable fashion. It is true that he was always subject to inner tensions, due mainly to the antagonism between his education and the demands of his profession. But in most cases Julian knew how to reconcile the principles on which he had been brought up with a realistic attitude towards the problems that he faced; until there came a moment when this happy continuity in his inner development was broken. The pattern of psychological tension no longer suffices to explain Julian's behaviour during the Persian campaign, which has rightly been pronounced to be the greatest problem of Julianic historiography.[7]

In all senses the Persian campaign was a failure. This failure, as Ammianus gives us to understand, was not so much the work of untoward fortune as the result of bad planning and worse execution. To use the same tactics as in Gaul was undoubtedly a mistake: the vastness of the Persian empire and the harshness of the weather during the summer months should have dissuaded Julian from planning an expedition on the model of his previous one—fighting for a few months of the year and then

---

[5] See Lib. XVII. 17: Ἀλεξάνδρου τοῦ φίλου τε αὐτῷ καὶ οὐκ ἐῶντος καθεύδειν. Cf. N. Baynes, 'Julian the Apostate and Alexander the Great', *Byzantine Studies*, 346–7, who brings evidence from the *Vita S. Artemii*. Cf. the golden medal showing Constantine and Alexander in profile (from the Cabinet des Médailles, BN, Paris).

[6] See Socr. III. 21. 7.

[7] 'Before it criticism sinks powerless, for it is a wonder-story and we cannot solve its riddle. The leader perished and the rest is silence': N. H. Baynes, 'Constantine's successors to Jovian: and the struggle with Persia', *Cambridge Medieval History* i, 1924², 81.

retiring to winter quarters.[8] But Julian was an excellent general,[9] as he had proved in his German campaigns, which were a good example of his ability to adapt his strategy to circumstances as they arose. Did he then lose his military touch, and if so, when, how and why? In Ammianus we read that, soon after Julian had left Antioch for the Persian expedition, while he was still at Circesium, he received a letter from Sallust in which the prefect of Gaul begged that the emperor should not expose himself to inevitable destruction by undertaking the expedition. Julian disregarded the wise advice of his counsellor and confidently continued on his way.[10] This incident is the first in a long series of analogous episodes which effectively illustrate Julian's progressive self-deception and estrangement from his counsellors. Soon the emperor came not only to disregard the opinion of experienced administrators and generals,[11] but also to despise all human knowledge and wisdom and even the art of divination.[12] After repeatedly ignoring the warnings of the Etruscan soothsayers, who vainly tried to dissuade him from undertaking the campaign, Julian pushed *hybris* to the extreme and defied the gods themselves:[13] as bad omens multiplied, the emperor set himself against Mars in an act of supreme defiance.

As Ammianus describes the growth of Julian's *hybris*, his narrative is increasingly pervaded by an atmosphere of doom. The accumulation of bad omens and gloomy hints, which anticipate Julian's death, creates a haunted climate which would suffice by itself to make us guess that at the end of all this some great catastrophe is awaiting the hero. But, as in a Greek tragedy, the catastrophe is not simply the outcome of a

[8] Commenting on Julian's lack of foresight in planning his campaign, Paschoud (Zosime, *Histoire nouvelle* II(1), p. xxii n. 3) remarks that Julius Caesar, who projected a similar invasion of Persia, estimated that his expedition would last three whole years (cf. Dio Cass. 43. 51. 1).

[9] Amm. XXV. 4. 11.

[10] Amm. XXIII. 5. 4–5.

[11] Amm. XXIV. 6. 5; 7. 3–4.

[12] Amm. XXV. 2. 7–8. An interesting parallel to Julian's behaviour is provided by Alexander who, relying on the philosophers of his entourage, disregarded the advice of the Chaldean magi, who had warned him against entering Babylon, cf. Diodor. XVII. 112. 1–5; Arrian, *Anab.* VII. 16. 5–6.

[13] Amm. XXIV. 6. 17. This point was not missed by Augustine, who repeatedly refers to Julian's ὕβρις during the Persian campaign: *Civ. Dei* IV. 29; V. 21.

collision between an innocent being and blind external forces. Ammianus is careful to present the change in Julian's fortune as the direct result of his change in attitude. There is a relation of cause and effect between the two, just as in the earlier parts of the narrative Julian's prodigious good fortune is presented as deriving from his wisdom and piety. As Ammianus' account of Julian's life unfolds, it seems as if the historian is gradually losing confidence in his hero. A first sinister note is struck in the middle of Book XXII as Julian prepares to leave Constantinople: 'elated by his successes, Julian now felt more than mortal aspirations'—'ultra homines iam spirabat' (XXII. 9. 1). But this clear allusion to his plan to invade Persia is not pursued any further. On the contrary, during the early period of Julian's stay at Antioch, Ammianus' remarks on his character are all favourable:[14] 'recognizing the hastiness of his somewhat excitable disposition, he allowed his prefects and associates freely to curb his impulses, when they led him away from what was fitting, by a timely admonition; and at times he showed that he regretted his errors and was glad to be corrected.'[15] This was a basic feature of Julian's nature which reappears in Ammianus' summary of the emperor's character: 'in disposition he was somewhat inconsistent, but he controlled this by the excellent habit of submitting, when he went wrong, to correction.'[16] What was it then that led Julian to belie over the last period of his life so conspicuous an aspect of his character, and when did he begin to behave in an authoritarian—almost an insane—manner?

Ammianus again is the source who can best help us if not to elucidate this problem, then at least to locate it within its chronological framework. His narrative suggests that Antioch was the place where things went wrong. It is significant that both Julian's entry into the city, and his departure are explicitly associated by the historian with death.[17] Doom is presaged through the multiplication of bad omens and calamities that afflict the empire right at the moment when Julian is feverishly preparing the campaign whose successful outcome will enable

[14] Amm. XXII. 9. 16 ff.; XXII. 12. 5.
[15] XXII. 10. 3.
[16] XXV. 4. 16.
[17] XXII. 9. 15; XXIII. 2. 5–6.

him to add 'to the tokens of his glorious deeds the surname of Parthicus'.[18] It is in this connection that Ammianus first alludes to the shaking of Julian's self-confidence; disregarding the political repercussions of his acts and giving free rein to that *levitas*, that was to prove so fatal to him, Julian pushed his religiosity to morbid extremes in order to ensure the happy outcome of an undertaking, which was opposed by at least half his army:[19]

He drenched the altars with the blood of an excessive number of victims, sometimes offering up to 100 oxen at once, with countless flocks of various other animals, and with white birds hunted out by land and sea: to such a degree that almost every day his soldiers, who gorged themselves on the abundance of meat, living boorishly and corrupted by their eagerness for drink, were carried through the squares to their lodgings on the shoulders of passers-by from the public temples where they indulged in banquets which deserved punishment rather than indulgence; especially the Petulantes and the Celts, whose wilfulness at that time had passed all bounds. Moreover the ceremonial rites were excessively increased, with an expenditure of money hitherto unusual and burdensome. And, as it was now allowed without hindrance, everyone who professed a knowledge of divination, the learned and the ignorant alike, without limit of prescribed rules, were permitted to question the oracles and the entrails, which sometimes disclose the future; and from the notes of birds, from their flight, and from omens, the truth was sought with studied variety, if anywhere it might be found. (Amm. XXII. 12. 6–7)

These are the first signs of extravagance in the previously temperate Julian, signs which betray the state of mind of a man falling increasingly under the domination of one idea: the defeat of Persia. This obsession is conveyed in a multitude of ways. The *solidi* that Julian now strikes, on which he appears in full armour and dragging a bound captive by the hair,[20] and the inscriptions set up all over Syria hailing the emperor as born for victory,[21] proclaim one and the same message. The dream of Persian

[18] Amm. XXII. 12. 2. For the calamities that afflicted the empire during Julian's stay at Antioch, cf. Amm. XXII. 13.

[19] For a good analysis of the different political and religious attitudes of East and West towards the Persian campaign, cf. D. Conduché, 'Ammien Marcellin et la mort de Julien', *Latomus* xxiv (1965), 359–80.

[20] Cf. J. P. C. Kent, *Roman Coins*, London 1978, No. 690.

[21] See above, p. 191.

conquest blunts Julian's political acumen: to keep his soldiers satisfied, he feeds them daily on large quantities of sacrificial meat, and lets them indulge in what they like even at the expense of civilians.[22] Any defeatist tendency within the ranks of the army is crushed before it is even manifested, while the only sure guarantee for the happy outcome of Julian's project is sought in his ever closer link with the supernatural.[23]

So much we can find in Ammianus: that Julian, at the moment of embarking on the Persian campaign, showed the first signs of an authoritarian behaviour which was to evolve in inverse proportion to his loss of self-confidence, and alongside his increasing obsession with the conquest of Persia. Julian himself, of course, makes much more important revelations about his mood at this time. Having now fallen under the spell of one major idea, he at first set out to prove that this was not the dream of a madman, but a reasonable ambition which had fired many a predecessor of his. In a work of apparently satirical intent Julian commemorated the feast of the *Saturnalia* for 362 by explaining to everybody how the political mission of the empire and its spiritual vocation were interdependent.

Julian's personal mixture of the Neoplatonic and Mithraic theologies serves as the background of this Menippean satire. Kronos-Saturn, reclining on a couch of gleaming ebony, presides over the council of the gods, gathered together in order to judge the merits of the Roman emperors. The dazzling blackness of his bed, which no eye can endure, symbolizes infinite time, a concept which Mithraists identified with the First Cause. Next to his father lay Zeus on a couch 'more brilliant than silver and whiter than gold' (X. 307cd), the two metals associated with Helios and Selene, while Rhea and Hera sat beside their husbands on thrones of gold. Quirinus and Heracles, the national gods of *Romanitas* and Hellenism, are the mediators between the immortals and their own descendants, Quirinus for Julius Caesar and all the Roman emperors, and Heracles for Alexander who, for obvious reasons, was the only Greek leader to take part in the contest for imperial supremacy.

[22] Amm. XXII. 12. 6–7; cf. Lib. XVIII. 168.
[23] See Amm. XXII. 14. 4; XXIII. 3. 2, 3. 7, 5. 8; Lib. XVII. 18; XVIII. 162, 172; XXIV. 35: τίνα εἰκὸς εἰρῆσθαι περὶ τούτου τοῦ τὰς ἁπάντων τῶν Ἑλλήνων ἐν τοῖς δύο ἔτεσι παρελθόντος θυσίας;

Julian's own divine ancestor, Helios,[24] also plays a decisive part in the satire. Thanks to him the unworthy emperors Commodus and Elagabalus are spared any biting criticisms, while Aurelian is dispensed from any further punishment, for the unjustified murders that he committed, by the personal intervention of the god whose cult the otherwise criminal emperor had made the State religion (X. 314a). Again, at the very end of the satire, when final judgement has been pronounced on each monarch, and special guardian deities have been allotted to those outstanding emperors who, after being short-listed, had stood before the tribunal of the gods and claimed the title of the best, Helios-Mithra appears as Julian's personal guide; while the hope for a better life awaiting the faithful adept of the god of light is expressed through a formula characteristic of the Eleusinian Mysteries—μετὰ τῆς ἀγαθῆς ἐλπίδος—often mentioned by Plato, taken over by the *Chaldean Oracles*, and constantly recurrent in Julian's own writings.[25]

In the upper region of the sublunary sphere, where Fate rules supreme, the deified Roman emperors hold their banquet. In a while they are all to appear one by one before the divine tribunal to be judged for their actions. And in his careful reconsideration of the policies of his predecessors Julian betrays his own preoccupations and allows us to formulate the questions for which he was so urgently seeking an answer from history. Above all the emperor needed to establish the axiom of the eternity and universality of Rome and to recall the felicity promised her by the gods: 'What other city began with 3,000 citizens and in less than six centuries carried her victorious arms to the ends of the earth?' (X. 320ab). But against this optimistic theme there also runs through the *Caesars* the sinister leitmotiv of Persia, the hereditary enemy, who is left undisturbed to pursue her arrogant policies. In his first panegyric Julian had observed, in a rather dispassionate academic tone, that:

The Persians in the past conquered the whole of Asia, subjugated a great part of Europe and had embraced in their hopes, I may almost

---

[24] Cf. Eunap. *Hist.*, fr. 24; see above, p. 179.

[25] Ἀγαθὴ Ἐλπίς in Plato, *Phaedo* 67c; *Rep.* 496e; etc.; in J. VIII. 180c; VII. 233d; *ep.* 89b. 298d; *ep.* 136; *ep.* 89a. 452c. See also Lobeck, *Aglaophamus*, 69 ff., and Cumont, *Lux Perpetua*, 401–5.

say, the whole inhabited world, when the Macedonians deprived them of their supremacy, and they provided Alexander's generalship with a task, or rather with a toy. But they could not endure the yoke of slavery, and no sooner was Alexander dead, than they revolted from his successors and once more opposed their power to the Macedonians and so successfully that, when we took over what was left of the Macedonian empire, we counted them to the end as foes with whom we must reckon. (I. 17cd)

But since then Julian had come a long way and he was now well able to grasp, and not only in intellectual terms, the state of mind of a Caesar crying upon hearing of the monuments erected to commemorate Alexander's exploits.[26] The Macedonian, who owes his presence among the short-listed Roman emperors to his having been the only one who ever succeeded in realizing what to the rulers of the Roman empire remained but a dream, has a few sarcastic remarks to make on the subject. Checking the misplaced arrogance of Julius Caesar, he reminds him of the 'Persian arrows': 'And if you think the conquest of Persia such a trifle, and disparage so glorious an achievement, tell me why, after a war of more than 300 years, you Romans have never managed to conquer even a small piece of that land beyond the Tigris, where the Parthians rule?' (X. 324d). Trajan's impressive, but abortive, attempt to conquer Persia only serves in this context to throw Julian's future achievement into relief.[27]

Perhaps the *Caesars* contains, if not the definitive answer to the enigma of the disastrous Persian campaign, at least a plausible explanation of it. Realizing that his religious and military policies were meeting with dangerously strong opposition at Antioch and elsewhere, Julian had begun to feel his self-confidence shaken. In the unfortunate state of mind in

---

[26] X. 322c; cf. Plut. *J. Caes.* 11. 5–6; Suet. *J. Caes.* 7.

[27] The superiority of the Persians was recognized by the Romans themselves; cf. M. Iunianus Iustinus, *Epit. Hist. Phil. Pomp. Trogi* XLI. 1. 7: 'soli ex omnibus gentibus non pares solum, verum etiam victores fuere.' On the other hand the exploits of Alexander were a persistent incitement to the Romans to follow his example (cf. V. Chapot, *La Frontière de l'Euphrate de Pompée à la conquête arabe*, Paris 1907, 379–80). By the end of the third century, this mixture of fear and ambition found its expression in an oracle which affirmed that no Roman emperor would ever advance further than Ctesiphon, Historia Augusta, *Carus* 9. 1: 'Hanc ego epistulam idcirco indici, quod plerique dicunt vim fati quandam esse, ut Romanus princeps Ctesifontem transire non possit, ideoque Carum fulmine absumptum, quod eos fines transgredi inperet qui fataliter constituti sunt.'

which he now found himself he reacted against disillusionment by questioning his principles and theories against the yardstick of tradition. But in doing so his perceptions were conditioned by the particular obsessions he had now developed to counter-balance his lost self-confidence. And as was to be expected, reflection on the history of the Roman state led Julian to what he had been seeking for: the vision of a peaceful universal empire to which Persia would be annexed. If the decision to attack Persia had already been made in Constantinople, it is only through the *Caesars* that we realize the degree of intensification reached by this theme in Julian's mind. 'Driven like a madman and consumed with tiny obsessions to begin with, he then came to the very depth of misfortune'[28] by actually embarking on the Persian expedition.

Yet through his constant references to Tyche—another great theme of the *Caesars*—we may detect Julian's greatest worry. Would Fortune invariably favour him as she had Augustus? (X. 330a.) The constant visits to the Tychaeon at Antioch[29] are surely a pointer to Julian's troubled state of mind over this period, while Alexander's bitter remark to Caesar about Pompey is equally characteristic: 'When he was deserted by Fortune, who had so long favoured him, you easily overcame him, thus unaided' (X. 323).

Equally important as a leitmotiv of the *Caesars* is the idea of piety. Julian, as he frequently proclaimed on his inscriptions, had been an invincible emperor so far,[30] and he felt that his piety was the only real pledge he could offer the gods, so that they continued to favour him. He expressed this *unconscious* feeling (for, surely, Julian never faced his devotion to the gods as a bargain) by allowing Marcus Aurelius to emerge as the winner of the contest (X. 335c). The philosopher-king, who had regarded the imitation of the gods as his only end in life (X. 333c), received the majority of their votes and was thus proclaimed the best Roman emperor. In heaven, where he had now gained full citizenship (X. 335d), Zeus and Kronos became his special patrons.[31]

[28] Greg. Naz. *or.* V. 8.
[29] XII. 346b; fr. 176; cf. Amm. XXIII. 1. 6.
[30] See above, p. 191 n. 127.
[31] In his admiration of Marcus Aurelius Julian went beyond all conventions, cf. Eutrop. X. 16. 3.

This was a genuine judgement on Julian's part.[32] The man who, elsewhere, had asserted in all sincerity that ruling over the whole *oikoumene*, Roman and barbarian together, was as nothing compared to the bliss of having gained some glimpses of the divine,[33] and who concluded all his speeches with a prayer for the salvation of his soul, only came to be whole-heartedly involved in the fortunes of the empire through the conviction that by doing so he was obeying the wish of the Immortals. In order to be able to consider his duty on earth as worthy of himself he had, once he had evolved a theocratical theory of kingship, to regard everything in the sublunary universe as potentially divine. But he never exiled himself completely into that universe, however strong his sense of commitment to the terrestrial city may have been. The point was soon to come when Julian ceased to make any concessions to the world in which he lived or to question his own hard-won values by exposing them to the harsh light of reality. Indeed, towards the end of his reign, Julian effectively became immune to the views, advice and criticisms of others, developing at the same time a strongly aggressive attitude towards whoever did not share his outlook and agree with his opinions. It is this streak in Julian's character that permeates the whole of his last literary composition, the *Misopogon*—

> ce rire amer
> de l'homme vaincu, plein de sanglots et d'insultes.[34]

'Raging against them all one by one [the members of the Senate of Antioch] as recalcitrant and stubborn, he composed an invective, which he entitled *The Antiochene* or *Misopogon*, in which he enumerated in a hostile spirit the faults of the city, including more than were justified.' If we believed Ammianus (XXII. 14. 2), we would conclude that the only motive behind the genesis of the *Misopogon* is wrath and that the work is a biased and exaggerated criticism of the historian's native city. Yet Julian seems to have conceived the composition of this work in quite a different light: under the impact of the disturbing discovery that in the eyes of his subjects he was a

---

[32] Cf. VII. 211d.
[33] VII. 222bc; cf. Plotinus, *Enn.* I. 6. 7.
[34] Charles Baudelaire, *Les fleurs du mal*, *LXXIX, Obsession*.

ridiculous and much hated ruler, he felt the urge to plead his cause before them; and in the *Misopogon* he saw his last hope of doing so convincingly. He had had a deep shock, and reacted against its unpleasantness by attempting an objective appraisal of his own person and policies. But in so behaving, Julian counted without himself. He disregarded that harsh element in his nature that he owed to his Dalmatian heredity, which education had superficially polished without softening, far less eradicating. Over a moment of frustration his uncle Constantine, whom Julian so much resembled, would resort to some act of supreme violence, of which he would later repent. Julian's deeply moral and cultured nature was still capable of experiencing the same fits of anger as his uncle, though he could not resolve them by means as drastic. Instead, he momentarily directed his rage against himself, and then let it burst against abstract notions, rather than against particular people, whom he felt unable to harm simply in order to indulge a personal emotion, however strong. Having been hurt and humiliated by the Antiochenes, Julian lost his sang-froid and, like a wronged child, he set out to tell them how bad they were and how good he was himself.[35]

The author's moralizing intention, the sarcastic tone of his remarks and the deep indignation to which the *Misopogon* owes its genesis, are all characteristics of conventional satire.[36] Yet the streak of personal passion in it is too strong and the occurrence of autobiographical passages too frequent for a 'satire de mœurs'. We are presented with an extraordinary text, impossible to classify within the conventional limits of any literary genre. In its pages the author justifies his past behaviour as

[35] O. Seeck had already noticed Julian's systematic self-praise in the *Misopogon*, *Geschichte des Untergangs der antiken Welt* iv, Berlin 1911, 243–4: 'Es gibt in der Literatur aller Länder und Zeiten wohl kein zweites Beispiel, das ein Schriftsteller seine eigenen Tugenden mit solcher Breite und Selbstgefälligkeit aufzählt, wie dies Julian in seiner Streitschrift gegen die Antiochener tut.' The *Misopogon* was published at the Tetrapylon of the Elephants near the Royal Street which served as an entrance to the palace (Malalas, *Chronographia* (Dindorf), p. 328), for Julian judged it necessary that the whole city should be in no doubt about his opinion of it.

[36] The ultimate object of the satire—the only literary genre that the Romans did not inherit from the Greeks (see Quintilian, *Inst. Or.* X. 1. 93 and Horace, *Serm.* I. 10. 65–6)—was the moral criticism and correction of society (Persius, Juvenal). The genre was often the vehicle for deep indignation and even wrath; cf. Juvenal, I. 45: 'Quid referam quanta siccum iecur ardeat ira . . .?'

both private and public man, professes his credo as a moral thinker and a statesman, and hints at the policy he is to follow in the future. Yet the *Misopogon* also contains a straightforward account of the events that caused the emperor and the citizens of Antioch to fall out with each other.

The indignation that Julian felt towards the members of the Antiochene Senate was inspired by their reluctance to assist him in putting an end to the corn scarcity that hit Antioch in 362.[37] Whether the councillors were ever in a position to co-operate with the policy that the emperor adopted is not to the point.[38] Julian believed that they could, and that it was out of indifference that they had not.[39] Naturally, such an attitude angered him. His anger was reinforced when he saw his sub-sequent efforts to solve the economic crisis being marred by the selfish speculations of the rich. As the Senate did nothing to terminate the scarcity, Julian fixed a maximum price for corn and ordered 40,000 measures of wheat from the neighbouring towns (XII. 369a). No sooner had the supplies arrived, than they disappeared from the market. Julian then offered the city large quantities of wheat destined for his own use (XII. 369b), but they too were immediately bought up by speculators and sold on the black market.[40] At this point Julian addressed bitter complaints to the *curiales* for their dishonest attitude (XII. 369d–370a).

That Julian did not understand that price control,

[37] The two main causes of the scarcity were a bad harvest (Amm. XXII. 13. 4; Lib. XVIII. 195; *ep.* 699. 3, referring to 362 as a particularly bad year) and the sudden increase in the population of the city, as Julian was accompanied by one of the largest Roman armies ever assembled. Zosimus (III. 13. 1) gives the number as 65,000. See Piganiol, *L'Empire chrétien*, 158 n. 3. Socrates (III. 17.2) is the only source that mentions the connection between the presence of Julian's troops in Antioch and the corn scarcity.

[38] Ammianus and Libanius clearly say that the *curiales* could not help Julian over the economic crisis (Amm. XXII. 14. 2; Lib. I. 126; XVI. 21 ff.). For a discussion of the question, see Petit, *Libanius*, 111 ff.; also Liebeschuetz, *Antioch*, 130 ff., who mentions in this connection the conflict between the city's interests and those of councillors as landowners and producers of corn, a point confirmed by Julian (XII. 350ab).

[39] XII. 368d.

[40] XII. 368d–369c. For a fuller discussion, based as well on the evidence of other sources than the *Misopogon*, and attempting to give an objective account of the situation at Antioch during the economic crisis of 362, see Petit, *Libanius*, 108–18.

unaccompanied by rationing, is not an adequate measure to halt food scarcity, is fully in character with a man who had a naïve belief in the basic goodness of human nature;[41] he was convinced that all that was needed to bring out the good elements in a man was the right *paideia*,[42] and accordingly had set out to be the educator of the entire *oikoumene*.

In the particular case of Antioch Julian had not tried to win the citizens to his cause by merely preaching abstract principles. In his desire not to be left behind by his predecessor,[43] he had befriended the city even before he set foot in it (XII. 367c), and had bestowed upon it a number of material favours.[44] Now he intended to increase its power and splendour still further, and possibly even had it in mind to make Antioch the capital of the empire.[45] But for a variety of reasons the city did not show any signs of gratitude towards the emperor. What appeared to Julian as the culmination of the Antiochenes' ingratitude was the way in which his efforts to settle the economic crisis were met: 'Those whom I have fed are ungrateful to me', he exclaims, referring to the ordinary people ($\delta\hat{\eta}\mu\sigma$), 'and as for the others, they hate me' (XII. 370b). The emperor was convinced that it was over the particular issue of the famine that the $\delta\nu\nu\alpha\tau\sigma\iota$ came to hate him,[46] but he suspected too that his devotion to the gods, his austere morals, even his love of justice and his humane and liberal attitude towards his subjects, had all contributed to his universal unpopularity in Antioch.[47] 'For

[41] In this Julian was unique. It is not possible to compare Diocletian's edict on maximum prices and Julian's measure, for, while Julian was dealing with an emergency that was confined to a limited area, Diocletian was inaugurating an economic policy with universal application. (See Diocletian's edict in M. Giacchero, *Edictum Diocletiani et collegarum de pretiis rerum venalium*, Genoa 1974.)

[42] See I. 9a; VII. 228; on Gallus, V. 271d–272a.

[43] Constantius had poured material benefits on Antioch: cf. I. 40d.

[44] XII. 366d. An enumeration of the favours that Julian bestowed on the Antiochenes is to be found in XII. 365b, 367d–368a, 370d–371a.

[45] XII. 367d; Lib. XV. 52, 53. Cf. Petit, *Libanius*, 200 ff., who, though announcing that he will attempt to detect Julian's motives for such a plan, confines himself to a discussion of the situation in Antioch from the religious point of view. Perhaps the real reason behind Julian's alleged plan was that whoever intended to fight Sassanian Persia needed Antioch as his capital.

[46] XII. 368c: τὸ δὲ δὴ μέγιστον, ἐξ οὗ τὸ μέγα ἤρθη μῖσος. Cf. Lib. XV. 76: Julian's treatment at Antioch may well have been responsible for Libanius' idea that the emperor was killed by a Roman.

[47] XII. 357d, 365d. For Julian's devotion to the gods, see specifically: XII. 344b: φοιτᾶς εἰς τὰ ἱερά, δύσκολε καὶ δύστροπε καὶ πάντα μοχθηρέ. Cf.

the man who wants to be bad considers as his enemy the one who does not allow him to be bad', Libanius observed, as he watched the Antiochene mob feast on the news of Julian's death. 'It is in the midst of such a crowd, enemy to the gods, that I have to live', he added sadly (*ep.* 1220. 3).[48] Even Julian hardly uses such bitter language when talking about the heavily Christianized city of Antioch—yet behind his relative moderation one detects a sadness much more pervasive than Libanius'.

Near Antioch, in the pleasant suburb of Daphne, stood the famous temple of Apollo, renowned for its colossal chryselephantine statue of the god, a copy by Bryaxis of that of the Olympic Zeus.[49] Before the emperor arrived in Antioch, he wrote a long letter to his maternal uncle Julian, whom he had appointed to the post of *Comes Orientis*, giving him minute instructions as to how special care should be taken to restore the temple to its original splendour.[50] He also took care to send one of his priests, Pythiodorus, who reached Antioch in time to organize the cult of the gods from the ritual point of view, before his own arrival.[51] Having made all these arrangements, Julian expected that everything would be perfect when the great moment of the annual festival of Apollo came. But reality disappointed him cruelly:

And I imagined in my mind the sort of procession it would be, like a man seeing visions in a dream, beasts for sacrifice, libations, choruses in honour of the god, incense and the youths there surrounding the shrine, their souls adorned with all holiness and themselves attired in white and splendid raiment. But when I entered the shrine I found there no incense, not so much as a cake, not a single beast for sacrifice. For the moment I was amazed and thought that everything was still outside the shrine and that you were waiting the signal from me, doing me that honour because I am supreme pontiff.

XII. 346bc. On his austere morals: XII. 342d–344a: ἀφεὶς δὲ τὴν σκηνὴν καὶ τοὺς μίμους καὶ τοὺς ὀρχηστὰς ἀπολώλεκας ἡμῶν τὴν πόλιν, ὥστε οὐθὲν ἡμῖν ἀγαθὸν ὑπάρχει παρὰ σοῦ πλὴν τῆς βαρύτητος. On his love of justice and humanity: XII. 343d, 353b, 354d–355a. On his 'pseudo-liberal' attitude: XII. 343cd.

[48] XII. 357d, 363a; see also Petit, *Libanius*, 200 ff.
[49] Amm. XXII. 13. 1.
[50] *ep.* 80.
[51] Lib. *ep.* 694. 6–7.

But when I began to enquire what sacrifice the city intended to offer to celebrate the annual festival in honour of the god, the priest answered: 'I have brought with me from my own house a goose as an offering to the god, but the city this time has made no preparations.' (XII. 361d–362b)

This incident made a deep impression on Julian. He hastened to express his indignation to the Senate in a long speech, in which he criticized the attitude of the city bitterly (XII. 362b–363c), but his words failed to evoke any response from the *principales*. It was otherwise, though, with the god who, confirming Julian's prophecy, 'forsook the suburb which for so long He had protected' (XII. 363c): during the night of 22 October 362, the temple of Apollo and the colossal statue of the god were completely destroyed by fire.[52] The emperor did not blame the Christians for the incident, which he seems to have regarded as an act of divine intervention punishing an irreligious city. He did not even express his personal feelings at the catastrophe. One would have expected a lamentation on the ruin of the temple, but Hellenism, and especially declining Hellenism, was too sacred and painful a topic for Julian to exert on it his rhetorical skill. *The Lamentation on the Temple of Apollo at Daphne* was for a man like Libanius to compose. And indeed he did the job brilliantly. As Julian confessed, his oration was 'such as no other man "of the stock of which mortals now are" could have composed' (*ep.* 98, cf. Homer, *Il.* A 272). Libanius' emotion at the disappearance of Bryaxis' masterpiece was deep and genuine as he wrote of the divine love (ἔρως) that a thing of beauty can at times kindle in a human heart. In what remains of his monody the rhetor has succeeded in conveying the aesthetic essence of Hellenism both in its unity pervading all aspects of life, and in its now threatened continuity. And yet it is only after reading this artful oration, where spontaneity of feeling is matched by a truly masterly prose, that we can fully understand the tragedy of Julian's life. For Libanius Hellenism was a set of cultural and aesthetic values, capable of inspiring in him the same nuance of adoration that a man like Synesius felt for the heritage of classical Greece.[53]

[52] Amm. XXII. 13. 1–3.
[53] Lib. XXX. 23, 42, 44–5, three passages that make clear that the author's attitude to Hellenism was one of purely aesthetic contemplation and mourning

These men, unlike Julian, worshipped Culture and stopped there. Yet in the whole of Antioch Libanius was the only man in whose company the emperor could feel somewhat at home,[54] as Julian himself complained in a melancholy passage in which he described the acute intellectual and moral isolation he experienced amidst the Antiochenes.

From what Julian tells us in the *Misopogon*, however, the actual burning of the temple of Apollo should be regarded as irrelevant to the causes that little by little induced the emperor to adopt a hostile attitude towards the Antiochenes. Their 'irreligiousness', frivolity and fanatic love of entertainment,[55] on the other hand, did estrange Julian increasingly,[56] though none of these habits would by itself have been adequate to arouse in his heart the feeling of 'ira', that Ammianus detected in him,[57] far less the hatred that, as Libanius for one was certain, Julian now felt towards the whole of Antioch.[58]

Julian believed that hatred was fully reciprocated by the Antiochenes.[59] When the emperor addressed a particularly vehement speech on the subject of Daphne to the *principales*,

over the 'cultural wreckage' that Hellenism was undergoing. See Liebeschuetz, *Antioch*, 11–12. See also Festugière, *Antioche*, 229–40; his point is valid only for Libanius and those who, like Libanius, embraced what Petit calls 'un paganisme moral et politique' (*Libanius*, 196), or 'littéraire', as Festugière prefers to qualify it (op. cit. 230 n. 3). As has been shown, such an attitude to Hellenism was entirely foreign to Julian and to the practising Hellenes of his circle.

[54] In XII. 354c Julian mentions Libanius as a friend of Hermes and of himself: Ἑπτὰ γάρ ἐσμεν οἵδε παρ' ὑμῖν ξένοι νεήλυδες, εἷς δὲ καὶ πολίτης ὑμέτερος, Ἑρμῇ φίλος καὶ ἐμοί, λόγων ἀγαθὸς δημιουργός, οἷς οὐδέν ἐστι πρός τινα συμβόλαιον, οὐδὲ ἄλλην ὁδὸν βαδίζομεν <ἢ> πρὸς τὰ τῶν θεῶν ἱερά, καὶ ὀλιγάκις, οὐ πάντες, εἰς τὰ θέατρα.

[55] On their irreligiousness: XII. 345a, 361b: πολλοὶ μὲν ἐγειρομένους ἄρτι τοὺς βωμοὺς ἀνέτρεψαν, οὓς ἡ πρᾳότης ἡμῶν ἐδίδαξε μόλις ἡσυχάζειν. On their fanatical love of entertainment: XII. 342b–d, 346ab, 351a, 357d–358a; cf. Herodian II. 7. 9: οἱ τὴν Ἀντιόχειαν κατοικοῦντες . . . σχεδὸν παρὰ πάντα τὸν ἐνιαυτὸν ἑορτάζουσιν ἔν τε τῇ πόλει καὶ κατὰ τὰ προάστεια; ibid. II. 8. 9. For the frivolity and insensitivity of the Antiochenes see also Lib. XXXV. 11; XXIII. 26–7 and *ep.* 739.

[56] Cf. the word ξένοι in XII. 354c.

[57] Amm. XXII. 14. 2: 'ira sufflabatur interna'; XXIII. 2. 4: 'nondum ira, quam ex compellationibus et probris conceperat, emollita.' After the departure of Julian, Libanius addressed an oration to the Antiochenes with the characteristic title Πρὸς Ἀντιοχέας περὶ τῆς τοῦ Βασιλέως ὀργῆς (*or.* XVI).

[58] Lib. XVI. 53.

[59] Ibid.: νῦν δὲ μισεῖ καὶ μισεῖσθαι πέπεισται ὁ Ἀπόλλωνος φίλος ὑπὸ τῶν Ἀπόλλωνος τροφίμων.

far from showing any signs of repentance for their professed
'atheism',[60] 'they chose another place than the Senate for
making their defence' (XII. 364a)—the market-place. Julian
also gives us to understand that those who composed vulgar
anapaests ridiculing his person, and sang them all over Antioch,
probably on the occasion of the New Year feast,[61] were incited
by the *principales*.[62]

The coarse jokes and slanders that were 'both uttered and
listened to throughout the whole city',[63] were mostly directed
against Julian's physical appearance, ascetic tastes and religious
devotion.[64] The emperor was deeply hurt by this attack on his
dignity, carried out by all classes in the city, and was confirmed
in his suspicion that Antioch now hated him (XII. 345c). The
venomous satire he now composed exploited those criticisms
that could easily be turned into pretexts for self-praise, but
refrained from commenting on what was self-evidently ridiculous about his person: his small stature, and the grand airs he
gave himself, which fitted so ill with his physical appearance.[65]
He sensed himself to have been immensely humiliated and his
embitterment was so much the greater for his feeling that it
was a city that he had benefited that had turned unanimously
against him.

It is on the subject of what Julian regards as 'the blasphemies'
against his sacred person (XII. 364a) that he first mentions the
collective punishment that ought to be inflicted on the city.
Starting from the punishment that they would have deserved—
execution—Julian proceeds through an anticlimactic structure

[60] XII. 363a. The main points of Julian's speech to the senators are reproduced
in the *Misopogon*, XII. 362b–363c.

[61] XII. 356c: οἱ δὲ ὑπ' ἐλευθερίας εἰώθασι κωμάζειν, ἀεὶ μὲν ἐπιεικῶς
τοῦτο ποιοῦντες ἐν δὲ ταῖς ἑορταῖς πλέον. Cf. Liebeschuetz, *Antioch*, 229.

[62] XII. 364a, of the *curiales*: ὑμεῖς [κατεδράματε ἐμοῦ] . . . ἐπὶ τῆς ἀγορᾶς
ἐν τῷ δήμῳ διὰ τῶν ἱκανῶν τὰ τοιαῦτα χαριεντίζεσθαι πολιτῶν. Libanius,
on the other hand, holds that a few foreigners only were responsible for the
disturbances (XVI. 31–3).

[63] XII. 364b; cf. 355d–356a.

[64] XII. 338d, 345cd, 355a, 364b ff. Cf. Amm. XXII. 14. 3; for the display of
black humour on the part of the Antiochenes, ibid. XXIII. 1. 5.

[65] See Amm. XXII. 14. 3: 'Ridebatur enim ut Cercops, homo brevi humeros
extentans angustos et barbam prae se ferens hircinam, grandiaque incedens tamquam Oti frater et Ephialtis, quorum proceritatem Homerus in immensum extollit.'
For Julian's iconography, see Calza, *Iconografia romana*, 364–91 and pls. CXXIV–
CXXXIII.

to assure the Antiochenes that he is not going 'to slay or whip or fetter or imprison or punish any of them' (XII. 364c). On the contrary, he grants them all the full right to go on ridiculing him in anapaestic verses, using even greater παρρησία. Refraining from inflicting on the city a physical sanction, which by its very nature would be partial and therefore unfair, Julian chooses to punish his undisciplined subjects by having recourse to a spiritual rather than simply moral sanction, which will apply to them all: he leaves Antioch, determined never to return again.[66]

Yet in the way in which Julian announces his departure, he lets us see all the damage that the attitude of the Antiochenes has done to his self-confidence: he will now move to another city, Tarsos in Cilicia, not because he is hoping that its inhabitants might like him, but because, according to his strict sense of justice, he feels that his subjects should share in turn in the bitter experience of his unpleasant manner (XII. 364d). This pathetic remark, which Julian intends to be sarcastic, is indicative of the way in which his self-confidence had been undermined, for it contradicts one of the main themes of the *Misopogon*—the emperor's attempt to prove how great his popularity was throughout the empire. He is never tired of emphasizing how much he is loved by the brave Celts, who had the opportunity to get to know him well over the years he spent in Gaul. Having pushed love for their leader to the very limits of altruism, they abandoned their homes and way of life for his sake and followed him to the end of the world (XII. 360c). His reputation as a brave, wise and righteous ruler, a skilful administrator and a formidable soldier, a man easy of access

---

[66] XII. 364d; Amm. XXIII. 2. 4: 'Cumque eum profecturum deduceret multitudo promiscua . . . loquebatur asperius, se esse eos asserens postea non visurum.' In the oration that he addressed to Julian on behalf of the Antiochenes (*or.* XV), Libanius grasped Julian's point: παίζεις, ὦ βασιλεῦ, πρὸς ἄνδρας ἀτυχοῦντας. τί φῄς; οὐ δημεύεις οὐδὲ σφάττεις οὐδὲ φυγαδεύεις, ἀλλὰ μισεῖς καὶ δυσμενεῖς νομίζεις καὶ καταλείπεις. τοῦτο δέ ἐστιν ἡ μεγίστη δίκη (55). Conversely, in the oration addressed to the Antiochenes, Libanius lets them understand that he believed that Julian, now full of wrath and hatred for the city, was bound to inflict serious punishments on it (XVI. 41). Implying that Julian was on the wrong side, even if his intentions were good (XVI. 23), he invited his fellow-citizens to show repentance before the irreparable happened: τούτων εἰ λέγοι τις βέλτιον, πρῶτος ὑπακούσομαι, εἰ δ' ἐνθάδε σιγήσας οἴκοι με κακῶς ἐρεῖ, θαυμάσεταί με τοῦ χειμῶνος ἅμα δάκρυσιν (XVI. 57).

and mild of temper, was spread throughout the empire by the Celts (ibid.); and Julian takes pleasure in contrasting their purity of heart and morals with the false and self-indulgent ways of the Antiochenes.[67] He claims that they influenced him as much as the tutors of his early youth (one of whom anyway was a Goth[68]), and they trained him to become a better person (XII. 350d); indeed their simple and frank ways had as great an effect on the formation of his character as the reading of Plato and Aristotle (XII. 359bc)—for it is primarily from these two masters that he derived his inability to mix with the licentious crowds and to consider material ease (τρυφή) as the happiest condition in life.[69]

It is interesting that in an autobiographical text Julian should juxtapose as formative influences 'the Hercynian forest' and Greek *paideia*, considering them of equal importance in the moulding of his character. The ἀμουσία of the boorish Celts (XII. 342a), which had provided him with an object of complaint when he was living in their midst,[70] he did not consider a mortal sin, for it was only a lack of intellectual refinement, and not a lack of respect towards the gods or the political traditions of the empire. But the ἀμουσία of the Antiochenes— the incompatibility of his notion of *paideia* with their ways of

[67] XII. 359cd, 342a.

[68] Mardonius: see above, p. 15 n. 10.

[69] XII. 359c: γέγονεν οὖν μοι μετὰ τὴν ἐκ παίδων τροφὴν ἥ τε ἐν μειρακίοις ὁδὸς διὰ Πλάτωνος καὶ Ἀριστοτέλους λόγων οὐδαμῶς ἐπιτηδείῳ δήμοις ἐντυγχάνειν καὶ ὑπὸ τρυφῆς εὐδαιμονεστάτῳ εἶναι (Lacombrade); the implication of the readings that Hertlein and Reiske suggest for this passage is that Plato and Aristotle are incompatible with the tastes of such people as the Antiochenes. On Julian's opinion of those who consider τρυφή as the highest goal in life, cf. XII. 356d. Τρυφή, in the sense of softness, luxuriousness, wantonness, is a highly pejorative term in Julian and Zosimus, who sometimes use it to denote simple material ease—a notion that a writer like Themistius conveys with the word ῥᾳστώνη. Behind this disagreement about the semantic content of two linguistic terms is to be found the divergence of two thought-worlds (cf. Dagron, T&MByz iii. 119). On the τρυφή of the Antiochenes, see XII. 339a: ἁβρότης βίου, ἁπαλότης τρόπου. XII. 340b: τρυφῶσα πόλις. XII. 342a–d; XII. 358a: τρυφερὰ καὶ πλουσία πόλις. XII. 359c; 365a: a reference to Ἀσσύριος πλοῦτος. XI. 365b. See D. Levi, *Antioch Mosaic Pavements* i, Princeton 1947, 206; 224, describing the personification of Τρυφή on two mosaics from Antioch; also Festugière, *Antioche*, 12.

[70] See above, pp. 66–7; cf. *ep.* 8: τὰ δ᾽ ἐμά, εἰ καὶ φθεγγοίμην ἑλληνιστί, θαυμάζειν ἄξιον. οὕτως ἐσμὲν ἐκβεβαρβαρωμένοι διὰ τὰ χωρία.

life—shocked him profoundly.[71] The barbaric ethos, Julian felt, had this at least in common with Greek philosophy: a healthy aversion to materialism.

This theme of the 'noble savage' had been canonized as a *topos* of ancient rhetoric; thus it was a question of taste and personal predilection whether one had recourse to it or not when talking about the Germans. Ammianus Marcellinus for one saw the ideal barbarians of the *Misopogon* as utter brutes, echoing in this the opinion of his fellow-Antiochenes.[72] Yet what is tragic is that when Julian idealizes his barbarians he is not consciously making use of a literary cliché. He believes what he says, and it is precisely on this idyllic image of the pure Celts that the bulk of his argument concerning his popularity as a ruler rests. Self-deception allows Julian to close his eyes to the real Celts as they are described by Ammianus, and this is precisely what makes him appear so pathetic in the *Misopogon*.

The emperor goes on to point out that the extraordinary affinities that link him with the Celts are not purely coincidental; for he is himself descended from the Mysians, a tribe which lives on the banks of the Danube (XII. 348d). As is to be expected, both he and his family display the major traits of the Mysian character; they are totally boorish, austere, awkward, insensitive to the charms of Venus and inflexibly attached to their ancestral traditions (ibid.). Julian's theory of Ethnic Gods and national characteristics thus provides a convenient starting-point from which he sets out in search of the reasons for the hostility that Antioch displays towards him. To his mind only heredity can be held to explain satisfactorily their mutual incomprehension and the deep contempt they felt for each other's manner (XII. 348b–349b).

Before ever setting foot in Antioch, Julian goes on to recall, he had prejudged its citizens. Having in mind that they were of Greek descent,[73] and following his theory of national characteristics, he had jumped to the conclusion that they would

[71] On the ἀμουσία and insolence of the Antiochenes, see Philostrat. *V. Apoll.* I. 14; 16–17; III. 58. Cf. Lib. XXIII. 27: ὦ Μουσῶν ὑμεῖς ἐχθροί, an apostrophe to his compatriots.

[72] Amm. XXII. 12. 6–7.

[73] XII. 367c and Lib. XI. 44–130, a long discussion of the mythology and history of Antioch, arguing for its purely Hellenic character.

conceive for each other 'the greatest possible affection' (XII. 367c). This expectation was founded on the assumption that he himself by personal choice, and the Antiochenes by right of birth, enjoyed a common culture (ibid.). Experience disappointed him, as he ingenuously confesses in the same passage where, of course, he avoids expressing his surprise at the discovery that practice can belie theory. After this realization, he prefers the road of self-deception, which will enable him to keep his theoretical edifice intact, to that of recognition of his fault, which would lead to a radical questioning of his way of thinking and of facing people. Posing as the arbiter of Hellenism, he convicts the Antiochenes of ἀμουσία (XII. 359c), rejects entirely any claims that they may have to Greek culture, and finds it only natural that they should have failed to understand and like him. Julian was able to treat the Antiochenes in this way and still remain consistent with his theory of national characteristics because he believed (with special reference of course to Christianity) that a race could become so degenerate as to reject its own culture—but then this race was condemned to doom.[74]

These qualities of the Antiochene temperament, which so much irritated Julian, their inability to control passion and their fundamental frivolity, are raised by him to the level of racial hallmarks. He supports this assertion by evidence drawn from Plutarch[75] and from contemporary history, which so effectively illustrates the moral gulf that separates the Celts from the Antiochenes (XII. 359d–360b). Naturally Julian blames himself for having expected that the Antiochenes would belie both their history and their contemporary reputation. 'In my folly I failed to understand aright from the beginning what the character of this city was, and this despite my having read no fewer books than any one else of my own age' (XII. 347a). Julian is not posing here. His outburst is sincere, for he is furious at having allowed himself to disbelieve what he had read in his books, and thus be led into a situation where he is exposed to ridicule and abuse.

Had he sincerely believed that the Antiochenes had reached the last stage of degeneration, Julian should have ignored them,

---

[74] See above, pp. 162–3.
[75] XII. 347b–348b, 358a–359a; cf. Plut. *Demetrius* 38; *Cato* 13.

refusing to take their criticisms so much to heart. But he was shocked, shaken and hurt by their attitude,[76] and went on trying to reassert his popularity with them by comparing them repeatedly not only with the Celts, but also with other Syrian cities, who had proved that they loved Julian more than their own sons.[77]

At the same time Julian puts a lot of energy into refuting the one assertion of the Antiochenes that cast radical doubt on his competence as a ruler: their accusation that he had turned the world upside down. The brutality with which this remark was formulated impressed Julian to such an extent that twice in the *Misopogon* he reproduced it verbatim:[78] 'Indeed I am not aware of turning anything upside down, either voluntarily or involuntarily' (XII. 360d), was his direct answer to the Antiochenes. But Julian felt that the point needed systematic refutation and so he devoted a substantial part of his satire to dealing with it. These are the apologetic pages of the *Misopogon* in which Julian attempts to rehabilitate his reputation as a good ruler. Childish provocations against the Antiochenes and tasteless self-praise are now abandoned; and the voice of a broken man is heard, whom a great and inexplicable misfortune has reduced to humility.

The ardent admirer of Plato, the indefatigable soldier of Mithra, had dreamed of a state founded on the principle of justice. In his capacity as emperor, he explained, he regarded himself as the guardian of law, the mediator between divinity, in the form of the Idea of justice, and humanity.[79] He knew, he remarked, that by assuming such a role, he would only gain enemies (XII. 354d–355a), but, confident in the teaching of

[76] Festugière seems to be the only one to have grasped the point of the *Misopogon*. 'Julien en fut blessé. Il se souvint à propos que cette tourbe indocile était ἄθεος. Ce dernier trait envenima la blessure. *Il n'en fut pas la cause première.* Tel est à mes yeux le fond du débat' (*Antioche*, 85, my italics); 'par dessus tout, les Antiochiens sont indisciplinés' (87); commenting on XII. 356d, Festugière remarks: 'ici se manifeste la vraie cause du ressentiment de Julien. Il a beau dire: "Puisque les dieux ne se formalisent pas d'une cité si indépendante et négligent de la punir, j'aurais bien tort de me fâcher et de m'emporter contre elle" (356d–357a). Au vrai il a été blessé. Et il parle avec l'amertume d'un être blessé' (88).

[77] XII. 361a; cf. 359c.

[78] XII. 360d: παρ' ἐμὲ τὰ τοῦ κόσμου πράγματα ἀνατέτραπται (σύνοιδα δὲ οὐδὲν ἀνατρέπων ἐμαυτῷ οὔτε ἑκὼν οὔτε ἄκων). XII. 371a: εἰκότως ὑμῖν φαίνομαι τὸν κόσμον ἀνατρέπειν.

[79] XII. 354d: ἐπὶ τῆς μεσιτείας αὐτοὺς ἐτάξαμεν. See above, p. 175.

Plato, he chose to aspire towards becoming 'the perfect champion of virtue.[80]

As a man striving towards such a goal, and aware of the greatest problem faced by any human society, that of the continuous antagonism between poor and rich, πένητες and δυνατοί, Julian chose to stand on the side of the former, yet without allowing himself to be deceived by the greediness and dishonesty often displayed by that class.[81] Thus in the lawcourts, he forced the rich to behave with moderation, but he also prevented the poor from making money by acting as informers (XII. 344a). His main preoccupation was how to guarantee that 'the poor should suffer no injustice whatever at the hands of the rich' (XII. 343a),[82] and he illustrated this attitude at Antioch when during the economic crisis he sought how best to offer assistance to the mass of the people who were being wronged (XII. 370b). After having behaved in such a way he cannot understand why, rather than being regarded as a benefactor, he is treated with such hostility:

> What, I ask, is the reason of your aversion and your hatred of me? For I know well that I have done no terrible or incurable injury to any one of you individually or indeed to your city as a whole; nor have I uttered any disparaging word, but I have even praised you ... and I have bestowed on you all the advantages that you could reasonably expect from a man who desires to be, within the limits of his power, the benefactor of humanity. (XII. 366cd)

This is the complaint of an honest man who has been misunderstood and wronged. 'Why, in the name of the gods, am I treated with ingratitude?' (XII. 370c) is the phrase that recurs like a leitmotiv throughout the *Misopogon*. Yet Julian never remains for long in this helpless mood. His embitterment alternates with righteous indignation at the spectacle of the ungrateful crowd: he will stop acting as an arbiter in the city's internal conflicts and, 'entrusting the whole matter to the care

---

[80] XII. 353d–354a: τέλειος ... νικηφόρος ἀρετῇ (or ἀρετῆς), a quotation from Plato, *Leg.* 730d. A theme that had acquired almost obsessive dimensions in Julian's mind: cf. III. 100c; II. 81a and *Leg.* 728a.

[81] Cf. Lib. XVIII. 183: καὶ οὐ τοῖς μὲν πλουτοῦσιν ἠναντιοῦτο καὶ δίκαια λέγουσι, μετὰ δὲ τῶν πενομένων καὶ ἀναισχυντούντων ἦν.

[82] Cf. III. 90d. Ammianus often congratulates Julian on this trait of his policy, XV. 5. 15; XVIII. 1. 1.

of Adrasteia', he will for ever turn his face away from Antioch (XII. 370b).

The citizens ought, Julian suggests, to remember how his brother Gallus had behaved a few years ago, when over a similar crisis a riot had broken out in their city. They ought to recall too the punishment then inflicted (XII. 370c) and, making the obvious comparison, understand how just, humane and conciliatory a ruler Julian is. After the parallel has been drawn, the emperor announces solemnly that he will not punish, but simply ignore, his ungrateful subjects. This sensational declaration is exceptional not only by the standards of the fourth century, but especially in view of the context in which it is found. And yet, in reality it epitomizes the spirit of theocracy: far from being lenient, it is the most terrible of punishments, for it means that by averting his face from Antioch the representative of God on earth deprives the city of divine protection, and literally 'entrusts it to the hands of Adrasteia'.

Julian lived in a century that witnessed the triumph of abstract thinking. As he showed in Antioch, he could think of human beings exclusively in terms of mental categories: he regarded the population of the city as forming a perfect organic unity[83] and found all classes equally disgusting, because they all felt towards him the same hatred and ingratitude. His natural response to such a situation was to inflict a collective punishment. Yet, in acting so, Julian inflicts more suffering upon himself than upon those whom he punishes, for he has to admit that he has now renounced one of the dearest illusions of his youth. In Gaul, when Constantius' agents attempted to stop him from helping the unprivileged classes, the Caesar had thought that to die in defence of such a cause would have been a noble fate: 'To me at least it seems a disgraceful thing . . . that I should abandon my post as defender of the miserable when my duty is to fight against such thieves with the help of the God who posted me here' (*ep.* 14. 385c). The enthusiastic

---

[83] XII. 356a: ταύτης ὑμῖν ἐγὼ τῆς ὁμονοίας συνήδομαι, καὶ εὖ γε ποιεῖτε μία δὴ πόλις ὄντες τὰ τοιαῦτα. XII. 357d–358a; also 370b: τὴν πόλιν δὲ εἶναι τὰ πρὸς ἐμὲ γνώμης μιᾶς. Julian's evidence contradicts Lacombrade (*Julien* II(2), 151) and Petit (*Libanius*, 232), who see in the *Misopogon* an attempt on the emperor's part 'to divide the population of the city by raising the plebs against the bourgeoisie' (Petit, loc. cit.).

H

belief in his vocation which could elicit such a sentiment from Julian contrasts dramatically with the embitterment, weariness and disgust that possess him as he describes his abortive attempt to stand by the ἀδικούμενον πλῆθος in Antioch: 'I knew even then that in acting like this I would not please everybody, yet I could not care less, for I thought it was my duty to assist the mass of the people who were being wronged' (XII. 370b). If the idea expressed in these two passages is the same, the spirit and the tone in which it is uttered reveal two very different human beings.

Through the pages of the *Misopogon* there speaks a profoundly disillusioned man,[84] one who had had the opportunity to discover for himself that an enormous gap separates theory from practice and that the most humane intentions and liberal ideas can prove disastrous in application.

Over the issue of the economic crisis—to Julian's mind the factor that really united the whole city against him (XII. 368c) —the emperor first became fully aware of the universal hatred that was felt for him. Yet, confident in his divine right, he did not foresee the issue and did nothing to stop discontent from being publicly expressed; he even refrained from taking any drastic measures once the protests against him reached a climax. But as he watched the rising flood of hostility, Julian clearly pondered upon the problem of how much liberty may properly be allowed to the people. The word ἐλευθερία, used always with a sarcastic nuance as a synonym for anarchy, occurs again and again throughout the *Misopogon*, and significantly enough concludes it.[85]

In the course of analysing what the notion of liberty means to the Antiochenes, and how it is put into practice by them, Julian appropriately recalls the famous passage in the *Republic*, where Plato discusses the problem of how easily a democratic regime may degenerate into a tyranny. Indeed, the emperor

[84] For Julian's acute sense of failure over this period of his life especially in the religious field, see *epp.* 84 and 98. 399d.

[85] 343c: ἡδὺ γὰρ ἐν πᾶσι τὸ ἐλεύθερον, 343d: ἔργῳ δὲ ἐᾶν ἡμᾶς εἶναι ἐλευθέρους, 345c: ἀλλὰ καὶ τὰ πρὸς τοὺς θεοὺς ἐλευθέρους εἶναι θέλοντας, 349c: πόλει . . . ἐλευθέρᾳ, 355b: τὸ γὰρ τῆς πόλεως ἦθος οἶμαι τοιοῦτον ἐστίν, ἐλεύθερον λίαν, 355c: οὕτως ἡ πόλις ἐστὶν ἐλευθέρα, 356b: δεῖ τὰ πάντα ἐλευθέρους εἶναι, 356d: τῶν θεῶν περιορώντων οὕτως ἐλευθέραν τὴν πόλιν, 371b: τῆς ὑμετέρας ἐλευθερίας, etc.

reproduces Plato's description of a democracy on the point of collapse, not only in the spirit of his words, but also down to the most insignificant detail. In order to illustrate the state of excessive freedom which he found in Antioch, he borrowed even the examples, similes and sarcasms of the Platonic text:

MISOPOGON

τὸ γὰρ τῆς πόλεως ἦθος οἶμαι τοιοῦτον ἐστίν, ἐλεύθερον λίαν, σὺ δὲ οὐ ξυνείς, ἄρχεσθαι αὐτοὺς μετὰ φρονήσεως ἀξιοῖς; οὐδὲ ἀπέβλεψας ὅση καὶ μέχρι τῶν ὄνων ἐστὶν ἐλευθερία παρ' αὐτοῖς καὶ τῶν καμήλων; ἄγουσί τοι καὶ ταύτας οἱ μισθωτοὶ διὰ τῶν στοῶν ὥσπερ τὰς νύμφας· οἱ γὰρ ὑπαίθριοι στενωποὶ καὶ αἱ πλατεῖαι τῶν ὁδῶν οὐκ ἐπὶ τούτῳ δήπου πεποίηνται, τῷ χρῆσθαι αὐταῖς τοὺς κανθηλίους, ἀλλ' ἐκεῖναι μὲν αὐτὸ δὴ τοῦτο κόσμου τινὸς ἕνεκα πρόκεινται καὶ πολυτελείας, χρῆσθαι δὲ ὑπ' ἐλευθερίας οἱ ὄνοι βούλονται ταῖς στοαῖς, εἴργει δὲ αὐτοὺς οὐδεὶς οὐδενός, ἵνα μὴ τὴν ἐλευθερίαν ἀφέληται. οὕτως ἡ πόλις ἐστὶν ἐλευθέρα.

(355bc)

REPUBLIC

τὸ μὲν γὰρ τῶν θηρίων τῶν ὑπὸ τοῖς ἀνθρώποις ὅσῳ ἐλευθερώτερά ἐστιν ἐνταῦθα ἢ ἐν ἄλλῃ, οὐκ ἄν τις πείθοιτο ἄπειρος. ἀτεχνῶς γὰρ αἵ τε κύνες κατὰ τὴν παροιμίαν οἷαίπερ αἱ δέσποιναι γίγνονταί τε δὴ καὶ ἵπποι καὶ ὄνοι, πάνυ ἐλευθέρως καὶ σεμνῶς εἰθισμένοι πορεύεσθαι, κατὰ τὰς ὁδοὺς ἐμβάλλοντες τῷ ἀεὶ ἀπαντῶντι, ἐὰν μὴ ἐξίστηται, καὶ τἆλλα πάντα οὕτω μεστὰ ἐλευθερίας γίγνεται.

(563c)

As the two texts unfold, the similarities become more striking:

Ὀρθῶς οὖν ὑμεῖς τοῦτο εἰδότες, ὅτι δεῖ τὰ πάντα ἐλευθέρους εἶναι, πρῶτον ἐπετρέψατε ταῖς γυναιξὶν ἄρχειν αὐτῶν, ἵνα ὑμῖν ὦσι λίαν ἐλεύθεραι καὶ ἀκόλαστοι, εἶτα ἐκείναις ξυνεχωρήσατε ἀνάγειν τὰ παιδία, μή ποτε ὑμῖν ἀρχῆς πειρώμενα τραχυτέρας, ἔπειτα ἀποφανθῇ δοῦλα.

(356bc)

Ἐν γυναιξὶ δὲ πρὸς ἄνδρας καὶ ἀνδράσι πρὸς γυναῖκας ὅση ἡ ἰσονομία καὶ ἐλευθερία γίγνεται, ὀλίγου ἐπελαθόμεθ' εἰπεῖν.

(563b)

Ἔνθεν οἶμαι συμβαίνει μάλα ὑμῖν
εὐδαίμοσιν εἶναι πᾶσαν ἀρνουμένοις
δουλείαν, ἀπὸ τῆς εἰς τοὺς θεοὺς
πρῶτον, εἶτα τοὺς νόμους καὶ
τρίτον τοὺς νομοφύλακας ἡμᾶς.

(356d)

κἂν ὁτιοῦν δουλείας τις προσφέρηται,
ἀγανακτεῖν καὶ μὴ ἀνέχεσθαι; τε-
λευτῶντες γάρ που οἶσθ᾽ ὅτι οὐδὲ
τῶν νόμων φροντίζουσιν γεγραμ-
μένων ἢ ἀγράφων, ἵνα δὴ μηδαμῇ
μηδεὶς αὐτοῖς ᾖ δεσπότης.

(563de)

τοὺς δὲ ἄρχοντας μὲν ἀρχομένοις,
ἀρχομένους δὲ ἄρχουσιν ὁμοίως
ἰδίᾳ τε καὶ δημοσίᾳ ἐπαινεῖ τε καὶ
τιμᾷ.

(562d)

What is most revealing about the *Misopogon*, though, is
Julian's careful avoidance, not only of reproducing, but even
of alluding to the one paragraph in Plato's discussion that
describes with astonishing accuracy the manner in which things
developed in Antioch: 'When a democratic city athirst for
liberty gets bad cupbearers as leaders, and is intoxicated by
drinking too deeply of that unmixed wine, then, if its governors
are not extremely mild and gentle with it, and do not dispense
the liberty unstintedly, it chastises them by accusing them of
being foul oligarchs' (*Rep.* 562d).

It was only at that stage that Julian realized that he had been
a 'bad cupbearer'—that once he had poured out to the city 'the
unmixed wine of liberty in too large quantities', it was inevitable, unless he continued being over-lenient, that the city
would turn against him and accuse him of being a tyrant
(XII. 357a). Julian must also have tried to find in the pages of
Plato what measures, if any, were to be taken, after the balance
had been shifted. But what he found there was disturbing:
anarchy would be succeeded by tyranny.[86] 'The people, trying

---

[86] Plato, *Rep.* 562b: Ἆρ᾽ οὖν καὶ ἡ δημοκρατία ὁρίζεται ἀγαθὸν (ἐλευθερία),
ἡ τούτου ἀπληστία καὶ ταύτην καταλύει. 564a: Ἡ γὰρ ἄγαν ἐλευθερία
ἔοικεν οὐκ εἰς ἄλλο τι ἢ εἰς ἄγαν δουλείαν μεταβάλλειν καὶ ἰδιώτῃ καὶ
πόλει. 569bc: Ὁ δῆμος φεύγων ἂν καπνὸν δουλείας ἐλευθέρων εἰς πῦρ
δούλων δεσποτείας ἂν ἐμπεπτωκὼς εἴη, ἀντὶ τῆς πολλῆς ἐκείνης καὶ
ἀκαίρου ἐλευθερίας τὴν χαλεπωτάτην τε καὶ πικροτάτην δούλων δουλείαν
μεταμπισχόμενος . . . Τί οὖν . . . οὐκ ἐμμελῶς ἡμῖν εἰρήσεται ἐὰν φῶμεν
ἱκανῶς διεληλυθέναι ὡς μεταβαίνει τυραννὶς ἐκ δημοκρατίας, γενομένη τε
οἷα ἐστίν;

to escape the smoke of submission to the free, would then fall into the fire of enslavement to slaves, and in exchange for that excessive and unseasonable liberty would earn the harshest and bitterest form of slavery—servitude to slaves' (*Rep.* 569bc). This last phrase stuck in Julian's mind. He had already used it to illustrate his own fate when Caesarship was thrust on him (V. 273c); but that it could one day be applied to describe the condition of those under his rule was a thought that he preferred not to entertain.

Yet how real was this parallel? Could ἐλευθερία and ἀναρχία have kept their meaning intact in a world that saw the extinction of the city-state as an autonomous political institution?

The loss of liberty at the level of the *polis* was to some extent outweighed in Roman and Byzantine times by the authorities' initially tacit grant of certain privileges, which enabled the people to continue to express their opinions. One of the commonest ways in which public opinion was articulated was through the *acclamations*, chanted in places of public entertainment, theatres, hippodromes or circuses. Now that the old democratic channels of individual self-expression had disappeared, the acclamations allowed the people to show their contentment or to communicate their claims and grievances to the governor or emperor.[87] In the fourth century this spontaneous means of giving voice to public opinion was associated with the old Greek ideal of παῤῥησία—freedom of speech—a word which reappears with astonishing frequency in the political and even religious vocabulary of pagan and Christian writers alike.[88] It was the notion of παῤῥησία that provided the ideological background of the acclamations, allowing the needs of everyday life to be expressed in the language of a tradition. Yet often the acclamations were used only as a pretext for the expression of the crudest ambitions of individuals or political

---

[87] On acclamations, see Th. Klauser, *RLAC* i. 220 ff. In connection with Antioch, cf. R. Browning, 'The riot of A.D. 387 in Antioch', *JRS* xlii (1952), 17–18, where evidence from the Codes is provided for acclamations as a legitimate means of expressing public opinion.

[88] On παῤῥησία, see E. Peterson, 'Zur Bedeutungsgeschichte von *Παρρησία*' *Reinhold–Seeberg–Festschrift*, Leipzig 1929, i. 283–97; also Murray, *Περὶ Βασιλείας*, 199 ff.

factions; for once the people had been incited by demagogues,[89] legitimate protest could easily degenerate into a riot.[90]

This was not as unusual in late antiquity as it was in classical Greece. There στάσις consisted in a conflict between citizens and, being an internal affair of the *polis*, had a pronouncedly political character, even if the pretexts for its outbreak often appeared to be unconnected with any factional interests. In late antiquity, on the contrary, στάσις was always directed against the ἐξουσία, the powers-that-be. Its causes were religious and, more often, economic, connected with some pressing problem of everyday life, the imposition of a new tax,[91] or famine; but the political factions who occasionally used the misery of the people as a lever in order to arouse disturbances, did not, as in the classical period, form organized bodies with explicit political aims and foreign affiliations. Late antique στάσις was a fairly common phenomenon;[92] it can by no means be described as the civil malady of which Aeschylus and Plato speak, and which in the context of the classical *polis* was a dynamic expression of the spirit of anarchy[93] in the Platonic sense of the word.

What happened under Julian in Antioch was not a *stasis* by either classical or late antique standards. But the state of anarchy that spread through the city, and was neither repressed nor culminated in a riot, could only have occurred in a classical town. It corresponds to Plato's description of a collapsing democracy, but it is extraordinary that any imperial town should have behaved thus in the fourth century. Yet the behaviour of the Antiochenes sufficiently shows that they recognized in Julian—who faced them as a perfectly autonomous and

---

[89] According to Libanius, in Antioch the people were led by a group of men who, next to their occupation in the theatre, acted as a claque, XLI. 9. See Liebeschuetz, *Antioch*, 208–19, 240 ff., 258.

[90] See Lib. XIX. 27 ff.

[91] Browning, art. cit. 14–15.

[92] For an analysis of the nature of *stasis* in late antiquity, see Lib. XIX. 8–11. The sophist is careful to place such a στάσις only in Ῥωμαίων βασιλείας τὸν χρόνον (11). In another passage (XXII. 5–6), describing the riot of 387, Libanius gives a summary definition of στάσις in late antiquity. Cf. Amm. XIV. 7. 5–7. On στάσις from the fourth to the sixth century, see J. R. Martindale, 'Public disorders in the late Roman empire, their causes and character', unpubl. diss. (B.Litt.), Oxford 1960, 63–100.

[93] Plato, *Rep.* 470; Aesch. *Eum.* 976–87.

free city in the classical sense—an anachronistic leader, and, though unconsciously, responded by behaving in an equally anachronistic way. By February 363 Julian was in an *ἀναρ-χουμένη πόλις* in the classical sense of the word, since no single remedy would suffice to bring the citizens back to order. No open *stasis* was declared against him, and no clear demand was addressed to him, once he had met the original claims of the citizens.[94] Thus the situation in Antioch in 363 was the opposite of the one that developed during the famines of 354 and 387. One should try to understand the process by which Antioch descended into anarchy. Julian's 'unkingly' behaviour,[95] in the sense of his democratic attitude towards the people, his paganism, his sobriety and his lack of any sense of humour[96] irritated the Antiochenes, so that they failed to show towards him as an individual the respect they instinctively felt in a general sense towards the person of the emperor. To their mind this particular monarch was a freak, and it was thanks only to his exceptional and unkingly ways that he was not a 'despot' too (XII. 343cd). He professed a tolerance whose limits the Antiochenes could test, once they knew that, whatever the issue, they were unlikely to incur more damage than they themselves were causing to Julian. As for Julian, he acted like the sorcerer's apprentice by unleashing through his too liberal policy forces which he was subsequently quite unable to control, and at the same time remain faithful to his democratic principles. He chose to stick to those principles, for he was absolutely convinced of their universal validity;[97] but he realized that in Antioch he had failed to put them into effect in the right manner, and this led him to question his own capacities as a ruler.

Throughout his political career Julian had proved repeatedly

---

[94] XII. 368c–369c. Compare an analogous case in Rome, where Julian dealt successfully with a famine, Mamert. 14. 1–2; cf. above, p. 83.

[95] Amm. XXII. 7. 3; XXII. 14. 3; XXV. 4. 18; see also above, pp. 35, 113

[96] See the criticisms of the Antiochenes on the matter: XII. 349ab; 349d; 350d, 360b; according to Eunapius, they were particularly graceful and humorous people: *V. Phil.* XVI. 2. 2: καὶ ὁ πάντες οἱ Συροφοίνικες ἔχουσιν κατὰ τὴν κοινὴν ἔντευξιν ἡδὺ καὶ κεχαρισμένον, τοῦτο παρ' ἐκείνου (Λιβανίου) λαβεῖν μετὰ παιδείας ἔξεστιν.

[97] See Julian's profession of faith in the *Misopogon*, 353d–354a (a reproduction of Plato, *Leg.* 730d), 354bc (cf. *Leg.* 729b), 365d: Ἡμῖν μὲν οὖν ἐδόκει ταῦτα καλά, πραότης ἀρχόντων μετὰ σωφροσύνης'.

that he was aware of the importance of the classical Greek concept of καιρός, the one opportune moment in politics that the statesman must detect and grasp to the profit of his enterprise.[98] The καιρός or καιροί that presented themselves to Julian during his stay in Antioch had been missed, as he himself recognizes in the concluding paragraph of the *Misopogon*: 'I myself am responsible for all the wrong that has been done to me, because I showered favours on men whose hearts knew no gratitude. And this is the result of my own folly and not of your ἐλευθερία' (XII. 371b). The examples Julian provides to illustrate this statement show that over a series of incidents he had done the wrong thing when he could by effective action have prevented the situation from reaching the extremes that it had by February 363.[99] Had Julian not, as a result of his stay in Antioch, lost confidence in his own capacities as a statesman, had he not understood that he had lost the battle, he would not have deserted the ἐλευθέρα πόλις. He would have persevered in finding a way of remedying the situation by trying to invent new methods of applying the political principles that he defends in the *Misopogon*.

Until he reached Antioch, Julian had experienced no major inner upheaval. The important events of his life—his initiation in the mysteries, his appointment as Caesar, his proclamation as Augustus and his entry into Constantinople as sole emperor—occurred only after he had had the time to prepare himself psychologically. More importantly, they were all positive events and Julian knew how to cope with happiness and success, for his was not an essentially hybristic nature. He also knew how to submit to misfortunes which he had not provoked himself;[100] but he was unable to face failure. In Antioch he suddenly realized that his policies had failed, indeed that in the eyes of his

---

[98] On καιρός as a crucial concept in fifth- and fourth-century BC Athenian politics, and its long semantic development in Roman and Byzantine times, see Lamer, *Καιρός, RE* x. 1508–21. For Julian's classical conception of the principle, see above, p. 76 n. 130; p. 176 n. 58.

[99] The result of such a policy is stated in the following sentence: ὃν [δῆμον] οὕτως ἐποιήσαμεν τρυφᾶν, ὥστε ἄγων σχολὴν ἀπὸ τῆς ἐνδείας τοὺς ἀναπαίστους εἰς τοὺς αἰτίους αὐτῷ τῆς εὐθηνίας ξυνέθηκεν (XII. 365b).

[100] For Julian's realization that he was able to, endure both misfortune and success with equanimity, see VI. 260b; for his awareness that *hybris* is the constant companion of success, see VI. 257ab.

subjects he was a ridiculous and even much hated ruler. His self-confidence abandoned him. And in the miserable state of mind in which he now found himself he felt the need to forget about a highly unsatisfactory present by diving into his past.

The details Julian provides in the *Misopogon* of his educational curriculum, the eulogies he bestows on his masters and on the companions of his youth, exceed by far the apologetical requirements of the moment. Here is somebody who lingers over his dearest memories, for they alone can console him. The man who was convinced that he was hated by an entire city needed to remember how deeply he was loved by a whole race, but also by the few individuals who came in close contact with him over the period of his growth. In this context he is even led to regret the one great lack in his life, that of a mother who died too young, when Julian was only a few months old (XII. 352bc). Yet from such recollections only a limited amount of consolation could be drawn. His digressions into the past and systematic self-praise could help him to bolster his opinion of himself, but could do nothing to change the mind of the Antiochenes—a tragic impasse for a man who was particularly concerned about his popularity and needed to be loved and admired by his subjects,[101] against whom his principles prevented him from using force.

Julian knew that he had been mercilessly ridiculed, and yet he still hoped that he might command respect and admiration, if he were to achieve some exceptionally glorious deed. The military sphere, in which he had proved himself, was the only possibility left for a man who was conscious of his failure elsewhere. Through his long-meditated campaign against Persia he might yet regain his self-confidence. His gods would help him to repeat Alexander's deeds, and then his maligned Hellenism would surely appear in the eyes of all as the only true religion, the only cult under which the Roman empire could prosper, thus confirming its claim to eternity.

At the moment when he composed the *Misopogon*, Julian still kept all his religious enthusiasm intact. Thus, when at Antioch he saw everything about him falling apart, when he reached the painful realization that he had failed as a statesman, his spiritual

---

[101] XII. 350d–353d. On Julian's excessive love of popularity, see Amm. XXII. 14. 1; XXV. 4. 18.

core was still unharmed. At the same time as the *Caesars*, he could compose the *Hymn to King Helios*, a work whose pages emanate an extraordinary sense of serenity and otherworldliness; in the midst of his preparations for the Persian campaign, when he was identifying more and more with Alexander, he could still face Marcus Aurelius as the supreme model who had fought and won a much more important battle than had the Macedonian.[102] Once again in Persia, during the last hours of his life, when he could see to what dangers he had exposed his army, and possibly guessed how tragic a future was dawning for the empire; when, through the extraordinary lucidity with which the touch of death may gratify even the dullest of mortals, he could contemplate the failing of his dream; still he departed with the serene conviction that he was called to union with heaven and the stars, and that during his passage on earth he had performed his mission conscientiously, regardless of whether he had succeeded or failed.

As a statesman Julian had indeed failed. His Hellenism and *Romanitas* led him to treat his subjects in too democratic a fashion, which proved both anachronistic and incompatible with the theocratic conception of kingship that his sense of reality had enabled him to evolve. His ideal of *paideia*, which as a theoretical construction seemed so coherent and in tune with the spirit of the age, did not prescribe how to deal with political situations such as the one that arose at Antioch. Faulted by his experience, Julian turned to the Persian campaign. There he could have the satisfaction of marching in the steps of Alexander the Great.[103] He became irresistibly attracted by the charismatic figure of the man who throughout late antiquity was regarded not only as the ideal leader of men, but also as the champion of Greek *paideia* abroad—a warrior and a civilizer, whom many a Roman emperor had dreamed of imitating. Increasingly mesmerized by an Alexandrian vision of Persian conquest, Julian found it more and more difficult to maintain contact with reality, till at the last he became totally

---

[102] See above, p. 200.

[103] The Antiochenes, realizing that the Persian campaign was Julian's major preoccupation, and recognizing also the great importance that he attached to it as a means of recovering his own self-confidence, attacked him on this point as well with particular malignity, cf. XII. 344b.

estranged from his own historical and human milieu. His initial loss of self-confidence was now followed by a state of over-confidence in his own capacities, during which he suspended self-criticism and ignored the advice of others. One more step and Julian crossed the confines of *hybris*.

Yet privately, Julian found in his ideal of *paideia* the full justification of his existence. Nor was this missed by posterity: the judgement of history may have seen in Julian an emperor of extraordinary goodwill and a man of many talents, who, for various reasons, failed to fulfil his ambitious plan; but legend, which is the language of the heart and the imagination, fully sanctioned the memory of the man, who lived seeking, striving and suffering, by making of him either a demon or a saint.[104]

---

[104] Lib. XVIII. 304. See my ' '*O 'Ιουλιανὸς τοῦ Θρύλου*', *Athena* lxxvi (1977), 103–54.

EPILOGUE

An oracle cited in the *Historia Augusta* had long foretold 'ut Romanus princeps Ctesifontem transire non possit', and indeed, Julian did not manage 'eos fines transgredi ... qui fataliter constituti sunt'.[1] Instead, he died in Phrygia of Mesopotamia,[2] as Apollo had prophesied in a dream,[3] and just after capturing Seleuceia, thus fulfilling yet a third oracle, delivered to him as he embarked on the Persian campaign:

> But when, brandishing your sword, you will have subjected
> the Persian race as far as Seleuceia,
> then, hurtling you through the tempestuous movements
> of the cosmic orbits, a fiery chariot will carry you towards
>   Olympus.
> Freed from the distressing wretchedness of human bonds,
> you will arrive in the ancestral halls of ethereal light,
> from which you had wandered away to be joined to mortal
>   body.[4]

According to Ammianus, the thirty-two year old emperor saw his untimely death as the 'summum praemium' with which the gods rewarded his piety,[5] and—presumably remembering the oracular verses—passed away in the serene belief that he was called to union with heaven and the stars,[6] thus anticipating his imperial apotheosis. Yet at the same time Julian welcomed death for a more mundane reason, for he saw it as the heavenly 'munus' bestowed upon him that he might be spared the 'arduae difficultates'[7] destined to be Jovian's heritage.

With Julian's death his dream of Persian conquest, his religious plans and the most ambitious aspect of his administrative reform, the revival of the municipalities, were all doomed. Thus, 'measured by the rigorous standards of the historian, Julian

---

[1] See above, p. 199 n. 27.
[2] Amm. XXV. 3. 9.
[3] Zonaras, XIII. 13 (Dindorf iii. 216).
[4] Eunap. *Hist.*, fr. 26.
[5] Amm. XXV. 3. 15.
[6] Ibid. 22.
[7] Ibid. 16.

achieved singularly little', as Professor Browning has rightly remarked. 'Yet his fate moved men's hearts and minds, and in spite of his failure he was not forgotten.'[8] The paradox of history which ensured the perpetuation of Julian's memory in Byzantium deserves some further investigation.

The vivid fear that Julian's educational and religious programme had inspired in the hearts of Christians was not easily forgotten even when the 'Apostate' was no longer there to pursue his reforms.[9] The efficiency with which he had carried out his policies during his short reign, his menacing behaviour towards the Christians and above all his untimely and mysterious death,[10] all these contributed to Julian's demonic reputation in Christian eyes; he was indeed the very incarnation of evil. Those who had lived through his reign naturally wished to commemorate their deliverance from it. Drawing a little on their experience, and a good deal on their imagination, they began to evolve the legend that carried the emperor's fame as far away in space as those western lands that Julian had known, loved and freed, and as far in time as the present day: only a few decades ago, Greek grandmothers could still be heard in remote Cappadocian villages telling a new generation of the atrocities committed by the 'Apostate' and of the just punishment inflicted upon him by the heavenly powers.[11]

Yet, apart from the initial fear and horror, that gave birth to the legend of Julian and kept his memory green in the Byzantine underworld, there were other reasons too why Byzantium chose to remember this emperor. As much because of his exalted conception of imperial power as by virtue of his especial respect for the dynastic ideal—an emotion that

---

[8] Browning, *Julian*, 221, 224.

[9] For the fear that Julian inspired in the Christians, see Greg. Naz. *or*. V. 19; 26.

[10] Who it was who killed Julian was never discovered. For several conflicting theories, see Amm. XXV. 3. 6; Lib. XXIV. 21; Socr. III. 21. 12; Zonar. loc. cit., p. 215.

[11] For Julian's legend see R. Nostitz-Rieneck, 'Vom Tode des Kaisers Julian: Berichte und Erzählungen', *Stella Matutina* xvi (1906–7), 1–35; R. Förster, 'Kaiser Julian in der Dichtung alter und neuer Zeit', *Stud. z. vergl. Literaturgesch.* v (1905), 1–120; N. H. Baynes, 'The death of Julian the Apostate in a Christian legend', *Byzantine Studies*, 271–80; my article in *Athena* lxxvi; R. Braun–J. Richer, (edd.), *L'Empereur Julien: de l'histoire à la légende (331–1715)*, Paris 1978; and J. Richer (ed.), *L'empereur Julien: de la légende au mythe (De Voltaire à nos jours)*, Paris 1981. Also I. Hahn, 'Der ideologische Kampf um den Tod Julians des Abtrünnigen', *Klio* xxxviii (1960), 225–32.

remained vital to the ethos of the Eastern empire—[12] Julian had belonged to the first truly Byzantine dynasty.[13]

No less Byzantine in character was the emperor's attachment to tradition, while his habit of justifying contemporary institutions by tracing them to their remotest historical and even legendary origins was enthusiastically adopted by his successors: Justinian was to make a point of deriving the Roman *imperium* not just from Augustus, but from Aeneas himself.[14] Like Julian, Constantine Porphyrogenitus considered respect for tradition to be the first duty of an emperor, and saw its neglect as the mark of ἀπαιδευσία on the part of the *basileus*. A propos of Romanus I, who gave his grand-daughter to marry the king of the Bulgars, the emperor born in the purple offers the following explanation:

The lord Romanus, the emperor, was a common, illiterate fellow, and not from among those who have been bred up in the palace, and have followed the Roman national customs from the beginning; nor was he of imperial and noble stock, and for this reason in most of his actions he was too arrogant and despotic (αὐθαδέστερον καὶ ἐξουσιαστικώτερον); and in this instance he neither heeded the prohibition of the Church, nor followed the commandment and ordinance of the Great Constantine, but out of a temper arrogant and self-willed and untaught in virtue and refusing to follow what was right and good, or to submit to the ordinances handed down by our forefathers, he dared to do this thing.[15]

If Porphyrogenitus' views on tradition and dynasty seem remarkably close to those of Julian, he also offers what might be described as a commentary on his theory of national characteristics. In a revealing section of his book *De administrando Imperio*,

[12] See S. MacCormack, 'Roma, Constantinopolis, the emperor and his Genius', *CQ* N.s. xxv. (1975), 145. For a characteristic anecdote illustrating the attachment to the dynastic ideal in Byzantium, see Liutprand of Cremona, *Antapodosis*, III. 37.

[13] 'Bred in Cappadocia, at Athens and in Phrygia', Julian 'was the first Byzantine emperor', G. Mathew, *Byzantine Aesthetics*, London 1963, 50. We should not forget that, some time before the tenth century, Julian's remains were transferred from Tarsus to Constantinople, where he was laid to rest to the north of the Church of the Holy Apostles next to the other members of the Second Flavian dynasty (Constantine Porphyrogenitus, *Cerem.* ii. 42 (Niebuhr) i. 646, and Zonar. XIII. 13 (Dindorf) iii. 216).

[14] D. Zakythenos, Βυζάντιον. Κράτος καὶ Κοινωνία. Ἱστορικὴ ἐπισκόπησις, Athens 1951, 30.

[15] Constantine Porphyrogenitus, *De administrando Imperio* (ed. G. Moravcsik,

he dwells on the reasons why the Roman emperor should never, yielding to political necessities, 'ally himself by marriage with infidels';[16] 'for each nation has different customs and divergent laws and institutions, and should consolidate those things that are proper to it and should develop out of the same nation the associations for the fusion of its life.'[17]

Just as dear to the Byzantines as Julian's political principles were his views on the relationship of Imperium to Sacerdotium.[18] For, contrary to what happened in the West, in Byzantium 'after the defeat of iconoclasm, the sacerdotium was left almost unmolested in the exercise of its function of expounding the true doctrine', while conversely, 'the sacerdotium never made an open attempt to usurp the functions of the imperium.'[19] Βασιλεία and ἐκκλησία were interdependent in the Eastern empire,[20] just as Julian had conceived them to be. In the words of the patriarch Antony II, 'Imperium and the Church are interconnected and united, and it is not possible to separate the one from the other.'[21] Julian would have agreed completely. The law on education had been a natural product of this way of thinking. And if, even among Julian's allies, this law aroused vigorous opposition, that was only because the time was not yet ripe for such cultural totalitarianism. When Justinian forbade pagans to be teachers,[22] nobody dreamed of criticizing him.

Indeed Julian was an Easterner able to identify himself with Roman values to the point where he could call the Greeks 'our kinsmen' (*C.G.* 200a), and reject the view that the Romans

trans. R. J. H. Jenkins), Washington 1967², 13. 149–58.

[16] *De administrando Imperio*, 13. 175 ff.

[17] Ibid. 175 ff.

[18] For Justinian's classical definition of the relationship between Sacerdotium and Imperium, see *Nov.* IV, *praef.* (= *Corpus Iuris Civilis* iii (ed. R. Schoell and W. Kroll), Berlin 1954, 35–6): Μέγιστα ἐν ἀνθρώποις ἐστὶ δῶρα Θεοῦ παρὰ τῆς ἄνωθεν δεδομένα φιλανθρωπίας, ἱερωσύνη τε καὶ βασιλεία, ἡ μὲν τοῖς θείοις ὑπηρετουμένη, ἡ δὲ τῶν ἀνθρωπίνων ἐξάρχουσά τε καὶ ἐπιμελουμένη, καὶ ἐκ μιᾶς τε καὶ τῆς αὐτῆς ἀρχῆς ἑκατέρα προϊοῦσα καὶ τὸν ἀνθρώπινον κατακοσμοῦσα βίον.

[19] See F. Dvornik, *Early Christian and Byzantine Political Philosophy* ii, Washington 1966, 840; cf. S. Runciman, *The Great Church in Captivity*, Cambridge 1968, 62.

[20] Runciman, op. cit. 61.

[21] See F. Miklosich–J. Müller, *Acta et Diplomata Graeca Medii Aevi Sacra et Profana* ii, Vienna 1862, 191.

[22] *C.Just.* I. 5. 18. 4; I. 11. 10. 2.

were the same race as the Greeks (X. 324a). By thinking in Greek of the empire as Roman, Julian was well ahead of his times. Until the very last day of its existence the Byzantine state considered itself as 'the Roman Empire',[23] and this extraordinary sense of political and national continuity survived so well that the Greeks today call themselves Ρωμιοί whenever they wish to convey a full awareness of all the characteristics that make them a particular race.[24] The complement of this ideal of the fusion of Greeks and Romans, anticipated by Julian, is to be found, in appearance at least, in the panegyric that an orator of the fifteenth century addressed to the emperors Manuel II and John VIII Palaeologi at a moment of great national distress. The anonymous rhetor highlights the vocation of Constantinople and the manifold achievements of the Greeks and the Romans, presented as one people under the name Ρωμ-έλληνες. The great theme of the grandeur and superiority of the two races that had ruled the Mediterranean world for millennia runs right through the lengthy oration, hammering home in every possible way the contrast with the contemporary situation. Thus, it was right at the moment when the Byzantine empire fell that an anonymous panegyrist coined the neologism Ρωμέλληνες to denote the Byzantine race.[25] In the fourth century, Julian had already anticipated this *hapax*, but in a different and fuller sense from the one in which the Byzantine world realized it, for, although the Byzantines thought of themselves as Graeco-Romans, in fact they were Romano-Christians. 'Dans la théorie politique de Byzance, *l'idée romaine* reste jusqu'à la fin vivante. La *pax Christiana*, superposée à la *pax Romana*, rend plus grande encore la nécessité d'un empire universel. *L'Hellénisme fut relégué au second plan.*'[26]

---

[23] *Inter alia*, see I. E. Karayannopoulos, ''Η πολιτική θεωρία τῶν Βυζαντινῶν', *Βυζαντινά* ii (1970), 39.

[24] For the names Ρωμαῖος, Ρωμαϊκός, Ρωμανία in connection with Byzantium, see D. Zakythenos, *Βυζαντινὴ Ἱστορία 324–1071*, Athens 1972, 13–14. See also N. Politis, ''Έλληνες ἢ Ρωμιοί', *Λαογραφικὰ Σύμμεικτα* I, Athens 1920, 122–33. For an amusing list of the respective characteristics of Έλληνες and Ρωμιοί, P. Leigh Fermor, *Roumeli*, London 1966, 107–13.

[25] 'Ἀνωνύμου Πανηγυρικὸς εἰς Μανουὴλ καὶ Ἰωάννην Η' τοὺς Παλαιολόγους' in S. Lambros, *Παλαιολόγεια καὶ Πελοποννησιακά* III, Athens 1926, 152.

[26] See D. Zakythenos, 'Étatisme byzantin et expérience hellénistique', *Byzance: état-société-économie*, London 1973, 669.

In the creation of this transformed Hellenism, which played so important a role in the intellectual life of the Byzantine empire (though as a linguistic and cultural rather than as a religious phenomenon), Julian had his part, and the Byzantines recognized it. His writings were always regarded as models of Greek prose style,[27] so that as distinguished a personality as Arethas of Caesarea in the tenth century produced an edition of them in order to make them accessible to a wider public.[28]

Thus some of Julian's tangible achievements, together with certain aspects of the spirit he stood for, survived him by many centuries. Indeed, as an individual Julian bore as little resemblance as possible to the type of the classical man. His indifference to sex and his stern asceticism are in tune with an age which saw the growth of Christian monasticism. In classical Greece Julian would have appeared as tragic and isolated a curiosity as Hippolytus, but because he lived in a world where asceticism was the fashion we are not surprised by him.[29] His was the divided personality of a man who lived between two ages, and in whose career we can perceive just as clearly his debt to the ancient world as his claim to citizenship in the new. No contemporary historian set himself to write of Julian the innovator; but the emperor's ardent struggle to perpetuate the spirit of the Greek and Roman traditions was recognized by two of the most important spokesmen of *Romanitas* and Hellenism in the fourth century: in words which, appropriately enough, look both to the past and to the future, Ammianus wrote that: 'the remains and ashes of Julian . . . ought not to be looked on by the Cydnus, though it is a beautiful and limpid stream, but they should, so that the perpetuation of his noble deeds be assured, be washed by the Tiber, which cuts through the eternal city and flows by the memorials of the deified emperors of old';[30] while Libanius thought that it would have

---

[27] For evidence, see J. Bidez–F. Cumont, 'Recherches sur la tradition manuscrite des lettres de l'empereur Julien', *Mém. de l'Acad. royale de Belgique* lvii (1898), 25–6.

[28] See H. Grégoire, 'Les manuscrits de Julien et le mouvement néo-païen de Mistra: Démétrius Rhallis et Gémiste Pléthon', *Byzantion* v (1929–30), 735.

[29] To the late antique man Hippolytus himself had become an object of admiration. Cf. Libanius' rhetorical question about Julian: οὐ σωφρονέστερος μὲν Ἱππολύτου . . .; (XVIII. 281); see also XXIV. 37.

[30] Amm. XXV. 10. 5.

been juster if the remains of Julian were to repose in the Academy next to those of Plato, and, like the great philosopher of old, be honoured by the sacrifices of the endless generations of youths and teachers still to come.[31]

[31] Lib. XVIII. 306.

SELECT BIBLIOGRAPHY

PRIMARY SOURCES*

ALBINUS, *Epitoma*, ed. and trans. P. Louis, Rennes 1945
AMMIANUS MARCELLINUS, *Res gestae*, ed. (1) C. U. Clark, Berlin 1910–15; (2) J. C. Rolfe, London 1935–9 (with English translation)
ARISTIDES, AELIUS, *Orationes*, ed. W. Dindorf, Leipzig 1829
——— —— *Orationes* XVI–LIII, ed. B. Keil, Berlin 1898
ASCLEPIUS, ed. A. D. Nock, trans. A.-J. Festugière, *Corpus Hermeticum* II, Paris 1960[2]
Chaldean Oracles, Oracula chaldaica, ed. and trans. E. des Places, Paris 1971
CLEMENT OF ALEXANDRIA, *Stromata*, ed. O. Stählin, Berlin, Books I–VI 1960[3], Books VII–VIII 1970[2]
Codex Iustinianus, ed. P. Krueger, Berlin 1906[8]
Codex Theodosianus, ed. P. Krueger and Th. Mommsen, Berlin 1954[2]
CYRIL OF ALEXANDRIA, *Contra Iulianum*, PG 76
DAMASCIUS, *Vita Isidori*, ed. C. Zintzen, Hildesheim 1967
Demegoria Constantii, ed. G. Downey and A. F. Norman, *Themistii Orationes* III, Leipzig 1974
DIOGENES LAERTIUS, *Vitae philosophorum*, ed. H. S. Long, Oxford 1964
EUNAPIUS, *Historia*, ed. C. Müller, *Fragmenta Historicorum Graecorum* IV, Paris 1951, 7–56
—— *Vitae Philosophorum*, ed. J. Giangrande, Rome 1956
EUSEBIUS OF CAESAREA, *Praeparatio Evangelica*, ed. K. Mras, Berlin 1954–6
—— *Tricennalia*, ed. J. Heikel, Leipzig 1902
—— *Vita Constantini*, ed. F. Winkelmann, Berlin 1975
GREGORY OF NAZIANZOS, *Historica*, PG 37
—— *Orationes* IV–V, PG 35
HIMERIUS, *Declamationes, Orationes*, ed. A. Colonna, Rome 1951
IAMBLICHUS, *De mysteriis Aegyptiorum*, ed. and trans. E. des Places, Paris 1966
—— *De vita Pythagorica*, ed. L. Deubner, Stuttgart 1975[2]
—— *Protrepticus*, ed. H. Pistelli, Leipzig 1888
JULIAN (EMPEROR), *Opera*, ed. (1) F. C. Hertlein, Leipzig 1875–6;

* Excluding inscriptions.

(2) J. Bidez, G. Rochefort, C. Lacombrade, Paris 1924–64 (with French translation); (3) W. C. Wright, London 1913–23 (with English translation)

JULIAN (EMPEROR), *Contra Galilaeos*, ed. K. J. Neumann, Leipzig 1880

—— *Epistulae, leges, poematia, fragmenta*, ed. J. Bidez and F. Cumont, Paris 1922

LIBANIUS, *Opera*, ed. R. Foerster I–XII, Leipzig 1903–27

LUCIAN, *Opera*, ed. K. Jacobitz, Leipzig 1836–41

MAMERTINUS, *Gratiarum Actio*, ed. R. A. B. Mynors, *Panegyrici Latini* III, Oxford 1964

MARINUS, *Vita Procli*, ed. J. F. Boissonade, Leipzig 1814

MENANDER, ed. L. Spengel, *Rhetores Graeci* III, Leipzig 1856

ORIGEN, *Contra Celsum*, ed. M. Borret, Paris 1967–76

Panegyrici Latini, ed. R. A. B. Mynors, Oxford 1964

Παραστάσεις Σύντομοι Χρονικαί, ed. T. Preger, *Scriptores originum Constantinopolitanarum* I, Leipzig 1901

PHILOSTORGIUS, *Historia Ecclesiastica*, ed. J. Bidez, Berlin 1972²

PHILOSTRATUS, *Vita Apollonii*, ed. C. L. Kayser, Leipzig 1871

PLATO, *Opera*, ed. J. Burnet, Oxford 1900–7

PLOTINUS, *Enneades*, ed. P. Henry and H.-R. Schwyzer I–III, Paris 1951–73

PLUTARCH, *Moralia* (various editors) I–VI, Leipzig 1929²–78²

—— *Vitae*, ed. and trans. R. Flacelière *et al.* I–XV, Paris 1957–79

PORPHYRY, *Ad Marcellam*, ed. W. Pötscher, Leiden 1969

—— *Contra Christianos*, ed. A. von Harnack, *Abh. der kön. preuss. Akad. der Wiss., Phil.-hist. Kl.* I (1916)

—— *De Abstinentia, De antro Nympharum*, ed. A. Nauck, *Porphyrii Opuscula Selecta*, Leipzig 1886²

—— *Epistula ad Anebonem*, ed. A. R. Sodano, Naples 1958

—— *Vita Plotini*, ed. Henry and Schwyzer, *Plotini Opera* I, Paris 1951

PROCLUS, *In Platonis Cratylum Commentaria*, ed. G. Pasquali, Leipzig 1908

—— *In Platonis Parmenidem*, ed. V. Cousin, Paris 1864

—— *In Platonis Rempublicam Commentaria*, ed. W. Kroll, Leipzig 1899–1901

—— *In Platonis Timaeum Commentaria*, ed. E. Diehl, Leipzig 1903–6

—— *Theologia Platonica*, ed. H. D. Saffrey and L. G. Westerink, Paris 1968–

SALUTIUS, *De Diis et Mundo*, ed. and trans. G. Rochefort, Paris 1960

SOCRATES, *Historia Ecclesiastica*, ed. R. Hussey, Oxford 1853

SOZOMEN, *Historia Ecclesiastica*, ed. J. Bidez and G. C. Hausen, Berlin 1960²

SYNESIUS, *Epistulae*, ed. A. Garzya, Rome 1979

SYNESIUS, *De regno*, ed. N. Terzaghi, Rome 1944
TATIAN, *Ad Graecos*, ed. A. J. Goodspeed, *Die ältesten Apologeten*, Göttingen 1914
THEMISTIUS, *Orationes*, ed. G. Downey and A. F. Norman, Leipzig 1965–74
THEODORET, *Historia Ecclesiastica*, ed. L. Parmentier, Berlin 1954[2]
ZONARAS, *Epitome historiarum*, ed. C. Dindorf, III, Leipzig 1870
ZOSIMUS, *Historia Nova*, ed. (1) L. Mendelssohn, Leipzig 1887; (2) F. Paschoud, Paris 1971–

SECONDARY WORKS

ATHANASSIADI, P., 'A contribution to Mithraic theology: the Emperor Julian's *Hymn to King Helios*', *JThS* xxviii (1977), 360–71
—— ''O 'Ιουλιανὸς τοῦ Θρύλου', *Athena* lxxv (1977), 103–54
BARNES, T. D., 'A correspondent of Iamblichus', *GRBS* xix (1978), 99–106
BAYNES, N. H., *Byzantine Studies and Other Essays*, London 1955
BIDEZ, J., 'Le philosophe Jamblique et son école', *REG* xxxii (1919), 29–40
—— *La Tradition manuscrite et les éditions des discours de l'empereur Julien*, Gand–Paris 1929
—— *La Vie de l'empereur Julien*, Paris 1930
BIDEZ, J.–CUMONT, F., 'Recherches sur la tradition manuscrite des lettres de l'empereur Julien', *Mémoires couronnés et autres mémoires publiés par l'Acad. Roy. des Sciences, des Lett. et des Beaux Arts de Belg.* lvii (1898), [1–156]
—— —— *Les Mages hellénisés. Zoroastre, Ostanès et Hystaspe d'après la tradition grecque* I–II, Paris 1938
BOWERSOCK, G. W., *Julian the Apostate*, London 1978
BOWIE, E. L., 'Greeks and their past in the Second Sophistic', *P & P* xlvi (1970), 3–41
BROWN, P. R. L., *Religion and Society in the Age of Saint Augustine*, London 1972
BROWNING, R., *The Emperor Julian*, London 1975
CALZA, R., *Iconografia romana imperiale da Carausio a Giuliano (287–363 d.C.)*, Rome 1972
CHADWICK, H., *Origen: Contra Celsum*, Cambridge 1965[2] (Introduction)
—— *Early Christian Thought and the Classical Tradition: Studies in Justin, Clement and Origen*, Oxford 1966
CUMONT, F., *Textes et monuments relatifs aux mystères de Mithra* I–II, Brussels 1896–9

CUMONT, F., *Sur l'authenticité de quelques lettres de Julien*, Gand 1889
—— *Les Mystères de Mithra*, Paris 1913³
—— *Les Religions orientales dans le paganisme romain*, Paris 1929⁴
—— *Lux Perpetua*, Paris 1949
DAGRON, G., 'L'empire romain d'Orient au IVème siècle et les traditions politiques de l'hellénisme: le témoignage de Thémistios', *T & MByz* iii (1968), 1–242
—— *Naissance d'une capitale: Constantinople et ses institutions de 330 à 451*, Paris 1974
DIELS H. (ed.), *Die Fragmente der Vorsokratiker* I, Berlin 1961¹⁰
DODDS, E. R., *Pagan and Christian in an Age of Anxiety*, Cambridge 1965
DVORNIK, F., *Early Christian and Byzantine Political Philosophy. Origin and Background* II, Washington 1966
ENSSLIN, W., 'Kaiser Julians Gesetzgebungswerk und Reichsverwaltung', *Klio* xviii (1923), 104–99
Entretiens Hardt, Le Culte des souverains dans l'empire romain xix (1972)
FESTUGIÈRE, A.-J., *La Révélation d'Hermès Trismégiste* I, Paris 1950²
—— *Antioche païenne et chrétienne*, Paris 1959
FOWDEN, G., 'Pagan Philosophers in Late Antique Society: with Special Reference to Iamblichus and his Followers', unpubl. diss., Oxford 1979
GIBBON, E., *The Decline and Fall of the Roman Empire* (ed. J. B. Bury) II, London 1909
GILLIARD, E. D., 'Notes on the coinage of Julian the Apostate', *JRS* liv (1964), 135–41
GLADIS, C., *De Themistii Libanii Juliani in Constantium orationibus*, diss., Breslau 1907
GORDON, R. L., 'Mithraism and Roman society: social factors in the explanation of religious change in the Roman empire', *Religion* ii (1972), 92–121
GRABAR, A., *L'Empereur dans l'art byzantin*, Paris 1936
GRÉGOIRE, H., 'Les manuscrits de Julien et le mouvement néopaien de Mistra: Démetrius Rhallis et Gémiste Pléthon', *Byzantion* v (1929–30), 730–6
HADOT, P., 'La fin du paganisme', *Histoire des religions* (ed. H. C. Puech) II, Paris 1972, 81–113
HALSBERGHE, G. H., *The Cult of Sol Invictus*, Leiden 1972
JAEGER, W., *Paideia: The Ideals of Greek Culture* I–III, Oxford 1939–1945
—— *Early Christianity and Greek Paideia*, Cambridge, Mass. 1961

JONES, A. H. M., *The Greek City: from Alexander to Justinian*, Oxford 1940
—— *The Cities of the Eastern Roman Provinces*, Oxford 1971²
—— *The Later Roman Empire 284–602* I–III, Oxford 1964
—— *et al.*, *The Prosopography of the Later Roman Empire A.D. 260–395*, Cambridge 1971
JULLIAN, C., *Histoire de la Gaule* VII–VIII, Paris 1926
LABRIOLLE, P. de, *La Réaction païenne: étude sur la polémique anti-chrétienne du Ier au VIe siècle*, Paris 1934
LEMERLE, P., *Le Premier humanisme byzantin: Notes et remarques sur enseignement et culture à Byzance des origines au Xe siècle*, Paris 1971
LEWY, H., *Chaldaean Oracles and Theurgy: Mysticism, Magic and Platonism in the Later Roman Empire* (ed. M. Tardieu), Paris 1978²
LIEBESCHUETZ, J. H. W. G., *Antioch: City and Imperial Administration in the Later Roman Empire*, Oxford 1972
LOBECK, C. A., *Aglaophamus sive de theologiae mysticae Graecorum causis, libri tres*, Königsberg 1829
MAGIE, D., *Roman Rule in Asia Minor* I–II, Princeton 1950
MARROU, H.-I., *Histoire de l'éducation dans l'antiquité*, Paris 1965⁶
—— *MOYCIKOC ANHP: étude sur les scènes de la vie intellectuelle figurant sur les monuments funéraires romains*, Rome 1964²
MASAI, F., *Pléthon et le platonisme de Mistra*, Paris 1956
MAU, G., *Die Religionsphilosophie Kaiser Julians in seinen Reden auf den König Helios und die Göttermutter*, Leipzig–Berlin 1907
MAZZARINO, S., *Aspetti sociali del quarto secolo*, Rome 1951
MILLAR, F., 'P. Herennius Dexippus: the Greek world and the third-century invasions', *JRS* lix (1969), 12–29
MOMIGLIANO, A. (ed.), *The Conflict between Paganism and Christianity in the Fourth Century*, Oxford 1963
NILSSON, M. P., *Geschichte der griechischen Religion* II, Munich 1974³
NOCK, A. D., *Conversion: the Old and the New in Religion from Alexander the Great to Augustine of Hippo*, Oxford 1933
—— *Essays on Religion and the Ancient World* I–II (ed. Z. Stewart), Oxford 1972
PETIT, P., *Libanios et la vie municipale à Antioche au IVe siècle après J.-C.*, Paris 1955.
PIGANIOL, A., *L'Empire chrétien (325–395)*, Paris 1972²
RÉMONDON, R., *La Crise de l'empire romain de Marc Aurèle à Anastase*, Paris 1964
ROCHEFORT, G., 'Le Περὶ θεῶν καὶ κόσμου de Saloustios et l'influence de l'empereur Julien', *REG* lxix (1956), 50–66
—— 'La démonologie de Saloustios et ses rapports avec celle de l'empereur Julien', *REG* lxx (1957), pp. xiii–xv

ROSTOVTZEFF, M., *The Social and Economic History of the Roman Empire*, Oxford 1957²

SATHAS, S. N., *Documents inédits relatifs à l'histoire de la Grèce au Moyen-Age* VII, Paris 1888

SCHWARTZ, W., *De vita et scriptis Iuliani Imperatoris*, Bonn 1888

SEECK, O., *Geschichte des Untergangs der antiken Welt* IV, Berlin 1911

SMITH, A., *Porphyry's Place in the Neoplatonic Tradition: a Study in post-Plotinian Neoplatonism*, The Hague 1974

STEIN, E., *Histoire du Bas-Empire* I, Bruges 1959

TURCAN, R., *Mithras Platonicus: Recherches sur l'hellénisation philosophique de Mithra*, Leiden 1975

WARREN-BONFANTE, L., 'Emperor, God and Man in the IV century: Julian the Apostate and Ammianus Marcellinus', *PP* xix (1964), 401–27

ZAKYTHENOS, D., *Byzance: État-Société-Économie*, London 1973

INDEX

Usage rather than consistency has been the criterion in transcribing Greek names and the titles of Julian's works. Modern scholars are not indexed and ancient authors are listed only when specifically discussed in the text.

revival, 111; benefited by Julian: 83;
her place in Julian's life, 51; her
tribute of honour to Julian, 51;
Julian goes to, 46; Julian leaves
Athens, 52
Attic rhetoric: as a formative influence
on Julian, 29
Attis: identified with Heracles,
Dionysus and Helios, 147; in Salutius,
155; symbolism of, 144 ff.
Aurelian, emperor: founder of the cult
of *Sol Invictus Exsuperantissimus*, 178,
198
aurum coronarium: and Julian's legislation, 105

Babel, myth of: interpreted by Julian,
165
Basil of Caesarea: and Greek culture,
10, 19; ignored by Julian, 127
Basilina: Julian's mother, 14, 15;
Christian, 18; her untimely death
regretted by Julian, 223; Julian
founds Basilinoupolis in her memory,
107 n. 96
Byzantinism (Julian's), 227 ff.; and
cities, 109–10, 121; and imperial
ideology, 16, 62, 64, 76, 113–14,
166–7, 171–81, 192; and ritual, 189–
91
Byzantium: and Greek culture, 4 n. 9,
10–12, 19, 171–2; tribute of honour
paid to Julian by, 227 ff.

Caesarea of Cappadocia: Julian's
hatred of, 107, 109
Callixena, pagan priestess, 186
Carterius, friend of Julian, 43
Celsus, apologist: on Hellenism and
Christianity, 3, 4, 80
Celsus, *consularis* of Syria: fellow student
of Julian at Athens, 51
Celts: Julian's attachment to, 71–2,
210–11; their ἀμουσία, 210–11; their
love of Julian, 209–10; wilfulness of,
196
Chaldean Oracles, 7 n. 18; and Julian,
144, 145; and Neoplatonism, 5, 136,
143; and theurgy, 6
Cheiron, Centaur: educator of
Asclepios, 168
Christ: and Dionysus, 133–4; and
Helios, 153; as Logos, 150

Christianity: and Julian, 24–7, 133–4,
161 ff.
Chrysanthius of Sardis: a true Hellene,
127–8; adept of theurgic Neoplatonism, 32; high priest of Lydia, 185;
serves Julian as model for the
ἐπιστήμων θεουργός, 33–4
chrysargyron: exemptions from, 104; not
remitted, 105
Claudius Gothicus, emperor: alleged
founder of second Flavian dynasty,
62, 64; worshipper of Helios, 180
Clement of Alexandria: on Greek
culture, 3; on *paideia*, 154 n. 130
collatio lustralis see chrysargyron
Commodus, emperor: in Julian's
Caesars, 198
Como: Julian secluded at, 45–6
Constantia (Maiouma) in Palestine:
Julian's hatred of, 107
Constantine I, emperor: and Alexander
the Great, 193 n. 5; and Christian
dogma, 141; and Naissos, 82;
criticism of his policies by Julian, 83;
embraces Christianity, 13; his *hybris*,
172; invests bishops with power,
184–5; similarities with Julian, 202;
worshipper of Helios, 179
Constantine Porphyrogenitus, emperor:
on tradition, dynasty and national
characteristics, 228–9
Constantinople: Julian adorns her,
108; Julian sits with senators of, 109;
Julian studies at, 27; Julian's
attachment to, 108; Julian's triumphant entry as Augustus into, 89
Constantius II, emperor: accused by
Julian, 83, 85; and Helios, 179; and
Julian's education, 14; and Julian's
panegyrics on, 61 ff.; breaks with
Julian, 75–6; demolisher of temples,
172–3; dies, 87; his envy of Julian,
70; honoured by Julian once dead,
89; Julian marches against him, 77
ff.; legislation on municipalities, 100
ff.; orders Gallus' execution, 45;
recalls Julian to Milan, 45, 52; recalls
legions from Gaul, 71; style of his
laws, 104
Corinth: Julian addresses a letter to, 86
curiae: and Julian's legislation, 103 ff.;
decline of, 100 ff.